Electrifying Anthropology

Also Available from Bloomsbury

Caravans, Hege Høyer Leivestad
Homely Atmospheres and Lighting Technologies in Denmark, Mikkel Bille
*Uncertainty and Possibility: New Approaches to Future Making in
Design Anthropology*, Sarah Pink, Yoko Akama and Shanti Sumartojo

Electrifying Anthropology

Exploring Electrical Practices and Infrastructures

Edited by
Simone Abram, Brit Ross Winthereik and Thomas Yarrow

With illustrations by Anjan Sarkar

BLOOMSBURY ACADEMIC
LONDON • NEW YORK • OXFORD • NEW DELHI • SYDNEY

BLOOMSBURY ACADEMIC
Bloomsbury Publishing Plc
50 Bedford Square, London, WC1B 3DP, UK
1385 Broadway, New York, NY 10018, USA

BLOOMSBURY, BLOOMSBURY ACADEMIC and the Diana logo are trademarks
of Bloomsbury Publishing Plc

First published in Great Britain 2019

Cover design by Tjaša Krivec
Cover illustrations by Anjan Sarkar

A catalogue record for this book is available from the British Library.

Library of Congress Cataloging-in-Publication Data
Names: Abram, Simone, editor. | Winthereik, Brit Ross, 1973- editor. | Yarrow, Thomas,
1977- editor. | Sarkar, Anjan, illustrator.
Title: Electrifying anthropology: exploring electrical practices and infrastructures / edited by
Simone Abram, Durham University; Brit Winthereik, IT University of Copenhagen;
Tom Yarrow, Durham University; with illustrations by Anjan Sarkar.
Description: London; New York: Bloomsbury Academic, 2019. | Includes bibliographical
references and index.
Identifiers:LCCN2019002793(print)|LCCN2019015661(ebook)|ISBN9781350102651
(ePUB) | ISBN 9781350102668 (ePDF) | ISBN 9781350102644 (hardback)
Subjects: LCSH: Electrification–Socialaspects.|Electricpowerconsumption–Social
aspects. | Electric power production–Social aspects.
Classification: LCC HD9685.A2 (ebook) | LCC HD9685.A2 E566 2019 (print) |
DDC 333.793/2–dc23
LC record available at https://lccn.loc.gov/2019002793

ISBN: HB: 978-1-3501-0264-4
ePDF: 978-1-3501-0266-8
ePub: 978-1-3501-0265-1

Typeset by Deanta Global Publishing Services, Chennai, India

To find out more about our authors and books visit www.bloomsbury.com
and sign up for our newsletters.

Contents

Figures

All chapters containing art are contributed by Anjan Sarkar.

Contributors

Simone Abram is Professor of Anthropology at Durham University and co-director of the Durham Energy Institute. She directs the innovative interdisciplinary MSc in Energy and Society at Durham University, and from 2016 until 2021 she is a co-investigator at the UK National Centre for Energy Systems Integration.

Gretchen Bakke holds a PhD from the University of Chicago in Cultural Anthropology. Her work focuses on the chaos and creativity that emerge during social, cultural and technological transitions. She is a former fellow of Wesleyan University's Science in Society Program and a former Fulbright fellow, and she is currently a guest professor at IRITHESys at Humboldt University – Berlin. Her book *The Grid* was selected by Bill Gates as one of his top five reads of 2016.

Leo Coleman teaches anthropology at Hunter College, City University of New York. He is the author, most recently, of *A Moral Technology: Electrification as Political Ritual in New Delhi* and the editor of *Food: Ethnographic Encounters*.

Jamie Cross is a senior lecturer in social anthropology at the University of Edinburgh. His current research focuses on the social–material politics of electrification and solar energy in contexts of global poverty. He is the author of *Dream Zones* (2014, Pluto Press).

Casper Bruun Jensen is a specially appointed associate professor at Osaka University. He is the author of *Ontologies for Developing Things* (Sense, 2010) and *Monitoring Movements in Development Aid* (with Brit Ross Winthereik) (2013, MIT) and the editor of *Infrastructures and Social Complexity* with Penny Harvey and Atsuro Morita (Routledge, 2016). His present work focuses on knowledge, infrastructure and practical ontologies in the Mekong river basin.

Joshua Kirshner is a lecturer in human geography in the Department of Environment and Geography at the University of York. His current research focuses on developing people-centred and justice-based approaches to sustainable energy. He was recently a co-investigator on a project that examined energy access amid sociopolitical conflict in urban Mozambique, supported by the British Academy.

Tristan Loloum has a PhD in social anthropology (EHESS, 2015) and an MSc in Integrated Planning (Lleida, 2010). He is currently a research engineer at the University of Tours and honorary research fellow at Durham University (Anthropology Department). Specializing in the study of heritage, tourism and social change, his latest research addresses the 'cultural politics of energy', questioning the role of energy tourism, industrial heritage and art sponsorship in the public understanding of energy and the influence of energy corporations.

Nathalie Ortar is Senior Researcher in anthropology at the École nationale des travaux publics de l'État (ENTPE). Her research interests focus on the meaning of dwelling as well as on the consequences of energy transition in daily life and its moral and symbolic implications.

Canay Özden-Schilling is an anthropologist of capitalism, energy and technology. She is a postdoctoral fellow in Data Sciences and Society and a lecturer in Anthropology at Johns Hopkins University. Canay received her PhD from the Massachusetts Institute of Technology in 2016. She is currently completing an ethnographic book on electricity trading in the United States.

Sarah Pink is Professor of Design and Emerging Technologies, and Director of the Emerging Technologies Research Lab at Monash University, Melbourne, Australia. Her research is interdisciplinary, international and interventional, and has recently focused on questions relating to the design and use of emerging technologies (such as autonomous driving vehicles). Her recent collaborative books include *Uncertainty and Possibility* (2018) and *Anthropologies and Futures* (2017).

Marcus Power is a professor of human geography at Durham University. His research interests include critical geopolitics and the spatialities of (post) development; visuality and popular geopolitics; energy geographies and low-carbon transitions in the global South; and China–Africa relations and the role of (re)emerging development donors in South–South cooperation. He is author of *Geopolitics and Development* (Routledge, 2019).

Hiroki Shin is a research fellow in the Department of History, Classics and Archaeology, Birkbeck College, University of London and the co-investigator of the research project 'Material Cultures of Energy'. His recent publications include 'Energy/Culture: A Reading Guide for Historical Literature', *Science Museum Group Journal* (2018); and, with Rebecca Wright and Frank Trentmann, *Power, Energy and International Cooperation: A History of the World Energy Council, 1923–2018* (Oekom, forthcoming).

Brit Ross Winthereik is Professor in the Department of Business IT at the IT University of Copenhagen. She has published widely in anthropology and science and technology studies (STS) on information infrastructures, ethnographic methods, environment, organization and accountability. She is lead investigator of the research project 'Data as Relation: Governance in the Age of Big Data'.

Thomas Yarrow is an associate professor in social anthropology at Durham University. His research uses an ethnographic approach to explore the 'social life' of expertise. He is particularly interested in everyday interactions through which professional knowledge is produced, the personal and ideological commitments that propel this work and the routine ethical dilemmas that arise. He has explored these issues through research in the UK and Ghana in a range of professional contexts, including international development, heritage conservation, electrical engineering and, most recently, architecture. His most recent book is *Architects: portraits of a practice* (Cornell University Press 2019).

Acknowledgements

This collection explores the infrastructures that have become part of our lives by considering electricity as a form of life that enables certain life forms while making others more difficult. It grew out of a Wenner-Gren sponsored workshop at Durham University in 2016, in which scholars working across anthropology, science and technology studies, geography, history, design and cultural studies met to pursue an interest in electricity's socio-materiality. This collection also includes contributions by scholars not present at the workshop.

The editors would like to express their thanks to Durham Energy Institute for workshop support, especially Lynn Gibson; the Anthropology Department at Durham University; Dr Christopher Crabtree at Durham University for facilitating a hands-on energy workshop during our Wenner-Gren meeting; Sandra Bell for support and advice throughout the process; and Lea Enslev at ITU Copenhagen for editorial assistance.

The editors would also like to thank the guest speakers who generously gave their time to participate in the original workshop, including Dominic Boyer, Dominique Desjeux, Annette Henning, Maja Hojer Bruun, Atsuro Morita, Sophie Bouly de Lesdain, Lea Schick, Laura Watts, Mike Anusas, Cymene Howe, Antti Silvast, Tanja Winther, Elaine Forde, Catherine Alexander, Taras Fedirko, Andres Luque Ayala and Ben Campbell.

Current thinking – an introduction

Simone Abram, Brit Ross Winthereik and Thomas Yarrow

Introduction

Since the nineteenth century, electricity and its various infrastructures have proliferated to the point where they now reach into every aspect of contemporary life. Whereas the first industrial revolution was helped along first and foremost by the steam engine, electricity was centrally implicated in the second (the rise of Fordist modes of production in the early twentieth century), and it is now inextricable from far-reaching and profoundly transformative socio-technical transformations. After a third industrial revolution associated with automation, 'Industry 4.0' is now being promoted strongly by European governments and industrial manufacturers, to connect producers and consumers through real-time digital networks (Bundesrepublik Deutschland 2014; EEF 2016). At the same time, counter-pressures to limit anthropogenic climate change caused by burning fossil fuels imply decarbonizing the energy system and, not least, decarbonizing electricity grids and transport systems. These pressures problematize the workings of electricity grids and the need to balance supply and demand, adapt to intermittent and distributed supplies, rethink electricity storage and work out how all this is to be financed in distributed, competitive and international markets. All of this raises doubts about the future of existing mass-generation infrastructures and demonstrates that any transition to more sustainable living is neither linear nor purely technical.

Changes in infrastructure have significant effects on the everyday lives of people living in industrial societies as well as those who do not. Electrification of transport and heating, for example, may generate forms of electricity dependence that would have been unimaginable just a short time ago. In short, the majority of people in Europe and America, at least, live in what we might term an 'electromagnetic field' to which they have become thoroughly habituated and whose scope is growing.

While it is pervasive – though by no means universally available or accessible – electricity nonetheless has qualities that make it recede from view: it participates in daily routines familiar to the point they are taken for granted (Pink 2011); it is channelled by infrastructures designed to conceal their workings; and it is known through expert technical vocabularies with which few non-specialists are conversant, as well as through poetry and popular language. For scholars of the social sciences, the internalization of electrical metaphors to the imagination of 'the social' is not new, yet it produces its own lacunae (Coleman, this volume). *Electrifying Anthropology* aims to render electricity visible and interesting – a matter of concern to social sciences and the humanities. It seeks to pursue this aim by rendering electricity socially and materially lively and by placing electricity firmly amid everyday practices and politics. *Electrifying Anthropology* thus explores how electricity is not merely a resource for social life but also part and parcel of infrastructures in which people live. Taking inspiration from the growing field of infrastructure studies, we adopt a broad approach to infrastructures; the book points to electricity and electric infrastructures as phenomena increasingly embedded in the ordering systems, including the ontologies, by which we live.

Electrifying Anthropology demonstrates how ethnographic approaches to electricity may illuminate and transform an already spectacular scene of research on energy, infrastructures, identity, history, language, communication and more. Analytically, we seek a subaltern approach to electricity production and use, which includes relativizing forms of authority and expertise that consider electricity as first and foremost a technical issue. Our discussion of electricity, as will be clear, is produced by the simultaneous ethnographic specificity and analytical variation presented. Framed by the deceptively simple question of what electricity actually is, we trace the multiplicity of practices by which it is produced, consumed, (re)-invented and transformed.

Situating electricity

Central to our approach is the proposition that electricity-in-practice is not a singular kind of thing, but a very varied phenomenon. The book collects chapters that explore electricity as tied into social and material infrastructure that can sometimes be sites of controversy. Studying electricity in a comparative way means paying attention to the language, metaphors, classification systems and devices used to deal with it in our daily lives as well as in engineering and policy work. It also means that readers who consider themselves to be 'technical experts' or 'social experts' must adopt an agnostic perspective on what electricity is, where it can be found or how it can be researched.

The approach taken in the chapters departs in key respects from the two broad approaches taken in the past. Engineers, on the one hand, have sought to define how electricity can be used, in terms that have mostly isolated technical and infrastructural considerations from the 'social contexts' of various users, as well as from their own epistemic practices (Marvin, Chappells and Guy 1999; Rial and Danezis 2011). Social scientists, in contrast, have tended to focus on 'social context' specifically in relation to practices of consumption, in terms that do little to describe how electricity materializes in technical and infrastructural terms (Shove and Walker 2014; Miller, Iles and Jones 2013). Here, in contrast, we are inspired by a small body of existing work that seeks to describe and analyse electricity-in-practice with attention to infrastructural, epistemic, political and material elements (Winther 2010, 2012; Rupp 2016; Wallenborn and Wilhite 2014; Anusas and Ingold 2015; Boyer 2015; Schick and Winthereik 2013) to add renewed impetus to efforts to move beyond binary framings of electricity as a variously 'social' or 'technical' entity. Such work has been inspired by social studies of science and technology and by the anthropological approaches intrinsic to the debates around actor–network theory (Law 1986; Law and Mol 2002; Jensen 2010; Holbraad and Pedersen 2017; Yarrow et al. 2015).

Contributors to the volume come from a range of conceptual and disciplinary traditions, including anthropology, science and technology studies (STS), geography and history, but are unified by the collective aim to better understand how electricity is formed and what it forms. Rather than treat this as a stable or singular object, we demonstrate how electricity implicates people in diverse forms of subjectification and objectification that reflect and reconfigure the lives of those involved, including through concerns with identity, emotion, ideology, language, ethics and knowledge.

Our efforts to understand how electricity is activated through specific articulations of concepts, practices, meanings, materials and infrastructure build on various conceptual approaches, as we demonstrate how electricity is involved in understandings, practices and concerns as diverse as life itself. Our borrowings are deliberately and unapologetically broad and do not, in the final analysis, resolve across chapters. Borrowing from some classic literatures, including on religion (Durkheim 1968), totemism (Lévi-Strauss 1962) and kinship, helps resituate classic concepts and insights.

Electricity's manifestations are so diverse and abundant that we inevitably have to deal with a broad range of conceptual approaches, but our efforts towards a more syncretic understanding have developed through close dialogue with one another and with a number of literatures. Broadly inspired by post-human thinkers (Hayles 1999; Pickering 1992), we pay close empirical attention to the various ways in which the 'social' and 'technical' elements of electricity are inter-defined, imbricated and distinguished. Electricity, which is not strictly a source of energy, but rather a medium of energy transmission, can bring about material and social changes in contexts as diverse as nervous systems or modes of organizing societies. Without thinking about electricity as and in materials, we fail to see how 'it' shapes ontologies and is shaped by them in return (Bille and Sørensen 2007).[1] In rejecting binary distinctions between the social and the material, we also have to think about the relationship between electricity's material properties and its manifestations in social and political worlds.

Extending recent interdisciplinary work on infrastructure (Furlong 2010; Chalfin 2016; Harvey et al. 2016), we highlight how electricity divides and connects through the material circumstances and technical arrangements that enable certain modes of stabilization and commodification. This focus brings to light a number of practices that have received limited attention and, by the same token, extends the conceptual repertoire of existing work: electrical infrastructures matter in specific ways as responses to the evanescent qualities of electricity itself.

What this volume seeks to add to the existing literature is a number of ethnographic studies and descriptions of electricity. From the case descriptions of how electricity is multiply enacted, the contributors offer vocabularies and concepts that can energize our scholarly and conceptual thinking around electrification of social life and infrastructures and raise a series of questions: How can the host of new roles for electricity in social and cultural life be acknowledged? How can we speak about 'it' in its own right, acknowledging that electricity is not one thing and not even 'a thing' (Bakke, this volume)? Through attending to electricity practices in many different places, the chapters all offer alternative vocabularies to engineering language. The question is whether, taken as a whole, they also provide the contours of a new grammar for analysing electricity.

All of the analyses walk a fine line between seeking not to lose the knowledge that science has already gathered and staying true to all the things we do not know much about, such as electricity's political agency and the richness of action at the edges of electricity networks. A real strength of the contributions is that they manage to steer clear of a division between a 'real', scientific version of electricity on the one hand and a socially and culturally constructed version on the other. Instead they are seen as intertwined. If, as Kirshner and Power claim (in this volume), 'energy infrastructure materializes state power and authority', then once again our attention to the materialities of electricity and its equipment remains crucial, but how to attend to it remains problematic. As they argue, Ferguson alerted us many years ago to the reliance of 'anti-politics machines' on the presentation of political projects as technical procedures (1990, see also Abram 2005), and our drive is patently not to reduce complex socio-technical worlds to apolitical technological problems. Focusing on material things may carry related risks, however. Jensen (this volume) points to Jane Bennett's focus on the many and diverse actual material things that make up something as complex as the infrastructure of an electrical grid and her arguments that these must be understood as heterogeneous networks of objects. But as Jensen argues, Bennett's approach ignores the observation that 'things and people are *all* internally heterogeneous, since all are shaped by emergent relations, entanglements and arrangements'. Instead, Jensen suggests taking as a departure point Isabelle Stengers' (1999) refusal to purify the force of things or the actions of people.

Articulations of electrification

We now outline some of the developments – recent and less so – that have made electricity matter in new and pressing ways. Before electricity became a consumer good, experimentation with electricity had taken place for centuries. It was in the nineteenth century that engineers reached the basic theoretical understanding of electricity that we continue to use today and, around that time, expertise on electricity began to solidify. Ever since then, electrical applications have continued to develop, and electrical installations have grown and transformed. In much of the so-called developed world (although with notable exceptions), several decades of increasingly large-scale power-generation installations removed electricity generation from the domestic and communal domains towards a national or international scope. Increasingly large coal-fired power stations with huge cooling towers were built onto transmission networks, massive nuclear power stations loomed large on some coastal horizons and electricity pylons drew patterns on the landscape, holding electricity generation at a distance high above and beyond the everyday and very far from its domestic consumers.

Recent attempts to include more renewable-energy sources in electricity grids, fuelled, among other things, by green societal transitions, have helped to bring electricity down to a human scale and highlight the parallel histories of domestic and community-scale generation. Pioneers of alternative electricity systems showed how to build DIY solar heating and electrical mini-grids,[2] enabling enthusiastic independent householders to adapt their own dwellings. Since then, manufactured household technologies like solar panels or heat pumps have caught up and have dropped in price, enabling non-experts to install their own generation equipment at home, in small businesses or community groups. Wind turbines, solar panels, heat pumps, incinerators that turn waste into electricity, battery packs and electric vehicles are some of the electric technologies that facilitate everyday interaction with electricity generation and help make electricity a matter of increased public concern. These developments put questions about electricity grids centre stage in our ethnographic approach.

Electricity demands a unique kind of infrastructure: of networks, links and grids at contrasting scales and dimensions (from circuit boards to international power cables), requiring harmonization, surveillance, maintenance and management between states, geographical regions and commercial and public institutions and between citizens and economies of all kinds. Electricity can be bought, sold, stolen and generated, captured and transformed (Golden and Min 2012; Min and Golden 2014). It is generated, distributed and used locally and across global connections that are physical, virtual, economic and political and often ambivalent (Arora 2009). A growing body of ethnographic readings has helped contextualize these ambivalences and confront technical and political assumptions about 'consumers', 'customers', 'prosumers', 'users', or 'providers' (Jakobson 2007; Wilhite 2008, 2012; Rupp 2016; Ulsrud et al. 2015). Such work reveals how electricity is not a single stable technical object in need of added social context. Rather, electricity is located and produced through bodies, materials, concepts and technologies and is propelled by various logics, as Cross (this volume) makes abundantly clear.

While in the twenty-first century electricity is changing in infrastructural impact and is gaining public attention, electricity is also increasingly politically charged (Summerton 2004; Breslau 2011). Concerns about electricity are starting to overshadow debates about oil (both in terms of its environmental consequences and in relation to oil as a finite resource), as the technical and social consequences of the shift to renewable sources emerge. In particular, the materialities of renewable sources of electricity are bringing in widely distributed generation capacity that values new supply chains, primary resources and geopolitical structures, while placing quite different demands on national energy grids that call for new thoughts about the government of electricity.

Throughout much of the later twentieth century, Western electricity users have largely been able to access as much electricity as they can pay for. Behind this plenitude lay a complex system of grid management, ensuring that instantaneous supply and demand could be matched. This relied on large-scale producers and consumers (i.e. industrial consumers) entering into agreements, such that large power stations could be managed as demand switched through diurnal and weekly cycles from industrial uses to domestic uses. We need not go into details of grid histories or technologies here, but suffice it to say that the demise of large-scale manufacturing in much of Europe and the United States and the move from large power stations to smaller, dispersed generating equipment raise complex challenges for the operation of a grid.[3] Electricity infrastructures, policies, systems and markets vary considerably between countries, but general trends are being seen across the globe towards competitive markets for electricity rather than purely state-owned and operated infrastructure and towards increasingly finely distributed generation. Changes to infrastructure are also neither singular nor linear. Even as generation is increasingly dispersed, grid connections have been undergoing their own form of globalization, becoming less nationally focused – not only through international inter-connectors that join grids but also through electricity markets that allow for trade across national boundaries. In some cases, grids are better connected between nations than within.[4] In this context, citizens' assumptions about accessing abundant electricity at any time are now being questioned.[5]

In contrast, in many non-Western countries, electricity supplies have been intermittent and often unpredictable. Access to grid energy becomes entangled in political structures that often distribute supplies unequally. Kirshner and Power (this volume) argue that electricity has been used in developing states as a means of state control. Cross (this volume) shows how provision of electricity has been integral to notions of modernization and development for the Indian state, for example. The coming of electricity 'lines' and the provision of 'current' through these lines articulate the social politics of rural life. Talking about 'current' in this context offers a discourse that spans well beyond electricity itself, 'rich with allegorical or metaphorical possibilities for talking about modernity and development, life and death, kinship and fraternity, love and sexuality' (Kirshner and Power, this volume). When the current fails and where it is not supplied, electrical infrastructure highlights its absence and the exclusion of some from the benevolence of the state.

For electricity consumers, messages are more mixed than ever. Manufacturers urge us to consume more – more gadgets, more appliances, more electrical activity. (Some) governments urge consumers to reduce their consumption, while consumer organizations want lower prices to bring people out of energy vulnerability. These forces conspire to create maximizing customers out of cost-insensitive consumers, while pushing the unreflective consumers of yesteryear to become aware of their consumption (Brown 2015).

For the engineers and economists largely tasked with rebalancing a transforming grid, the idea of pricing as a means to change behaviour is appealing. Hence the idea of 'smart grids' and 'smart metres' has become extremely popular among policy makers and industry as a technical solution to emerging grid problems (Marvin, Chappells and Guy 1999; Rial and Danezis 2011; Nyborg and Røpke 2015). Making consumption visible has been seen as a first step towards achieving this, but while the search has begun for the rational households that will adjust their consumption patterns and help balance the load in an overheated system, there are numerous complications. One of them relates to the ways people are figured in the system, imagined either as reflexively adjusting to pricing mechanisms (and being in charge of consumption) or as resistant to change (and thus unresponsive) (Strengers 2012; Schick and Winthereik 2013). Another complication relates to the lack of attention paid by grid technologists to the actual material setup of energy supplies and the differences to be found between theorized models and lived practices, and between different systems, despite an emerging supply of knowledge on this theme.

These questions about changing electrical infrastructure matter now not least because so much of the world's population is increasingly dependent on electricity supply. Modern hospitals are so reliant on electricity that they are normally installed with dedicated emergency generators in case of grid failure, and they are prioritized when general electricity supply is restricted. In war zones, cuts in electricity supply, including cuts in diesel supply for generators that run autoclaves, ultrasound scanners, centrifuges and other hospital equipment, can hasten or cause deaths. The targeting of medical centres in recent conflicts (Herbermann and Fleck 2017) and a long history of wartime targeting of electrical infrastructure show how politically important electricity is, given the increasing dependence of all sorts of infrastructures on electric supplies.

Electricity is so pervasive in the centres of power that access to electricity is promoted by international organizations such as the United Nations as a kind of human right, a basic essential for 'civilized' life (Winther 2010). Access to electricity is indeed globally very uneven, both in terms of geographical spread and stability and security of service in particular states, and in terms of affordability of access, although some argue that, rather than a simple concern for equal access to restricted goods, claims such as the United Nations' contribute to a colonialist normalization of Western priorities (Shove 2003). Among energy vulnerabilities that are now recognized, lack of access or unreliable access to electricity has particular features that relate to the forms of electricity itself and the appliances, machines and plant that are used to generate, convey and use it. Yet paradoxically, for some Westerners, it is a life off the grid that is now an ideal.[6] Recognizing the degree to which grid connections are tied into specific sociopolitical and economic frameworks, those seeking alternative non-capitalist lifestyles may choose to go off the grid altogether. This does not necessarily mean rejecting electrical services, however, and as Forde shows, being technologically innovative in relation to electricity can be aligned with a rejection of grid connection, while it is also possible to overlook the provenance of components and their derivation from the markets that are being rejected (Forde 2016). Rejection of the grid can thus be a form of rejection of the political status quo. Indeed, as Luque-Ayala and Silver show, a spatial focus on electricity, and in particular an urban focus, shows how various forms of urban grid can become the site of protest as well as power (2016).

Summing up this historical section, we can say that after a century of domestication, electricity is socialized and politically embedded in ways that now require sustained empirical attention, including how its histories and futures are performed (Gupta 2015; Möllers and Zachmann 2012). One of the important tasks following from this is close study of *who* is doing this performing. Certainly, electricity has been brought to public attention as a concern, but it is also often dealt with by experts behind closed doors. Lack of transparency is not only a matter of who has the technical expertise or whether electrical matters can spark publics into being (Marres 2014). It is also a matter of how particular historical renderings of electricity have spurred our current thinking. As others have already pointed out, just because certain practices have become naturalized, this doesn't make them universal. Hardwired into our current thinking are demonstrations of electricity in which its dangers have been highlighted and in which a strong link between science and engineering has been performed (Schiffer 2005; Shamir 2013; French 2017). But with renewability high on some national and industrial actors' agendas (DONG Energy, now Ørsted, recently sold all its off-shore operations in Denmark and is investing massively in renewable-energy production in the UK), and with an IT and robotics revolution expected in some parts of the world, we need new resources for articulating what 'electrification' means.

The structure and themes of the book

In proposing an anthropologically informed approach to electricity, we acknowledge that different research methods materialize their research objects differently (Sovacool 2010). The book includes accounts that draw on historical methods, textual analyses, participant observation and interviews. In various ways, these are enlisted in the service of understanding what electricity is and what it means to those people who are the empirical focus of enquiry. Ethnography attunes attention to these empirical circumstances in specific ways, locating what people know or claim in relation to the practical circumstances of their everyday lives. Descriptions of what electricity 'is' are presented as necessarily indissoluble from considerations of where, when, how, who and by what means it is made to be so. Our ethnographic focus extends to the various experts involved in the production of electric knowledge and infrastructure as much as to the 'consumers', who are more routinely the subject of social scientific attention. While all accounts share a common understanding of the indissolubility of concepts from practice, different disciplinary, methodological and analytic commitments train attention in distinct ways. Taking a clue from Nye (1999), the contributors to this volume consider electricity as a participant in societal transformations on larger as well as smaller scales. As electricity is becoming a visible concern in people's lives and a new political force, we ask what are the emerging forms of interpreting, managing and imagining electricity and our future with 'it'? How do reconfigured electricity practices make electricity present in new ways, and what energy futures do these help to structure?

Gretchen Bakke's chapter offers us a way to address such questions, presenting an incisive analysis of the linguistic limits to our apprehension of the grammatical form of the indefinite. In Bakke's terms, electricity evades the nominative form of language and escapes the genitive: it is neither noun nor verb, yet European languages constantly urge a *thingization* of something so ephemeral as an electromagnetic field.

As Bakke shows, while anthropologists have embraced the idea that things are good to think with, its converse is that non-things are difficult to think at all. Electricity provides a challenge in being just such a non-thing. We barely know what electricity is, she argues, even if we are increasingly familiar with its effects (largely true for scientists as well as social scientists). As a result, we can talk about electricity's effects, but we often do this as if we are talking about electricity itself, which we are, in fact, not doing. Instead, popular discourse, for example, includes a plethora of metaphors applied to electricity, with *flow* being only the most common. Electricity does not flow; nor do electrons – this much is certainly known. When engineers talk about a *flow of charge*, on the other hand, they knowingly adopt the methods of physics and its use of models and metaphors that serve explanatory purpose without being direct representations of material phenomena.

Coleman's chapter continues the exploration of electricity as inspiration for language and brings metaphor firmly to the fore. As Coleman shows, early humanities scholars were not slow to adopt electrical metaphors and make them part of their vocabulary. For scholars of religion, in particular, the idea of an invisible force with palpable effects was enticing. In what Coleman describes as a 'scholarly pedigree in biblical criticism', analogies between mechanical and divine energy offered an attractive model, inspiring Durkheim's attempts to explain the 'forces' of social action. Indeed, Coleman describes a 'constant "signals traffic" between religion, natural science, and the burgeoning human or "moral" sciences' of the nineteenth and early twentieth centuries. A flourishing world of experimentation generated unified fields of positive science such as 'psychophysics', which built on the idea of energy and vital forces. Curiously, as Coleman notes, such unified science inquired into humans as biological organisms, including their thought processes and the development of the species. While the disciplines then gradually emerged as separate endeavours throughout the century, recent work on the Anthropocene, the period of time that has seen man-made planet-scale geological changes, brings holism centre stage across the human and physical sciences, thrusting scholars, again, into dialogue across, through or around disciplinary boundaries.

Bakke and Coleman are both concerned with approaching infrastructures as materializations of collectives that are both human and material. As Bakke explains, since it is easier to think and talk about things, a focus on materialities – concrete stuff of the grid, electrical appliances and so forth – makes electricity available through its effects. A focus on effects and on 'being affected' offers a way to shift the focus to relations rather than objects. Vinciane Despret, for example, has built on Haraway to think about being affected by something only partially within reach. In Despret's and Haraway's renderings, being affected is not about empathic relationships but about 'creating the possibility to inscribe oneself in a relation of exchange and proximity that has nothing to do with identification' (Despret 2016, 17).

Cross's chapter shows how, in contrast, electrical current can be good to talk about, and how talk about 'current' links local conditions to broader political debates. The visibility of grid infrastructure that supplies electricity to some and not others reminds people of the inequalities suffered on a daily basis among sectors of the Indian population, particularly in rural areas where geographical separation reinforces social segregations. The lights visible from dark houses make inequalities apparent and lend metaphorical richness to the language of power. Perhaps surprisingly, access to off-grid energy through India's solar revolution does not dissipate these disparities but reinforces the differences in access to different qualities of electricity, on or off-grid.

Sometimes the concrete description of a specific practice can illustrate this kind of inscription. Ortar transports us to a university city in the south of France, inviting us to take a sensual-ethnographic approach to the electrical. Focusing on the experience of riding her electric bike, Ortar unpacks the bike in terms of the effects riding it had on the organization of her day, the temporalities it invokes, hers-and-its bodily energy as a particular edge of the grid system. Ortar's account is of a relatively happy configuration of power and person, a benign encounter with varied infrastructures experienced through the sensuality of movement. The thematic focus in Ortar's chapter is on everyday experiences of electricity and on the embodied nature of 'living electrically'.

In contrast to inscribing bodies as situated edges of specific power grids, Shin's account of the changing charging systems for electricity use in Japan shows how technical expectations can foster outcomes that are far from benign. In contrast to the Insull-inspired use of metres to embed electricity in financial infrastructures in America, Japanese households were charged by the light socket. As people found ingenious ways to multiply their socket connections, they were criminalized by the systemic response to their creativity. Shin's chapter reminds us how access to energy services like electricity has been implicated in economic and political structures that entail punitive consequences. These early forms of rationing, in contrast to the classic Western rationing-by-price, not only make apparent the cultural forms of organization and institutionalization of electric services, but also illustrate the significance of the metaphors and models that are put in place to enact electrical effects. Shin's focus on relationality brings us closer to electricity and its hybridity and indicates an important theme for the book: infrastructures as set in time and space and as sites for experimentation.

Jensen also analyses part of an electrical infrastructure as he seeks to 'deal anthropologically with the force of things'. The construction of hundreds of dams along the Mekong River relies on many different kinds of models, but in particular it requires some convergence between hydrological river models and electrical and economic plans. His description of the models-in-practice shows us different ways in which the Mekong River can be known. The river is different in each model, becoming a kind of river-multiple, as it is known through multiple different and differently partial models. Model-makers themselves know the flaws of their models but rarely reject their explanatory power (cf. Abram, Murdoch and Marsden 1998). As models are used for planning purposes, they adopt electric ontologies and start to become about economic 'flows and currents'. In practice, as Jensen shows, the electric world is full of cuts, conversions and transformations. Models are restricted – therein lies both their value as models and their weakness as partial representations – but it is the promotion of some aspects over others that can have such deleterious and political effects. His point is not merely that models reveal some things and conceal others; rather, he draws attention to the process and politics by which some things are revealed through the concealment of others.

In their chapter, Kirshner and Power put it more bluntly: in sub-Saharan Africa, more specifically Mozambique, 'energy production and use translates into control over space, and energy and its supporting infrastructure becomes a means for states to express their authority, extend their reach and consolidate territorial control'. Using the tools of political economy, they argue that state control (or lack of control) of electricity grids has effects on relations between citizens and state, shaping forms of governance. State power and electric power are related, sometimes quite directly. Yet the state's efforts to control power (in both senses) are as uneven and incomplete as the country's electrical infrastructure. The state holds out the promise of providing electricity to the citizens, but its failure to deliver on the promise has the counter-effect of alienating large parts of the population. Kirshner and Power show how dams in Mozambique became the focus for competing factions during the civil war – they were defined as a symbol of the progress of high modernism, as a symbol of Portuguese colonial power or as a national asset vital to the success of a liberated country. The dam became a site of struggle precisely because of the link between electric power and political power on a geopolitical stage, a battle that played out through civil-war attacks on the transmission lines connecting the dam to the rest of the country as well as on the dam itself. The country's obligations to international contracts and the reflection of colonial history in the shape of the electricity infrastructure mean that the citizens see little benefit from the dam's productive power. Subsequent liberalization of the electricity network exacerbated this unevenness and reinforces the geopolitical pressures on the country's energy infrastructures. While United Nations and World Bank powers over the state continue to shape the electricity sector, the state's hold over citizens remains as uneven as their access to electricity.

Geopolitical considerations also figure in Özden-Schilling's chapter but in a somewhat different way. Given this broader reach of the grid of electricity generation, transmission, governance, political relations and financial flows, Özden-Schilling asks us to think about what she terms the 'big grid': the Grid beyond the infrastructure of the electricity grid itself. She shows us how US grid development has been intimately entwined with the development of the notion of 'big data', as scientists and engineers sought to address optimization problems. As the ability to solve these problems has developed, the opportunity to use that problem-solving has itself enabled rapid optimization techniques that have in turn afforded new financial trading opportunities in the electricity markets. While Özden-Schilling does not claim that big grids are the direct precursor to big data, she shows how grid-like thinking began to pervade engineering specialisms, and she shows us how the increasing scale of grid thinking permeates contemporary life through a description of a famous widespread blackout in the northeast United States. Özden-Schilling also ventures into the questions around the idea of a smart grid and the depth of socialization involved in imagining, preparing for and ultimately attempting to implement multiply-networked and agented grid systems.

The prospect of controlling integrated grids – that is, where control of supply to specific appliances or users is in the hands of system operators rather than in the hands of consumers/owners/users – raises far-reaching questions about the kinds of political-economy issues that electricity grids figure in. Kirshner as well as Power and Özden-Schilling point to the scale of work needed to consider the relations between centralization and dispersal, state control, regulation, financial investment or empowerment with respect to national electricity grids. Questions around (de)centralization of energy systems will not be tackled head-on by this book. However, the approach taken by Loloum is helpful in considering how particular institutions in the electrical system communicate desired perceptions of themselves. Loloum offers us an intriguing glimpse into the public promotion of the electricity world's biggest beasts: nuclear power stations.

By combining an experiential approach with the forthright statement of state scientific power that is the nuclear power station, Loloum reminds us of the placement of electrical infrastructure in the technological sublime. Dams such as those discussed in the chapters by Jensen and Kirshner and Power have long been central to this powerful aesthetic, with images of the Aswan and Hoover Dams carrying particular potency as images of modernity and progress in their time. Visiting dams or nuclear power stations as a tourist constitutes the visitor as a particular kind of subject, subject to the instrumental and symbolic safety procedures, checks and warnings that constitute a nuclear governmentality. Loloum also draws on David Nye's observations that the American technological sublime is destined to be experienced not by individuals but by groups of tourists joining excursions to view the great achievements of science fulfilled by the state and capital (1996). Nye's particular focus on the 'electrical sublime', through the dazzling electric lighting that stunned early audiences, highlights the cleanliness often associated with electricity as a form of power.

Électricité de France (EDF) and other companies enrol their infrastructure quite explicitly in the political project of public relations (PR), hoping to generate public support for investment in nuclear power. Notwithstanding the abundant pollution caused by electrical power plants, great efforts are taken to present electricity as clean and safe, particularly at that most notoriously risky location, the nuclear plant. The power to control such incipient danger only adds to the effect of awe and the frisson of averted danger for the spectator/ visitor, making the visit in many ways an archetypal tourism experience despite – or perhaps precisely because of – the extremely utilitarian design of the plant. The nuclear power station becomes a spectacle whose surface of scientific authority and engineering sophistication can be admired, while the painful and often exploitative chains and networks of supply of its resources are well hidden from view in a partial narrative of the kind highlighted here. Scholars of tourism are familiar with Goffman's notion of front-stages and back-stages, the performance of place and identity for tourism purposes and the partiality of the performance that tourists willingly, if not eagerly, experience. Variations of this partiality can be recognized in the presentation of electrical effects in the various models, narratives and discourses noted here.

Thinking through electricity

What might it mean to 'know' electricity anthropologically? In some sense, it is about having fuses and splices that don't match the epistemic practices through which electricity has been performed in science and engineering. It might also be about knowing that, as anthropologists, we are aware of the complexity in 'fixing it up', as Joni Mitchell puts it in the lyrics to her song 'Electricity' (1972). What kinds of expertise and knowledge relate to electricity, and how should we (mutually) approach those areas that we do not entirely understand? If our work is in redescribing electricity (see Lebner 2017), how might we access the various forms of knowledge without privileging any particular kind as we seek to explore diverse possibilities of meaning? Anthropology excels in considering diverse ways of knowing, but scientific expertise itself often poses a particular challenge, and this is exemplified in scientific and engineering expertise about electricity. This is not an easy challenge and raises a number of questions. For example, if we adopt the language of engineers, can we then think critically about the social and ethical assumptions built into engineering approaches? If we refuse the language of engineers and scientists, how do we acknowledge or incorporate their learning? If we reproduce the language of energy policy, where is the space for subaltern voices in setting energy agendas? How, in other words, do we find ways to discuss electricity that encompass knowledge about its technical capacities without capitulating to the socio-scientific implications of technical debates? How, as Bakke puts it, can we take electricity seriously in its own right (see also Holbraad and Pedersen 2017)?

As a whole, *Electrifying Anthropology* moves far beyond the creeping realization of how embedded electric power is in so many aspects of contemporary life. It moves beyond the idea of electricity as an immovable force, in the face of which our only option is to examine its 'impact'. True, we need power to enliven our appliances, travel around or communicate, but this power is deeply enmeshed in linguistic practices, power politics, geopolitical relations, metaphors and models of thought and so on. What the book offers is a set of potential trajectories for thinking about electricity and its effects, of tying the thoughts of social scientists to the builders of dams, the geopolitical negotiators to the person flicking a light switch or the tourist hopping on an electric bike. Applying electricity to social science helps us diffract electricity (Haraway 1997) and invigorate social science at the same time, challenging our most central assumptions and discourses and opening new fields for exploration.

Notes

1 We are painfully aware that our subaltern approach to electric metaphors is limited by and limited to the descriptions made possible by the English language (Mol 2014).
2 For example, in Britain at the Centre for Alternative Technology: https://content.cat. org.uk/index.php/how-cat-started (accessed 24 April 2017).
3 See www.ncl.ac.uk/cesi or www.ukerc.ac.uk for further information.
4 For example, the interconnector between mainland Scotland and the Orkney islands is too low-grade to transfer Orkney's abundant renewable-energy production; connections between mainland Greece and other European Union (EU) countries are better in some instances than connections to the Greek islands.
5 See Ward (2016).
6 See, for example, how communities in Canada seek alternatives to centralized supply http://lifeoffgrid.ca/.

References

Abram, S. 2005. 'Science/Technology as Politics by Other Means', *Focaal*, 46: 3–20.

Abram, S., J. Murdoch and T. Marsden. 1998. 'Planning by Numbers: Migration and Statistical Governance', in P. Boyle and K. Halfacree (eds), *Migration into Rural Areas: Theories and Issues*, 236–51. Chichester: Wiley.

Anusas, M. and T. Ingold. 2015. 'The Charge against Electricity', *Cultural Anthropology*, 30(4): 540–54.

Arora, V. 2009. 'They Are All Set to Dam(n) Our Future': Contested Development through Hydel Power in Democratic Sikkim', *Sociological Bulletin*, 58(1): 94–114. JSTOR, www.jstor.org/stable/23620837.

Bille, M. and T. F. Sørensen. 2007. 'An Anthropology of Luminosity', *Journal of Material Culture*, 12(3): 263–84.

Boyer, D. 2015. 'Anthropology Electric', *Cultural Anthropology*, 30(4): 531–9.

Breslau, D. 2011. 'What Do Market Designers Do When They Design Markets? Economists as Consultants to the Redesign of Wholesale Electricity Markets in the

U.S., in Charles Camic, Neil Gross and Michèle Lamont (eds), *Social Knowledge in the Making*, 379–403. Chicago, IL: University of Chicago Press.

Brown, W. 2015. *Undoing the Demos: Neoliberalism's Stealth Revolution*. New York: Zone Books.

Bundesrepublikk Deutschland. 2014. *The New High-Tech Strategy: Innovations for Germany*. Rostock: Publikationsversand der Bundesregierung. https://www.bmbf.de/pub/HTS_Broschuere_eng.pdf (accessed 24 April 2017).

Chalfin, B. 2016. '"Wastelandia": Infrastructure and the Commonwealth of Waste in Urban Ghana', *Ethnos*, 82(4): 1–24.

Despret, V. 2016. *What Would Animals Say If We Asked the Right Questions?* Minneapolis: Minnesota University Press.

Durkheim, E. 1968. *Les Formes élémentaires de la vie religieuse: Le système totémique en Australie*, 5ième ed. Paris: Presses Universitaires de France.

EEF. 2016. *The 4th Industrial Revolution: A Primer for Manufacturers*. www.eef.org.uk/fourthindustrial (accessed March 2017).

Ferguson, J. 1990. *The AntiPolitics Machine: Development, Depoliticization and Bureaucratic Power in Lesotho*. Cambridge: Cambridge University Press.

Forde, E. 2016. 'Planning Regimes On and Off the Grid: Low-Impact Dwelling, Activism and the State in West Wales', Doctoral thesis, Goldsmiths College (University of London).

French, D. 2017. *When They Hid the Fire: A History of Electricity and Invisible Energy in America*. Pittsburgh: University of Pittsburgh Press.

Furlong, K. 2010. 'Small Technologies, Big Change: Rethinking Infrastructure through STS and Geography', *Progress in Human Geography*, 35(4): 460–82.

Golden, M. and B. Min. 2012. *Theft and Loss of Electricity in an Indian State*. International Growth Centre Working Paper 12/0060.

Gupta, N. 2015. 'An Anthropology of Electricity from the Global South', *Cultural Anthropology*, 30(4): 555–68.

Haraway, Donna. 1997. *Modest_Witness@Second_millennium. FemaleMan©Meets_OncoMouse™: Feminism and Technoscience*. New York: Routledge.

Harvey, P., C. B. Jensen and A. Morita. 2016. *Infrastructures and Social Complexity: A Companion*. London & New York, Routledge.

Hayles, K. 1999. *How We Became Posthuman*. Chicago, IL: University of Chicago Press.

Herbermann, J. D. and F. Fleck. 2017. 'Attacks Depriving People of Urgently Needed Health Care', *Bull World Health Organization*, 95: 6–7. doi: 10.2471/BLT.17.020117 (accessed 24 April 2017).

Holbraad, M. and M. A. Pedersen (2017). *The Ontological Turn: An Anthropological Exposition*. Cambridge: Cambridge University Press.

Jensen, C. B. 2010. *Ontologies for Developing Things: Making Health Care Futures Through Technology*. Rotterdam: Sense Publishers.

Law, J. (ed.). 1986. *Power Action and Belief. A New Sociology of Knowledge*. London: Routledge.

Law, J. and A. Mol. 2002. *Complexities: Social Studies of Knowledge Practices*. Durham, NC: Duke University Press.

Lebner, A. (ed.). 2017. *Conventions of Organisation and Ethnographic Redescription: The Draw of Strathernian Conversations*. London and New York: Berghahn.

Lévi-Strauss, C. 1962. *Totemism*. Boston, MA: Beacon Press.

Luque-Ayala, A. and J. Silver (eds). 2016. *Energy, Power and Protest on the Urban Grid: Geographies of the Electric City*. Abingdon and New York: Routledge.

Marres, N. 2014. 'The Environmental Teapot and Other Loaded Household Objects: Reconnecting the Politics of Technology, Issues and Things', in P. Harvey, E. Conlin Casella, Gi. Evans, H. Knox, C. McLean, E. B. Silva, N. Thoburn and K. Woodward (eds), *Objects and Materials: A Routledge Companion*. London and New York: Routledge.

Marvin, S., H. Chappells and S. Guy. 1999. 'Pathways of Smart Metering Development: Shaping Environmental Innovation', *Computers, Environment and Urban Systems*, 23: 109–26.

Miller, C. A., A. Iles and C. F. Jones. 2013. 'The Social Dimensions of Energy Transitions', *Science as Culture*, 22(2): 135–48.

Min, B. and M. Golden. 2014. 'Electoral Cycles in Electricity Losses in India', *Energy Policy*, 65: 619–25.

Mitchell, J. 1972. 'Electricity' [song] from the album *For the Roses*. Hollywood, California: A&M Studios.

Mol, A. 2014. 'Language Trails: "Lekker" and Its Pleasures', *Theory, Culture & Society*, 31(2–3): 93–119. doi: 10.1177/0263276413499190.

Möllers, N. and K. Zachmann (eds). 2012. *Past and Present Energy Societies: How Energy Connects Politics, Technologies and Cultures*. New Bielefeld: Transcript Verlag.

Nyborg, S. and I. Røpke. 2015. 'Heat Pumps in Denmark – From Ugly Duckling to White Swan', *Energy Research and Social Science*, 9(September): 166–77. doi:10.1016/j.erss.2015.08.021.

Nye, D. 1996. *American Technological Sublime*. Cambridge, MA and London: MIT Press.

Nye, D. 1999. *Consuming Power: A Social History of American Energies*. Cambridge, MA and London: MIT Press.

Pickering, A. 1992. *Science as Practice and Culture*. Chicago, IL: University of Chicago Press.

Pink, S. 2011. 'Ethnography of the Invisible', *Etnologia Europaea: Journal of European Ethnology*, 41(1): 117–28.

Rial, A. and G. Danezis. 2011. 'Privacy-Preserving Smart Metering', in *WPES'11*, Chicago, 17 October 2011.

Rupp, S. 2016. 'Circuits and Currents: Dynamics of Disruption in New York City Blackouts', *Economic Anthropology*, 3: 106–18.

Schick, L. and B. Winthereik. 2013. 'Innovating Relations – Or Why Smart Grid Is Not Too Complex for the Public', *Science & Technology Studies*, 26(3): 82–102.

Schiffer, M. B. 2005. 'The Electric Lighthouse in the Nineteenth Century', *Technology and Culture*, 46(2): 275.

Shamir, R. 2013. *Current Flow: The Electrification of Palestine*. Stanford, CA: Stanford University Press.

Shove, E. 2003. *Comfort, Cleanliness and Convenience: The Social Organization of Normality*. Oxford and New York: Berg.

Shove, E. and G. Walker. 2014. 'What Is Energy For? Social Practice and Energy Demand', *Theory Culture & Society*, 31(5): 41–58.

Sovacool, B. K. 2010. 'The Importance of Open and Closed Styles of Energy Research', *Social Studies of Science*, 40(6): 903–30.

Stengers, I. 1997. *Power and Invention: Situating Science*. Minneapolis: University of Minnesota Press.

Summerton, J. 2004. 'Do Electrons Have Politics? Constructing User Identities in Swedish Electricity', *Science, Technology & Human Values*, 29(4): 486–511.

Ulsrud, K., T. Winther, D. Palit and H. Rohracher. 2015. 'Village-Level Solar Power in Africa: Accelerating Access to Electricity Services through a Socio-Technical Design in Kenya', *Energy Research and Social Science*, 5: 34–44.

Wallenborn, G. and H. Wilhite. 2014. 'Rethinking Embodied Knowledge and Household Consumption', *Energy Research and Social Science*, 1: 56–64.

Ward, A. 2016. 'Regulator Warns That Guaranteed Electricity May Come at a Cost', *Financial Times*, 12 December.

Wilhite, H. 2008. 'New Thinking on the Agentive Relationship between End-Use Technologies and Energy-Using Practices', *Energy Efficiency*, 1: 121–30.

Wilhite, T. 2012. 'Electricity Theft as a Relational Issue: A Comparative Look at Zanzibar, Tanzania, and the Sunderban Islands, India', *Energy for Sustainable Development*, 16(1): 111–19. doi:10.1016/j.esd.2011.11.002.

Winther, T. 2010. *The Impact of Electricity: Development, Desires and Dilemmas*. London and New York: Berghahn.

Yarrow, T., M. Candea, C. Trundle and J. Cook (eds). 2015. *Detachment: Essays on the Limits of Relational Thinking*. Manchester: Manchester University Press.

2

Electricity is not a noun

Gretchen Bakke

O body swayed to music, O brightening glance,
How can we know the dancer from the dance?

W. B. Yeats[1]

Not a thing, stolen

It begins with a theft. 'Early in the process of Soviet electrification,' writes Arkady Markin, a Soviet himself and chronicler of this era, 'two men were arraigned for stealing energy. Though they freely admitted to tapping somebody else's electric mains, they were acquitted on the following pretext: "The nature of electricity is unknown," said the judge. "When talking of electric current people take the word 'current' conventionally. A theft, however, implies that some definite object must be stolen, such as storage batteries, or wires." In response, the defense attorney crowed, having just won his case: "The courts cannot establish the fact of theft! Indeed," he continued, "can a smell, or air, or sound be stolen?"' (Markin 1961, 7).

The same story, again differently

In 2016, a power systems engineer in California repeated to me an explanation he had given his wife for the difficulty in assuring 100 per cent renewable power on any large-scale electricity system (a difficulty not acknowledged by those electricity retailers, who promise to sell such purity to customers for a small additional surcharge). 'Stand in the middle of a field,' said this engineer to his wife. 'At the other end of the field are a number of men, each equipped with an identical bass drum. This one we'll call coal; this one – nuclear; this one – natural gas; that one – wind, a last – solar. Imagine, one man, coal, begins to beat his coal drum, *bang bang bang*; add the natural-gas drum, *bang bang bang*, the nuclear, and the others, all the others, until the air is resonant with the same beat at the same rhythm.' 'Now,' he said, 'try to only listen to the one called wind.' It is as impossible to hear a single drum amid the cacophony as to separate out and use a single-sourced electron stream on a contemporary electric grid. Grids are made stable – culturally, fiscally, physically – by means of a mix of diverse energy sources feeding them (and, though this is not part of his story, also by a mix of diverse draws upon them; one listener is not enough, for when she sleeps, who will listen in her stead?).

As this single story intimates, understanding electricity presents a number of serious conceptual problems. It is, simply put, very difficult to think. Weirdly, it is easier to make, work with and design for electricity than it is to know it. We had dynamos aplenty for producing an electric current thirty years before anyone could figure out what to use it for and half a century before the intimate structures of the atom were divined. Even today, one can go to school and learn the physics, the math, the formulas, the drawing of circuits, but even then a gap persists, between laymen and experts, between a wife and a husband, between the legislator and system regulated, between the consumer and the producer.

The Soviet judge does right by this misunderstanding, by letting the gap rest, deeming it unbridgeable and thus beyond his capacity to enforce the law upon it. Capitalists, more eager in their pursuit of mastery, have also struggled mightily with electricity's intractabilities – How does one count what is indivisible? How does one store instantaneity? How might one enslave the lethal? How does one extract profit from a force? We are now 140 years into the era of domesticated electricity, and none of these questions have been resolved in a satisfactory way. Convention coupled with monopoly merged with the staid manageability of 'stock resources' (things that when we use them, we use them up) has worked well enough, but the mass integration of renewable sources of power is ripping convention apart. How electricity is understood and misunderstood, thus, matters a great deal to how future systems that make it and manage it are imagined, designed and built out.

Thinking with things, for better or worse

In 1963, Claude Lévi-Strauss wrote, in a small volume (not about electricity) that 'natural species are chosen [as "totems"] not because they are "good to eat" but because they are "good to think" (Lévi-Strauss 1963, 89). It was a seemingly simple turn of phrase initially designed to refute functionalist approaches to 'primitive' social and religious practices that claimed the opposite: that animals became symbolically important because they *were* good to eat.[2]

However, by the 1950s, as Lévi-Strauss was framing his dismissal of the 'good to eat' school of social analysis, it was becoming clear: first that certain animals held great symbolic import to certain peoples despite being irritating and not particularly tasty (most notably the mosquito); and second that symbolic categorizations had more to do with the relational matrices that certain animals functioned within than with their literal qualities. Lévi-Strauss's interest was not in literal social function. Rather, he suspected that relations between animals were, for humans, primarily tools for thinking about *other* systems of relations. Their function was symbolic and culturally particular. So, for example, a suckling pig, or mosquito, or tortoise each stood within a system of natural relations with other species of animals, and these become etched, by dint of familiarity, into the minds of the people who live in intimate proximity with them.

Though Lévi-Strauss's proposition relating to categories of mind that become modally inflected categories of culture has had a long and fruitful afterlife within anthropology,[3] what has been most remarkable is the staying power of the phrase 'good to think with'. It might well be true that animals are good to think with but only about half as good to think with as the notion that 'things' of various sorts are good to think with. Thus do we have: women are good to think with; autochthony is good to think with; satyrs are good to think with; science is good to think with; Bourdieu is good to think with; glaciers are good to think with; genes are good to think with; disabled people are good to think with; the body is good to think with; and so is pantomime, and the apocalypse, and birds, and zombies, and community and so on and so on, pretty much ad infinitum. [These examples are taken from the first two pages of hits on a Google search for 'good to think with'].

What unites all these things good to think with is that they are all *things* – material objects in the world – or they can be treated, linguistically, as things. Thus, as the phrase itself has multiplied, what has become most clear is that more than any of the particular instances in which it has been used, the notion that 'things are good to think with' has itself proven very good to think with. And if, at the beginning, in Lévi-Strauss's baptismal use of the phrase, he was not arguing so much that animals were better to think with than, say, varieties of nut but rather that it was their 'being good to think with' rather than their 'being good to eat' that made them important to human society, this nuance has largely been lost with time. If animals are 'good to think with', and I agree that they are, it is now implied by the phrase that they are *better* to think with than with some other sort of thing. The examples above, thus, imply that women are better to think with than men; glaciers are better to think with than puddles of water; the undead are better to think with than the dead; and so on. Though this comparative is never made specific, it is always implied by both the structure of the phrase and the arguments that follow from it.

But what of the other things – things infelicitous to thought? And, I think it's worth also asking, what sorts of thought are they infelicitous to? We do have a partial list of things that are particularly difficult to think with, thanks to our Soviet defence attorney: smell, air, sound and electricity, all things which failed, in the early 1900s, to achieve a certain decided materiality. The atom had not yet been proven. Air and smell could not yet be thought of as particulate, sound's impact had not yet been thoroughly thinged into a 'wave', and no-one had any idea what electricity was; materiality, even metaphoric materiality, did not stick well to these non-things – non-things, not nothings. For if 'we know that a theft has occurred', what we do not know is what has been stolen. The fact that we can call that-which-was-stolen by a name, *electricity*, doesn't seem to help in the least. The name, in this case, is insufficient to 'thingize', or legally materialize, a non-thing.

It turns out that to transform things that are bad to think with into things that are good to think with, we need not so much *materiality* as *measure*. A whiff of roses on the wind. A 10-volt battery. A cubit foot of air. A pulse of sound. We need containers for unwieldy, infelicitous, bad-to-think-with things. Linguistically, this tends to mean that we need the genitive case, which is charged with both possession 'a whiff OF roses' and the partitive 'SOME tea'. The genitive allows a noun to modify another noun: 'a pound of flesh'. But who are we, who need the genitive case? Benjamin Lee Whorf, a fire inspector and amateur linguist from New England, gave us a name: *Standard Average Europeans*, or, the people for whom the genitive case appears to be not only good for thought, but essential to it.

Of containers and turns of phrase

In Lévi-Strauss's initial offering, social context was an explicit part of the story. All humans, he ventured (in a later work), hang their logical systems on scaffolding made from existing, locally salient fields of relationship (Lévi-Strauss 1966). But though the fact of the scaffolding may be universal, its shape is not. What I venture here is that one aspect of Lévi-Strauss's own scaffolding which also held, more or less constant for the French-speaking, English-speaking, German-speaking and Russian-speaking anthropologists who would follow in his footsteps, was precisely a proclivity to think with things rather than with non-things. The more material these things, and the more divisible, the better they were for thinking with. One might even suspect that the drive to understand immaterial and poorly divisible things *as* material and divisible – the search, for example, for the particulate nature of smell or the atomic nature of electricity – is part of what makes cultures akin to Lévi-Strauss's own so odd.

This argument is not, in fact, my own. In the 1920s, a generation before Lévi-Strauss began troubling over the relevance of tasty animals to human thought, Whorf posited that speakers of Standard Average European have a very well-developed bias for thinking with things. His argument was that this also serves as a sort of mental blindness. They are very poor at thinking otherwise and thus tend to either misunderstand non-things or do what is syntactically necessary to make things of them.

Whorf had a vested as well as an intellectual interest in sorting out culturally specific tendencies to misconstrue physical phenomena. As a part of his day job as a fire inspector, Whorf amassed hundreds of reports about the circumstances surrounding fires and explosions, many of which were the direct result of human error or, more precisely, human categorical misunderstanding. He wrote:

> In due course it became evident that not only a physical situation *qua* physics, but the meaning of that situation to people, was sometimes a factor, through the behavior of people, in the start of a fire. … Thus, around a storage of what are called 'gasoline drums', behavior will tend to a certain type, that is, great care will be exercised; while around a storage of what are called 'empty gasoline drums', it will tend to be different – careless, with little repression of smoking or tossing cigarette stubs about. (Whorf 1956, 135)

Whorf's New Englanders who accidentally caused fires by acting incautiously around things like limestone, or water, or lead, or 'empty gasoline drums' did so, according to Whorf, because they did not expect limestone or water or lead or 'empty' anything to burn. The place of linguistic categorization and the behaviour that followed from it in incendiary situations led Whorf the socio-linguist to an examination of categories of thought and the relationships to the material world that they begat. 'Limestone', 'water' and 'lead', like 'space', 'time', 'milk', 'sand', 'money', 'coal', 'butter', 'rain', 'meat', 'electricity' and 'gasoline', are all mass nouns in Standard Average European (a category of Whorf's own making that refers more or less to all Indo-European languages). The critical uniting characteristic of these languages for Whorf was their reliance on 'large subsumations of experience by language' (Whorf 1956, 138). In English, mass nouns are marked by the lack of a plural form, there are no milks, only cups *of* milk (or cartons of milk, or udders of milk; here you can see the genitive creeping in). This lack of a grammatical plural insinuates a 'homogenous continua without boundaries' (Whorf 1956, 140). Milk without limit; space without bounds. Electricity, however, is harder to containerize than is milk. In fact, resisting containment is one of the most definite qualities of electricity, not only (or even especially) linguistically; it can't be physically stored either.

The 'storage' we do have (and here I am switching from problems of language to problems of physics) is not of electricity exactly, but of electrically driven mechanical processes that can be reversed to *re*generate an electric current. The most common of these is pumped storage. When there is too much water in the reservoir of a hydroelectric dam, some of the electricity that that dam makes is used to pump excess water uphill, to a second reservoir, where it sits until additional power is needed; then this water is allowed to flow, with gravity, downhill again, passing through a set of turbines at the bottom which generate a 'new' electric current. Batteries, which look a lot like little electricity boxes, or fuel cells, which look like big electricity boxes, are not ever full of electricity. There is no electricity in there. Rather they are filled with layers of chemicals that produce an electric current under certain conditions. Flywheels, which store kinetic energy for about sixty seconds, are literally everywhere on contemporary electric grids. These are wound by an electric current and they then reproduce an electric current as they unwind. It's not the *same* electricity; the first is spent in the winding, and the second is made in the unwinding. In every case, it isn't electricity that is stored but electricity that is used to create a mechanical or chemical capacity to produce electricity later.

So while there are lots of ways to imagine and speak about different sorts of containers for milk, just as there are main ways to actually contain milk, there is arguably no way to use the genitive – noun-modifying noun means – to talk about electricity. Something leaks over from the physical problems of storing electricity into linguistic means for talking about it. Technically, we can say, 'a kilowatt hour of electricity', but we don't. We say simply, a kilowatt-hour, or a volt or a charge. The unit of measure stands alone. Nor do we use the partitive form of the genitive case and say 'some electricity', as in 'hey man, I need some electricity to charge my phone'. No, we simply charge the battery; the 'charge' is equal to the capacity of the battery to hold it. In the case of electricity, the container utterly trumps its contents. This is in part because there are no contents; there is no electricity in a battery, just as there is no electricity in the reservoir behind a hydroelectric dam. This nowhereness (which might also be thought of as 'immediacy' or newness) causes electricity, as an abiding physical substance, to fade further from conceptual grasp.

A case in point

If anything *is* a box for electricity, it's the electric grid itself. The grid, as mechanism for making, transiting and using electricity, is too vast and rangy to look like a box, and it seems to be comprised of too many objects to count as an object itself, and it fails the test of portability that a 'box' hints at, but at least it is *full* of electricity.[4] This, then, is where things grow strange, and terminology begins to feel like a trip through the funhouse mirror. Despite the fact that the grid has come to stand in metaphorically – as a network – for infrastructural imaginings as a general category of thought, because electricity is so unlike the other things in our world, the grid hardly works like other infrastructures.

According to anthropologist Brian Larkin, an infrastructure is an 'architecture of circulation', built to 'facilitate the flow of goods, people, or ideas and allow for their exchange' (Larkin 2013, 328). In this way, well-designed, well-kept roads allow cars to flow efficiently through the densest of cities and across the least hospitable of natural terrains. Well-made pipelines move oil with liquid efficiency from the wilds of extraction to the refinery. Train lines bring coal to power plants. Libraries circulate books. The whole story of infrastructure would seem to be of a thing that doesn't move, in order that other things might speed summarily along.

At first glance, the electric grid does seem to work like this too, except for the fact that there are no 'other things'. Roads have cars, libraries have books, pipelines have oil – two terms, two nouns put into relationship to each other with an infrastructural logic of facilitation. Convention, not grammar, holds one still and moves the other. One can, thus, interact with a car or with a road, with a car not on a road and with a road devoid of cars. One can interact with a pipeline and, in tapping it, also interact with the crude pouring out of it into a bucket.[5] One can take a book from a library and never give it back. As with a 'box of rocks', with infrastructure, there are two separate and separable things in play, the infrastructure which doesn't move and the 'goods, people or ideas' it was designed to set into fluid motion. With an electric grid, however, there is nothing to separate out. It isn't a thing of wires (*qua* conduits) transiting electricity in a magical golden stream from power plant to lightbulb. The two are, rather, one and the same: the wires, the electromagnetic force; same, same.

Imagine a carefully placed row of dominoes; tip the first with your index finger, watch them fall. The force that fells each in turn is not separate, nor separable, from the dominoes. Without the tipping of one into the next, there is no falling line; and without the dominoes correctly placed, there is no push to be measured. The dominoes and the act of falling/pushing-the-next are the same. This is similar to how an electron stream works. A generator rips electrons from atoms; those electrons bump into the next nearest atom. In nestling up to that atom, they push some of its electrons away; these bump along to the next atom and do the same, and with the next the same, and the same, and the same all the way around the great loop of the grid. Electricity is this bumping along, this displacement of electrons by other electrons. Some substances, metals most especially, make this process of displacement easier, and these are what we tend to build conductors (wires) out of. Take away the conductive material, and the electricity isn't there.[6]

The first trouble, then, is realizing that electricity is coexistent with and inseparable from its infrastructure. Whatever form a grid takes, whatever its scale, whatever future technologies we dream up for it, however full of electricity it is, it will never be a 'container' for that electricity. This is no more possible than dreaming up a fancy box into which gravity might be poured and stored. Despite this, if history is any guide, there will be a solid tendency to figure electrical systems and components *as if* they were objects, as if they too were the sorts of infrastructures that might push the genitive into the world, materializing it and giving it form, just as cartons of milk make the genitive a real, tactile and memorable part of everyday life;[7] just as pipelines and parking lots grind grammar into landscape, disrupting migrating reindeer and peregrinating persons respectively. This mode of building electrical systems that feel like the genitive (what difference really, between a pipeline and a power cable, between a tub of yogurt and a battery?) attempts to materialize an accord between a system of things and electromagnetism – which follows none of the same rules nor any of the same physical laws. One result is, as one might expect, that misunderstandings and weird preferences proliferate and are built out, legislated or funded. To my mind, this is part of the grid's charm; it holds social desires, many of which are grounded in the wrong logic, in its form. These desires produce iterative breakdowns, as common-sensical wants for electricity systems and the functioning of these systems fail consistently to align. The grid is a misunderstanding machine; a machine that 'works in practice, but not in theory' (Alexandra von Meier, Personal Conversation, 2010).

Being in time

What is electricity then, if not a noun? If not a verb? If not thing, and yet in possession of an abiding material substance, with its own physical rules and its own infrastructural logics? If not a Deleuzian becoming? If not precisely a tool, with its killing capacity? If it is a being at all, it is a being in time. Electricity is now. The trouble then, is not just thinking in time, or thinking without a sense of that-which-purdures, can be stored, manipulated or stolen, but in designing an electricity system that takes these difficult-to-think-with features of electricity as the centre point of innovation. It happened once before, in the 1890s. When Samuel Insull, an early utility man in Chicago, learned to see the clock, he understood electricity in time and from this built up the grid as a monopoly enterprise, a big thing into which all the customers within a given geography were folded, not because of economies of scale but because of economies of temporal ordering. His customers mattered because of *when* they used power, not because of how much of they used. This model, once devised, became the standard operating procedure in every country attempting universal electrification.

Understanding the importance of the temporal grounds for electricity networks requires a quick dip back into physics and twentieth-century solutions to the intractability of electric power. Because electricity doesn't properly exist in space, a business aiming to make money of it must take one of two routes: it must sell *not* electricity but grids, or bits of grids (things), or it must manage temporal rather than spatial orders.[8] This has been true from the start.[9] Even Thomas Edison, who was quite savvy in turning the electric grid and its various components (lightbulbs, electric sockets, dynamos, wires, etc.) into marketable products, faded into ignominy in the mid-1890s precisely because he misunderstood the nature of electricity *as a product*. As he built the necessary infrastructure to make electricity a viable competitor on the home and office lighting market, what he saw was not its instantaneousness but a (mistaken) materiality akin to that of gas – a substance governed by the laws of fluid dynamics rather than those of electromagnetism. Historian Maury Klein explains that

> [Edison's] error [was] in using the gas industry as a model. Gas could be stored, which made it possible to produce on an orderly rational basis like other manufactured products. It could maintain reserves to meet peak requirements and level out demand over a twenty-four hour period. Not so electricity. It had

to be produced, sold, delivered, and used all at once, which meant that the plant supplying it needed the capacity to deliver the total maximum load demanded by customers at any given moment. (2010, 403)

In other words, the immediacy of electricity – that it could be no more stored in Edison's days than our own – meant that all the conventions of production and delivery well-known to markets, businessmen and capitalists in the late 1800s did not apply to the electricity business, and even Edison, who was both wily and brutally intelligent, didn't grasp this in productizing his force. As a result, despite popular perception, Edison's grid did *not* become the norm in North America; rather, the electricity system in use today is a mix of the alternating current grid developed by Nikola Tesla and brought to market by George Westinghouse in the late 1880s and a business model developed by Samuel Insull in Chicago in early 1900s.[10] Without Insull, who was unique in his understanding of the exigencies of electricity as a lethal, un-storable, intensely immediate, non-liquid non-thing and who structured a business around these constraints, the United States would have had elite light (the system Edison's grid was best suited to) in the form of private plants for wealthy customers, and industrial power for building and moving things, for much longer than it did.[11]

Insull's gift was the capacity to see time. His was not an immediate wisdom but developed over the course of decades of wrangling with the weird economics of an industry with an unstockpileable product. When, in 1892, Insull (a Brit by birth, and for years Thomas Edison's personal secretary) took over the management of Chicago Edison, it had much in common with electric companies sprouting up in urban America; it had, in Chicago's case, a single DC power plant (which could transmit power for about a mile) located in Loop, the densest part of the city.[12] This plant produced power at a single voltage – about 110 volts, or enough to run then state-of-the-art lighting – which was sold to businesses with large numbers of white-collar workers.

What this meant, practically speaking, was that Chicago Edison's 5,000 or so customers (in 1892) only used, and paid for, all the power the plant could make during the early evenings. When dusk settled over the city, every front-office clerk and every corner-office executive alike found themselves in need of artificial illumination. The demand for electricity then dropped off precipitously as offices closed up for the night and the last of the city's workers stepped aboard L trains bound for the suburbs, where they read by gaslight and ate food cooked with a gas flame. At night, in the Loop, when no one was at work; in the mornings; and for most of the day (most especially during the summer), Chicago Edison's sole power plant, fully capable of supplying its 3,200 kilowatts all the time, sat idle or was massively underutilized. As Insull once famously said: 'If your entire plant is only in use 5.5 percent of the time, it is only a question of when you will be in the hands of a receiver'. He needed a way to sell power the rest of the day, or his company would founder.

The problem was that the business strategy used by all the Edison franchises at that point to stay afloat was to sell, install and provide maintenance for private plants – tiny, privately owned grids. They had opted for the route of selling a thing, in this case, electric grids. While this was a wise tactic for maintaining solvency over the short term, over the long term, the multiplication of private plants further diminished the customer base for central-station power. When Insull first arrived in Chicago, the Loop was home to eighteen central-station electricity providers (including the Edison franchise he was to manage), plus another five hundred private plants (2010, 401).

These private plants, however, were in a critical way as limited as Insull's grid. Chicago's manufactories, for example, produced and used power during the day, turning their generators off at night; private plants in apartment buildings and luxury residences usually sprang into use in the evenings just as the bulb system in the business district was being shut down; streetlights – often municipally owned – only burned at night; and streetcars ran most intensively at dawn and dusk. Everybody was using their fairly expensive, almost identical infrastructure only part of the time because it was as cheap to produce their own power as it was to buy it from any centralized source.

What Insull wanted and strove to build was an infrastructure that would be the inverse of what he was saddled with. Instead of many little generating stations, with many owners, running intermittently, he wanted one that he owned and which ran all the time. In order to do this, he needed to acquire 'load' for each time period during the day.[13] He needed streetcar companies to buy from him at dusk and dawn, residential customers for the late evenings and early nights, municipal street lights for night-time, businesses for the late afternoons and early evenings and, most important of all, industry for midday. He wanted to make a lot more power, make it round the clock and to sell it all – every last watt.[14]

While it is easiest to see Insull as a narrow-minded monopolist (his empire would collapse in 1929, with Insull himself fleeing the country to escape corruption charges), I want to recuperate him here as something else. Insull built a monopoly out of electricity by securing control over the sole provision of a good in a particular territory; in this way, his activities were little different from those of the classic monopolies of his time: US Steel or Standard Oil. What set him apart was that he understood that, in order to do this *with electricity*, he would need to control a market that was primarily temporal in character. The hours of the day were the tranches of adversity. He did not see people or use or even land; he saw the need to engineer a constant consumption across a diurnal cycle. He needed a monopoly in order to capture twenty-four hours' worth of load.

This structure of monopolization of a temporally diverse customer base worked well in the United States until the early 1970s, when for technical and cultural reasons, the price of electricity began to rise and consumption to drop. Less than a decade later, in 1978, a piece of legislation called the National Energy Act made a tiny crack in the monopoly system that has, with time, computerization and further legislation, resulted in the dismantling of the utilities' control over the production of power. They have come apart. And as they shatter into bits (one can see it in every private wind farm and every home solar system), the structure Insull built up, which found profit in the control of consumption *in time*, has also been slowly dismantled without a wise replacement. Instead we've started to treat electrcity as a thing again, until today in the United States, it is treated in much the same way as gas, or coal or a box of bananas – able to enter market relationships designed for the sort of supply and demand comfortable from other commodity relations. The current moment is in this way utterly retrograde, with the genitive recolonizing discussions about electricity and renewably powered futures. The primary form this desire takes is the battery. As a thing, a battery would seem to catch a hold of electricity, objectivizing it and making it 'good to think with'.

Unwieldy

In the autumn of 2016, I had lunch with a small team of men in the unspectacular business of building high-voltage direct current power lines (HVDC). They are an upstart, a private company with ten employees who have decided to work around the utilities; they look for the cracks and seams in the existing power delivery system and aim to build these out. Right now, one big seam is the United States–Canada border and a giant resource that hovers just out of sight to most Americans above that line, the massive hydroelectric dams at James Bay in Northern Quebec. The goal of this company is relatively simple; they'd like to balance wind power with hydroelectric power wherever it is possible in order to create HVDC pipelines of renewable energy, one line at a time. Since electricity, with care, can be made to travel long distances with relatively little loss, 'near at hand' can be several thousand miles away, making the problem with Canadian hydro not the nine hundred miles that separate it from the wind farms of upstate New York, but the hardened politics of an international border.

The political–economic machinations of building a high-voltage power line are literally beyond my imagination. Hundreds of thousands of dollars slip like water from a leaky pipe into local economies; every wire requires substations, happy townsfolk and environmental and governmental stamps of approval as it runs through states, across borders, under bodies of water. Each takes years to negotiate and build, and all the capital is upfront. Investors have to sign on to things that a single town can slow or cause to grind to a halt. There are a lot of meetings at the beginning of every wire – years' worth of meetings. This lunch is one of them.

In a pause, between discussions of the desired wire, we are talking about cultural differences in R&D (research and development): Canada is very heavy on the D to the frustration of many of its scientists. The Massachusetts Institute of Technology (MIT), to no one's surprise, is exhibiting an extraordinary bias for the R. The CEO of this wire company launches into a story: the day before, he'd been at MIT talking to students about the future of grid technology, or rather they had mostly been talking to him – about batteries. Bigger, smaller, flow, anode-free, new chemistry here (cheaper), new chemistry there (longer-lasting), new chemistry everywhere. The promise, the research, the excitement was battery-promise, battery-research, battery-excitement. He shakes his head; so many bright minds all on one path. It's not that it's the wrong path so much as that its popularity exhibits the sort of bias that Whorf would have found unsurprising. These young researchers are trying to find a way to thingize electricity, in fact, and at a scale worth appreciating. They are trying to make it into something that *can be* stolen, or bought, or shipped, or traded or thought. Every way in which electricity defies easy categorization is soothed by batteries; they are exceptionally good to think with.

The line-builders, the men at the table, are trying to do something else. Hence the shaking of heads at the single-(battery)mindedness of the brightest, best-funded of youthful researchers. Building a line that allows for a marriage of wind power, which is variably produced, with hydroelectric power, which is not, involves thinking with electricity rather than trying to objectify it as means of getting it to behave like other things that are easy to think with. Premising grid reform on better battery technology, or (as Bill Gates dreams) on 'liquid solar', involves first converting it, in mind and, in fact, into a thing – an object, a liquid even – so that it might be managed within regimes of thought and structures of business comfortable for object-oriented institutions. This inevitably cuts much of electricity's native potential out from the new systems we are designing to utilize it. The history of electricity is littered with this precise battle between working with electricity's obduracy or pretending it is something it is not, and then working with pretence.

It's not that Insull has been forgotten; it's that given that grid reform is happening everywhere that has privatized generation and proclaimed high renewable-energy goals, there are two main routes into thinking grid reform. One privileges the box – a mode of conceptualizing electricity that relies strongly on the desire for electricity as a noun, a thing to be commanded and controlled and a hoped-for route of invention that will make electricity an orderable substance that it has never been. The other aims to build a stable, reliable infrastructure that takes the instantaneity of electricity as the starting point. This route does not attempt to hold power and make it work our way, but rather to let it go, to take electricity seriously in its own right. What this lunchtime conversation reveals is that both will likely be components of a twenty-first-century grid that relies on renewables like wind and solar. One, however, the one that makes electricity function like a noun, is generating a lot more excitement and attracting a lot more capital, making it all too easy to overlook that the conceptually more difficult route is both more innovative and holds more promise for a system's reform that feels like a good fit for the future.

It is not, then, simply that things are good to think with (à la Lévi-Strauss), but that we SAE folks prefer using things in order to think, to the degree that we make things out of non-things all the time. Indeed, according to Whorf, this is one of the primary things that we do with language, and then we forget that we have done it, treating these linguistic constructs as inalienable objects in the world with noun-like capacities to hold logical descriptors to them: a puddle of water, a gust of wind, a summer day, a 10-volt battery.

Be all of this as it may, there remains the problem that even if we think electricity *as if* it is a thing – a delimited material object in the world – it doesn't care. It continues to behave in most un-thing-like of ways. It is as immodestly indifferent to our metaphorizing modes of thought as it is to our laws or profit seeking. If however, we set aside the battery and its ilk for a minute, other solutions are forced to the fore. Or, as a young engineer in that same line company said (several weeks later) as he waved his hand dismissively in the direction of the future: 'Maybe in 25 years *they* will solve that storage problem.' His meaning was that that would be awesome, fantastic, game changing, but for now, as for the past 130 years (or the entire history of domesticated electricity), we'd best work with what we've got. Rather than premising systems design or business models on something that doesn't exist but feels good to the mind, it would be better to work with on the exigencies on the table. First among these is finding a way to get stock resources (coal, natural gas, oil, uranium) out of our electricity system without allowing that system, and the markets that make it, to tumble into ruin.

Notes

1 W. B. Yeats. 1961. 'Among School Children' from *The Poems of W. B. Yeats: A New Edition*, edited by Richard J. Finneran. Copyright 1933 by Macmillan Publishing Company, renewed © 1961 by Georgie Yeats. Reprinted with the permission of A. P. Watt, Ltd. on behalf of Michael Yeats. Source: *The Collected Poems of W. B. Yeats* (1989): 215.

2 See Lévi-Strauss (1963). See also the 'Totems – The Structural Study of Totemism' at http://science.jrank.org/pages/11480/Totems-Structural-Study-Totemism.html (accessed October 2014).

3 See, most notably, Mary Douglas' work on animals that stand between categories and by virtue of this fact alone become *not* good to eat, or 'unclean' (Douglas 1966) – for example, shrimp, which live in the sea but fail to have scales and fins and thus are not really fish; or pigs, which chew their cud (like cows) and yet have cloven hooves (like deer). How things fail to fit, and how these failures are made to matter symbolically, are worthy of consideration, as they reveal a great deal about the structures and values of a given culture. Douglas' point, which has become, increasingly, anthropology's point, broadened Lévi-Strauss's initial contribution. Animals are still good to think with, but this adheres as much to the ways in which relational matrices *fail* to be totalizing as it does to the actual systems of relationship these might describe (as between sorts of fish, for example, or between sorts ruminants).

4 There are teeny-tiny grids in use by the US military that involve flexible solar panels that roll out on a marching soldier's shoulders and, for example, wires that connect these to all the batteries that the solder carries. It still doesn't have the 'feel' of storage because power is being made by this system by means of an external fuel source (the sun).

5 See Woody (2016).

6 The exception, of course, is wild power, lightning, which proves that under extreme enough circumstances, almost anything can function as a conductor, but this is situation is not 'infrastructural'; it is what the infrastructure is designed to avoid.

7 Not just milk, but the tendency to manufacture containers (i.e. packaging) for many things that don't need it in order that the things themselves become 'contents' would

seem an additional interesting route of investigation into the ways in which grammatical biases and the made-world interact, with landfills full of the genitive for proof.

8   Rhythm is a management problem in all supply chains: getting the raw materials and labour force into place to make and move things to market at the right moment for consumption. *Making* electricity from fossil fuels is as subject to rhythmic disruptions, as is making any other product. Indeed, there are a surprising number of blackouts in the United States every year caused by jams on rail lines used to move coal to power plants. Once made, however, electricity is not subject to these sorts of interruptions or the machinations necessary to avoid them, the do-si-do of contemporary global commodity markets. From the user's point of view, electricity is binary, either there or gone; the light is on or it is off. This is an illusion based upon the instantaneousness of the link between production and use.

9   For a vastly expanded version of this argument, see Bakke (2016, 57–84).

10 All national grids, including the Soviet one, ran into the same issues solved in the United States by the combination of alternating current and a new sort of consolidation of markets around the clock, rather than over a certain geography. In many, but not all, cases, the Insull model was an important precursor to this understanding.

11 European grids developed differently (see Hughes 1983), but with time they too evolved into monopoly systems for large populations of temporally diverse customers. The difference is that as the monopoly system has been slowly dismantled in America since the late 1970s, in Europe it is has maintained; thus transitions towards renewables in the United States involve a lot more people trying to make a boxable product out of electricity, whereas in Europe, fewer people, at the tops of massive hierarchies are governing this process.

12 3,200-kilowatt DC power plant on West Adams Street, built in 1888.

13 Diversity here takes on a temporal twist; race, economic standing, gender – none of these matters for their its own sake to the governance of grids. They do matter, however, for their temporal qualities. If, for example, women are home during the day rather than integrated into the work force, they are able to alter the accounting necessary for both profit making and good grid governance.

14 It is worth noting that even this ideal cocktail of customers and times of day fails to provide significant night-time load. This remains a problem for our utilities today. Even taking into account public street lighting, electricity use drops off precipitously as people start to go to bed and only starts to creep upward again around 6 a.m. One of the reasons that electric cars have received such public praise is that they can be programmed to charge almost exclusively at night and thus provide that rarest of beasts – substantial midnight load. Insull, of course, gets no credit for the cars, but we can thank him for zealously promoting a rate structure that rewards night-time electricity use and for zealously promoting, including not only a rate structure that rewards night-time electricity use, but also home refrigerators and

hot-water heaters which, until the rise of the conservation movement in the 1970s, were phenomenally hungry appliances and even today remain – along with air-conditioning – the most electrically intensive items in a home (see Bakke 2016).

References

Bakke, Gretchen. 2016. *The Grid: The Fraying Wires between Americans and Our Energy Future*. New York: Bloomsbury.

Douglas, Mary. 1966. *Purity and Danger: An Analysis of Concepts of Pollution and Taboo*. London: Routledge.

Hughes, Thomas P. 1983. *Networks of Power: Electrification in Western Society*. Baltimore, MD: Johns Hopkins University Press.

Klein, Maury. 2010. *The Power Makers: Steam, Electricity, and the Men Who Invented Modern America*. New York: Bloomsbury.

Larkin, Brian. 2013. 'The Politics and Poetics of Infrastructure', *Annual Review of Anthropology*, 42(October): 327–43.

Lévi-Strauss, Claude. 1963. *Totemism*. Boston, MA: Beacon Press.

Lévi-Strauss, Claude. [1962] 1966. *The Savage Mind*. Chicago, IL: University of Chicago Press.

Markin, Arkady. 1961. *Power Galore: Soviet Power Industry, Past, Present, Future*. Translator Arthur Shkarovsky, publication of Translation 1961 (original date of publication unknown). Moscow: Progress Publishers.

Whorf, Benjamin Lee. 1956. 'The Relation of Habitual Thought and Behavior to Language', originally published in Leslie Spier (ed.), *Language, Culture and Personality: Essays in Memory of Edward Sapir*, 1941, reprinted in 1956, 134–59. Cambridge, MA: MIT Press.

Woody, Christopher. 2016. 'Drug Cartels Have Been Stealing Huge Amounts of One of Mexico's Biggest Revenue Sources', *Business Insider*, published online, 12 May. http://www.businessinsider.com/mexico-oil-theft-from-pipelines (accessed 5 February 2019).

Yeats, W. B. [1933] 1961. 'Among School Children', in Richard J. Finneran (ed.), *The Poems of W. B. Yeats: A New Edition*, 215. New York: Macmillan.

3

Widened reason and deepened optimism: Electricity and morality in Durkheim's anthropology and our own

Leo Coleman

Electricity appears, at first thought, to be both a novel and an intensely contemporary object of anthropological theorizing. But electricity provided nineteenth-century scholars of religion, including William Robertson Smith, William James and Émile Durkheim, with a scientific, positive vocabulary they could use to understand the force and reality of mystical experiences and 'strange' religious beliefs, which were just then perplexing anthropologists as much as the physics of electromagnetism was problematic for their scientific colleagues. Briefly put, scholars and spiritualists alike in the late nineteenth century made comparisons between divine powers or spiritual forces and electricity. Durkheim refined this comparison as he built a science of social forces, drawing on his own and his associates' readings of non-Western ethnographic material to assert a sociological connection between *ideas* of force (whether 'primitive' and religious or modern and scientific) and an underlying and more fundamental reality of social organization (founding the sociology of knowledge, in the process). Non-Western conceptions of moral power and magical efficacy, pre-eminently as expressed through the Oceanic term 'mana', provided an important model for Durkheim's grounding of theoretical ideas of force in experiences of a social order, and mana was itself often directly analogized to invisible and all-pervasive electricity, as the imagined force behind 'magical' feats.

This all lies, of course, deep in the history of anthropology. By the middle of the twentieth century, Robert Redfield could swiftly dismiss the idea that mana was some kind of 'spiritual electric' as outmoded and frankly ridiculous (1948, viii). Decades later, Rodney Needham characterized such comparisons, drawn from 'the experience of technological civilization', as nothing more than mistranslations of indigenous concepts (Needham 1976, 82). More recently, however, Oceanist and Indianist ethnographers (as I will discuss) have found in Durkheim's glosses of missionary ethnography and colonial observations a remarkable set of insights into general processes of 'ethical mediation' between persons and things, insights that provide a useful framework for understanding even contemporary ethnographic encounters with forces that are at once moral and material, simultaneously affecting our bodies and forming our connections to others.

To be sure, Durkheim's account of social force as a reality equal to physical forces like electricity drew on the technological terms of his nineteenth-century 'discourse network'. However, I turn to these scholarly episodes not out of historical motives alone, but also in order to explore how concepts of social force and *conscience collective*, developed through anthropological comparisons between electricity and religion, may still afford insights into contemporary energy infrastructures.[1] In short, I want to run the 'electrical analogy' between physical and moral concepts the other way and see what it produces now.

More narrowly, I return to the Durkheimian anthropology of social forces to better understand an aspect of energy infrastructures that I think has been underemphasized (as a matter of theoretical reflection) in the rich and ever-growing literature on their material, dynamic and indeed subject-forming powers (see Jensen, this volume). This is their central role in sustaining *human* collectives (if not always self-conscious ones), serving people – including anthropologists – as sites and objects for the elaboration and institution of collective or commonly held ideals and ideas about the world and about the beings and forces that populate it. Infrastructures are not only 'more-than-human' realities or besetting architectures of alienating power, but also often directly at issue when people come to ask how some collective 'we' does and should live in the world, shaping occasions for specific articulations of collective need and common interest. Public infrastructures depend upon judgements about what a given community shares – how it shares in and shares out common goods (see Anand 2017; Rogers 2015).

As Penny Harvey and Hannah Knox have suggested in their ethnography of road construction and the politics of uneven development in Latin America, ideals and values are not simply added to material infrastructures through some ideological imposition. Collective needs emerge and become real in socially dense encounters with material architectures, but also in reciprocal demands for the common goods that are associated with them – goods that legitimate their costs and burdensome installation in the first place, but that are frequently *not* realized through the construction or provision of infrastructures alone (Harvey and Knox 2015; cf. Harvey and Knox 2012). However, in their own and others' recent emphatic turn to study the materiality of infrastructures, and in particular with the current ethnographic emphasis on the hidden and technical 'operational processes' that form infrastructures (Harvey, Jensen and Morita 2017, 4), we have perhaps lost sight of the wide range of 'political and moral investments [that] people make in technical forms' (Jensen and Morita 2015, 85). This is a common consequence of paradigm shifts, of course – novel relations and even whole new entities are brought into view, while other and still-active associations fade from analytic attention. In ways that are challenging for these contemporary turns, for Durkheim, social ties were most real, most effective, in their conceptual and formal elaboration rather than in their material or bodily concretion, leading him to ask how, in the flux of social life, people sense, grasp and rework the 'force congealed in the techniques we use' (Durkheim 1995, 214). In its moral orientation, this is not a question that can be answered only by an expert account of the operational processes that make a given technique effective for a particular end.

I come to these problems from my own longitudinal study of electrification as a legal, political and material topic of concern in New Delhi across the twentieth century (Coleman 2017). Over the past century, moral and political questions of the good or evil that electrification might bring, and how it would act to reform or damage collective life, have frequently been posed by citizens and politicians in India's capital city. My research in the history of electrification in India thus provoked ethnographic questions about the dynamic relation between material infrastructures and collective languages of legality, legitimacy and rights. In this chapter, however, I will focus on the theoretical and anthropological issues that disciplinary comparisons of electrical and moral forces have raised, rather than the pressing moral – and ecological – ones presented by the current politics of urban technological systems (see Kirshner and Power, this volume).

Automatic reactions

Infrastructures and communications networks (conveying material energies along with information, and provoking expectations and imaginations) have recently been defined anthropologically as being comprised of 'things and also the relations between things' (Larkin 2013, 329) – relations which may be legal, or informational or poetic. On these terms, infrastructures may be said to entangle entities 'that we might be inclined to view as "natural," "social," and "spiritual"' (Jensen 2015, 25) and to obviate any such *a priori* distinctions between them. This latter move allows the tracing of emergent ontologies and further enables us 'to rethink all-too-human histories of power and enablement' (Boyer 2015, 532).

However, as ethnographers have long observed, infrastructures also provoke judgements from people nearby, animating concerns about the forms of life and the proliferating relations fostered by their concrete existence and the energies or messages they convey. For instance, to take a classic example of anthropological attention to such things, Lévi-Strauss tells us that Indians in the Mato Grosso of Brazil 'mistook' the buzzing of a telegraph line for the noise of wild bees at work and brought down the poles in search of honey, interrupting communications between settlers in their territory. He goes on, however, to flesh out this reported association. Through their interpretation of the buzzing of these energized lines, he implies, the Indians rightly associated this infrastructure with the never-benign intentions of settlers and missionaries. The latter, in their turn, used the telegraph to share news, mitigate their isolation and share fearful fantasies of vulnerability to the attacks of 'wild' Indians. Meanwhile, for the anthropologist, the dilapidation of the 'line' signified the futility of technological civilization and paradoxically heightened the ruined nature all about it – 'surprisingly enough the line adds to rather than detracts from the surrounding desolation' (Lévi-Strauss 1992, 272). One technological object was the singular vehicle for diverse thoughts about natural fecundity, human difference and moral evil. Through such judgements – and the arguments and assessments they might provoke – social fields are generated that pulse with strange powers not to be accounted for by a catalogue of actors and entities alone; infrastructures incite magical and metaphorical understandings, projecting what we naively take to be material facts into spectral realms of imagination in 'irreducibly indeterminate' ways (Sneath, Holbraad and Petersen 2009, 6).

Such multiply interpreted encounters with electrical infrastructures and devices were, further back in the history of anthropology, an important part of the context in which modern anthropological thought developed. In the later nineteenth century, there was a constant 'signals traffic' between religion, natural science and the burgeoning human or 'moral' sciences, including anthropology. At the same time as science plumbed the mysteries of nature and technology harnessed seemingly fundamental forces, this also provoked new revelations and shaped what William James called, at the time, the 'contemporary vagaries' of religious experience (1917, 108) – by way of illustration, James cited one divine who exhorted his flock to 'attach the belts of our machinery to the powerhouse of the universe' (James 1917, 101).[2] Such analogies between mechanical and divine energy were not mere outbursts of enthusiasm, however. They had a scholarly pedigree in biblical criticism, which we can trace back to a novel scientific materialism and then forward again through their transformation into sociological concepts.

A decade before James delivered the lectures on which he based the *Variety of the Religious Experience* in Edinburgh (in 1901–2), the philologist William Robertson Smith had lectured in Aberdeen on ancient 'Semitic' religious rites, pursuing a then-scandalous historical and material accounting for fundamental religious phenomena. In addition to providing a historical and philological basis for biblical stories, Smith worked out a schema of evolutionary development in religious ideas. Smith sought to demonstrate how, in the evolution of human thought about natural forces, a spring became a shrine and ultimately a source of eternal life. To kick off his evolutionary schema, Smith explained the holiness of archaic sanctuaries and the operation of the sacred in the world as grasped by 'primitive' thought, as something essentially thoughtless, automatic, or mechanical: 'The mysterious superhuman powers of the god – the powers which we call supernatural – are manifested, according to primitive ideas, in and through his physical life, so that every place and thing which has natural association with the god is regarded, if I may borrow a metaphor from electricity, as charged with divine energy and ready at any moment to discharge itself to the destruction of the man who presumes to approach it unduly' (Smith 1972, 151).

Smith came by this electrical metaphor honestly, we might say – or at least sociologically. He was plugged in to the intellectual and scientific world of Edinburgh and Cambridge, in which experimentation and theorization on electrical phenomena was among the most prestigious of scientific endeavours. As an editor of the celebrated ninth edition of the *Encyclopædia Britannica*, he solicited articles on electrical forces from James Clerk Maxwell, the originator of the modern mathematical description of electricity (and, not incidentally, of a famous 'daemonic' thought experiment about entropy). Smith was also an intimate of James Frazer, from whom he solicited the famous pair of articles on totem and taboo for the same edition of the encyclopaedia – articles which do not, however, repeat the electrical analogy that Smith used.

This is too narrow a sociological frame, however, through which to assess the importance of Smith's passing analogy between religion and physics. Throughout Europe in this period, the already remarkable fruits of the new physical sciences, based on experimentation, manipulation of electrical forces and chemical bonds and precise measurement of physical reactions, promised a deeper understanding of humans as beings constituted of matter – an understanding that Smith, in his account of 'primitive' materialism, simply placed at the roots of human religious evolution. The 'discourse network' of the time period (to build on literary critic Friedrich Kittler's analysis) impelled investigations into the mysteries of selfhood and human subjectivity through the exploration of material processes, automatic recording, physical impulsions and synesthetic crossings between the senses (which revealed the shared physical basis and bodily location of all sensation and perception) (Kittler 1990, 206–336). Such researches dethroned metaphysical spirits, divine purpose and 'soul' from explanations of subjectivity and history alike. In human biology, this network can be traced back at least to Helmholtz's experiments on the speed of electrical impulses in nerve fibres, which spawned burgeoning fields, like psychophysics, that used new technical devices to produce precise measurements of mental and psychological phenomena (Schmidgen 2002). Indeed, psychophysics was adopted as a prime example of a new unified, positive science by the natural philosopher Ernst Mach, on whose philosophy Malinowski would later write a doctoral dissertation – laying the foundation for anthropology's own brand of materialism and functionalism (Young 2005, 83).

Energy, vital forces and automatic communication, whether discovered in frogs or postulated as the primitive human condition, seemed thus to promise a new unification of the natural with the human sciences, a veritable electrical monism in which mathematical physics, as the queen of all sciences, would govern inquiry into the human being as a biological organism, *including* his or her thought processes and development as a species. Beyond his direct appropriation of electrical terms from the elite intellectual culture of his day, however, Robertson Smith also innovated – in the very terms of this discourse network – by forging a metonymic set of connections (connections of contiguity) between religion, communities of worship and electricity-like forces. This set of connections allowed consideration of forces that flowed *between* persons and things and that could be manipulated – through ritual and symbolic practices – to localize and organize more diffuse, more plural, powers.

Forces and feelings

How discrete bodies were linked together to form a self-conscious collective was, of course, the main question in Émile Durkheim's late-nineteenth-century turn to religion as the central topic and testing ground for the new science of sociology. Influenced by his reading of Robertson Smith, Durkheim's larger project was indeed congruent with Smith's special interest in the forces which operated between persons and things. Durkheim had a broader mission, however, not only to 'explain the nature and origin of the forces which stimulate social action' (Jones 2005, 177), but also to reveal the 'logic of collective representations [as] the logic of logic – the foundation of all thought in social as distinct from mental life' (Lemert 2006, 16). An analogy between religious forces and electrical ones played a distinctive role in buttressing this more ambitious project – which moved beyond literal or metaphorical physics to define the distinctive properties of social relations as such.

In *The Elementary Forms of the Religious Life* ([1912] 1995), Durkheim defined religion in its elementary 'totemic' forms as being derived from the mental grasp (or representation) of an 'anonymous and impersonal' force that courses through beings and things and gives them power and life. Moreover, he defines this force through a comparison with electricity:

> 'When I speak of these principles as forces, I do not use the word in a metaphorical sense; they behave like real forces [*forces véritables*]. In a sense, they are even physical forces that bring about physical effects mechanically. Does an individual come into contact with them without having taken proper precautions? He receives a shock that has been compared with the effect of an electrical charge. … When [these forces] enter into a body that is not meant to receive them, they cause sickness and death by a wholly mechanical reaction' [*une réaction tout automatique*]. (1995, 192; 1968, 270–1)

This passage mirrors almost exactly Robertson Smith's borrowing of 'a metaphor from electricity' to understand beliefs about taboos surrounding holy precincts.[3] Whether the reference is direct or not, Durkheim ultimately takes his comparison in a very different direction than Smith does. For Durkheim, the totemic force is not a matter of primitive belief and even less so of automatic reaction to natural forces. It is real or true, and it is its very objectivity as a force in the world that is attested by the fact that it acts upon believers mechanically.

That is, the force of the totem arises not from a physical ground (or, even less so, pure primitive imagination) but from ritual practices that gather groups of people, a society, around the totem. 'Once … individuals are gathered together, a sort of electricity is generated from their closeness and quickly launches them to an extraordinary height of exaltation' (Durkheim 1995, 217). Most importantly, a mediating movement of thought grants the experience of collectivity a claim to truthfulness independent of individual beliefs or autonomic physical reactions. The forces generated in rituals are *known* as totemic, and their operation can be predicted and harnessed because there is a category of such forces which is constructed and shared, through collective experience, as a means of description and explanation of what the subject has been through.

This may appear to raise logical problems of priority and causality – what comes first, the congregation, the totem or the category? But the point is that an energy is felt in the processes of congregation that is neither a reflex of an encounter (as for Robertson Smith) nor only a secondary emanation of the association of bodies, their 'closeness', as in certain readings of Durkheim. Rather, this energy (or effervescence, to give it its proper name) is channelled in thoughts and represented in forms which grant it an objectivity greater than that held by the passing moment or the contingent states of the people gathered together. How the thoughts and feelings (sensations) provoked by this energy are shared and passed around (and down) is a secondary question – a matter of folklore, if you will – though it is certainly not as automatic as even Durkheim implies, in obeisance to the discourse network of his day. Indeed, at about the same time as he is writing *Elementary Forms*, Durkheim will formulate this question in a more challenging way: 'How, in fact, can a state of feeling be independent of the subject that feels it?' (1953, 82). This question specifies the sociological insight at stake: neither the congregation nor the totemic object is a thing in itself. Both are *collective* representations, and their reality is that of a shared idea or even, more precisely, a feeling that, *qua* idea or feeling, necessarily takes place in the inner world of the social person but does not find its origin or its truth there. Whether congealed in a social body or a thing or simply existing as a common property in the intellect of thinking subjects (and thought is always comprised in part of other thoughts that have been said or read between subjects), such representations become a personal means of understanding and organizing the forces of association on which human beings depend. To be clear, to call this a 'personal means' is not to say that the force itself has to be personified but rather that it provides the power for the self-realization, through internal and external relations, *of persons*.

Collective powers

Whatever the source of the electrical metaphors in Durkheim's own writing, he also draws heavily on an earlier study of magic by Marcel Mauss (his nephew) and Henri Hubert (Mauss [1903] 2001) for the distinctive notion of 'force' that underwrites this metaphor. Mauss and Hubert had found, in non-Western concepts like 'mana', an idea of a force that is a *physical* manifestation of experiences of ritual and congregation, which can be congealed in an object and also in-forms a shared and yet intensely personal *understanding* of power and efficacy. In their study of magic, then, the collective representation of social forces is more capaciously defined in ways that allow us to see what is elided or obscured by the perhaps still overly mechanical electrical analogy that Durkheim used.

Mauss and Hubert built their theory of magic from a detailed reading of ethnographers' and missionaries' accounts of 'primitive' beliefs and practices, especially Robert Codrington's description of Melanesian mana – the active element in 'native' magic, as he understood it – as a 'force altogether distinct from physical power, which acts in all kinds of ways for good and evil' (a definition already in circulation since 1877, when the Sanskritist Max Müller quoted it in a lecture based on his own correspondence with Codrington) (see Tomlinson and Tengan 2016, 3). That mana was already an idea, a 'theoretical' understanding of the operation of forces both upon bodies and also within social relations, was of central importance to Mauss and Hubert. In their critical dialogue with James Frazer's *The Golden Bough* (itself written in dialogue with Smith's work, as noted earlier), Mauss and Hubert criticized Frazer's wholly mechanical explanations of the operation of 'primitive' magic through the association of things and ideas. They pointed out that to perform or assist at a magical rite, howsoever mechanical it might be, people must hold an already complex idea – like mana – of the power or energy that is at the command of the sorcerer or officiant and that *affects* whatever associations magic achieves (Mauss [1903] 2001, 125–6).

What it meant to hold such an idea, and how one might describe the operation of such an idea in apparently rote performances of inherited formulae, however, remained a question. 'All magical affirmations, even the most spiritual of them, depend on a completely universal affirmation of magical power, which is itself contained in *mana*,' they wrote. Still, the theoretical understanding this affirmation involves is entirely subsumed in the practical uses to which it is put.

'There is nothing intellectual or experimental about it,' Mauss and Hubert insist, 'except the feeling of society's existence and society's prejudices' (Mauss [1903] 2001, 155). They conclude their argumentation with an explication of this last point in terms of the most characteristic idea of the *Année Sociologique* school: collective representations. Notions like mana reveal the 'categories' of collective knowledge, concepts inhering in human social experience and distributed and communicated by its processes, as distinct from both the Kantian categories, which are integral to individual understanding, and synthetic judgements that depend on a brute encounter with the 'outer' world (see Siegel 2006). Such collective categories are found in, and founded upon, a group's treasury of commonly held ideas, passed down through myth and education and reinforced by rituals that distribute – to specific persons – the forces they describe.

To indicate the distance between such collective, shared, social categories like mana, on the one hand, and individual knowledge, on the other, Mauss and Hubert quote some lines from *The Tempest*. After he has relinquished his magical powers and his dominion over his island, Prospero says, 'Now my charms are all o'erthrown,/And what strength I have mine's own;/which is most faint.' That is, Prospero's powers depended on the command of forces he learned or borrowed or extorted from others (most importantly, those of the enslaved Caliban and Ariel), not only his individual skill or intellectual energies. Mauss and Hubert comment, thus, that once Prospero has given up his claim to these political relations he loses also his magical – that is collective – powers, and becomes 'nothing more than an ordinary mortal and may as well burn his books' (Mauss [1903] 2001, 170).

The ideal of force

In the *Elementary Forms*, from the very outset, Durkheim builds on Mauss and Hubert's research into mana as a collective category of 'force', making this magical understanding, collectively constituted and commonly shared, the type and origin of all knowledge of energetic relations (Durkheim 1995, 9). Not only is the general 'idea of force … of religious origin', Durkheim further argues that the religious life in fact provided the very model from which the scientific concept of physical forces was derived. 'Religious forces are real, no matter how imperfect the symbols [such as totems] with whose help they were conceived of. From this it will follow that the same is true for the concept of force in general' (1995, 206). With this, Durkheim is saying more than just that parallel intellectual procedures can produce true knowledge of two different kinds of forces; the claim here appears to be that ideally scientific reason is enriched by sociological reason. Tutored by sociology, physical science will move beyond positive knowledge of discrete things composed of individual parts, animated by definite causes. As Durkheim puts a similar point elsewhere: 'To see society only as an organized body of vital functions is to diminish it, for this body has a soul which is the composition of collective ideals. Ideals are not abstractions, cold intellectual concepts lacking efficient power. They are essentially dynamic, for behind them are the powerful forces of the collective. They are collective forces – that is, natural but at the same time moral forces, comparable to the other forces of the universe' (Durkheim 1953, 93). This version of his argument is slightly more modest than that in the *Elementary Forms*, in its mere 'comparison' of – rather than equivalence between – social forces and the energies that govern the universe of matter.

Ultimately, however, this comparison and coordination of social and physical forces represents Durkheim's riposte to any mechanistic account of human thought and relation, whether an evolutionist history of developing mental forces or a psychological or biological automatism. Durkheim's newly defined and freshly visible *social* forces, evident in the totemic social organizations and in experiences of collective effervescence, are neither simply material nor only moral/spiritual. 'They bestride the two worlds' (Durkheim 1995, 224) created by a modern, materialistic constitution of knowledge that tries to explain the human animal on the basis of the physical processes happening inside individual specimens while placing morals, religion and purely mental facts aside as immaterial (to science). Durkheim rejects this division of attention and interest as, finally, unscientific, or at least unalert to the formative power of collective representations even within the physical reality of the material world as it is occupied and known by human beings. As Durkheim explains, 'Religion has borne reality whole within itself, the material world as well as the moral world, the forces that move both bodies and minds have been conceived in religious form' (1995, 225). The task of Durkheim's sociology, then, is to 'preserve man's distinctive attributes' even within positive and material descriptions of life and association and above all not to place these distinctive attributes 'outside experience' (1995, 448). This new science can encompass religion and science both, but only by being encompassed by religious modes of experience rendered into sociological form – which is to say, only by grasping the mobile force that binds persons to each other and enriches their association, their world and all its objects.

Both Durkheim and Mauss read William James and criticized his conception of religion as mystical (Baciocchi and Fabiani 2012). Still, a passage from the *Varieties of the Religious Experience* sums up nicely the main principle of the sociological science of religion that uncle and nephew constructed together over these years. 'The world interpreted religiously is not the materialistic world over again, with an altered expression,' James wrote. 'It must have, over and above the altered expression, a natural constitution different at some point from that which a materialistic world would have. It must be such that different events can be expected in it, different conduct must be required' (James 1917, 518).

A different constitution

Obviously, there are other analogies between energy and society now available to us that are less mechanical than the electrical metaphors on which Durkheim and his contemporaries drew. Current theoretical alternatives include anthropological reworkings of both biological energy and historical time in terms of open-ended and non-iterative processes like entropy or through the Deleuzian energetic metaphor of 'potential' (e.g. Barry 2015; Helmreich 2013). But the question of the distinct and different reality of social forces, as such, not merely their metaphorical properties, is uniquely at stake in Durkheim's writing on religious energies and their collective production. The phenomenal reality of social forces bears, finally, on their capacity to organize bodies and powers – their constitutional effects, as it were. To clarify the continuing importance of this point and how Durkheim makes it through his electrical analogies, it is perhaps necessary to dwell a bit longer with works that reflect on religion and its manifestations of power and order (before turning back to infrastructures).

A passage from Bhrigupati Singh's philosophical inquiry into his own ethnographic study of spirits, possession and the 'quest for life' in a village called Shahabad in rural India, provides a useful articulation of the key questions provoked, still, by Durkheim's anthropology and the place of electrical analogies within it. Singh, too, turns to Durkheim for his understanding of religion as, in Singh's gloss, 'an engagement with a vital animating principle, 'a kind of anonymous and impersonal force" (Singh 2014, 174). He notes that this Durkheimian account of religious force echoes the understanding of a Indian spirit medium of his acquaintance, named Kalli, who says that 'states of possession are akin to receiving an electric current'. Durkheim's 'remarkable formulation' of the reality of religious forces in just such electrical, tangible, even folksy terms, however, is for Singh all too quickly reduced by Durkheim to 'his signature form of the metaphysical: "the moral authority of society"'. Singh quotes Durkheim: 'The basic purpose of the religious engagement with life is to reawaken solidarity. … The cult really does periodically recreate a moral entity on which we depend, as it depends on us. And this entity does exist: it is society' (Durkheim 2001, 258). Singh goes on to comment: 'We may call this an exhausted formulation, or we may call it a spot ripe for recultivation. Innumerable anthropologists have shown how religion does not necessarily "reawaken solidarity." My question, though, is prior to that: Does anthropology necessarily "reduce" all energy to "the social"? Or is the social one among other dimensions of life?' (Singh 2014, 174).

Singh thus very elegantly follows Durkheim's move from 'supernatural' energy or vital force to a grounding, force-generating 'social', and on Deleuzian grounds he refuses this trajectory – preferring to keep 'force' alive, plural, proliferating and unbounded by social or even bodily organization (as well as leaving open the possibility that spirits and other such entities are something other than emanations or representations of social relations between human beings). Faithful to his Deleuzian inspiration, Singh declines to 'negate' Durkheim's grounding of forces in human associations and rather seeks to continue beyond the point where, he argues, Durkheim stops – 'moral authority', 'society' – to move conceptually into 'other dimensions' of life, where other forces propagate novel potentials of relation and action beyond the merely human, or beyond those already given in a particular state of society.

Singh's account of religion as a force that opens outward beyond 'the social' and beyond 'moral authority' into other dimensions of 'life' has a real ethnographic power. It reminds me of the urgency with which I was instructed by a man I met once at a Gujarati shrine, about the 'love' [*prem*] that he felt for the saint buried there, love which he received back from the saint, and about which he asked me if I felt it, too. Sitting with him and others as an apparently spontaneous rite of spirit possession got underway in the gardens, I did indeed feel moved. I understood that this love gripped him and others and drew them as devotees to the shrine, where they were convinced of the power of the saint by the love they received in return. Certainly something other than mere congregation, aggregation of bodies, around the displaced reality of a transcendent 'society' was at stake there.

However, Durkheim's discussion of totemism and force can be reread to place the emphasis less on the reduction to 'the' social that Singh objects to, and to stress instead the reality of the common consciousness of force that is attested to by his informants and my own, in their own idiom of electricity or of love and the moral force of the attestation itself. Society as such is not the only 'real' at stake for Durkheim. Religious forces are 'real' too, and felt as such. In fact, the claimed reality of religious forces appears, in some respects, to be more important to Durkheim than their putative reliance on a hypostatized society pre-existing their emanation. While certainly the collective with its moral authority is a central prop of Durkheim's thought, read together Durkheim and Mauss – the latter especially – figure the collective as itself formed of a force which relates; meanwhile, specific societies only gain what formal reality they have through knowledge of those relations.

That is, the force of relation is what is real and what is felt; society is in a sense only a name for it – love or electricity will serve just as well. Indeed, since this experience of force is both personal and shared, it is frequently the case that social forces are thought and recognized as the public form of 'elements borrowed from our psychic life' (Durkheim 1995, 368) – like love – or on the basis of analogies drawn from our experience of the technological and material objects that also populate our experiences. In his or her dealings with others, the subject experiences an inner feeling of an impulsion or obligation coming from outside; on this basis discrete persons can name and recognize as real the forces that link the community together and by so doing also grant that community discernible form. Such a form-giving force is what mana is, though its recognition is by no means always easy or pleasant, nor need it always sustain life (Siegel 2006).

Bruno Karsteni nicely explains the role played by this inner 'feeling' or awareness of moral forces, within Durkheim's own thought. In late writings on moral experience and the objectivity of moral values, Durkheim probes 'the existence of a little-known dimension of internal experience, one that cannot be explained by subjective resources alone and imposes itself on the subject in a way that nonetheless remains attached to that subject – that is, feeling; [he] also offers a new way of looking at *things*, namely, in terms of the 'feeling' that gets mixed into and 'enriches' them. ... What is at issue here is quite literally the *auctoritas* of certain things, an attribute that inheres in their being as things' (Karsteni 2012, 31).

Durkheim's sociology, on this reading, is not an attempt to reduce all force and power to the moral authority of *a* society, and all religion (or law) to a solidarity-producing mechanism; nor is he insisting on the 'ideal' rather than the 'material' constitution of the world, with moral forces simply added to a mute and material nature and all the interest staying with the moral action (Greenhouse 2011). Rather, his sociology can be read as a science of collective forces that are real and consequential, that are *felt*, that inhere in things as we relate to them with others, but that we can only ever grasp by analogizing them to something else: God, perhaps, or love, or, for we moderns, something more physical, 'like receiving an electric current'.

The analogy between moral and electrical force that Durkheim makes, finally, is itself a kind of value judgement about the reality of social power itself, and its distribution both between and within bodies. The comparison between physical and moral forces is a way of insisting upon the phenomenal reality of social forces as they are *felt* in congregation, at sacred sites, in prayer, and also (as I have argued elsewhere) in the political rituals of modern states and before great material installations and institutions. Such feeling is both logically and phenomenally prior to – which is to say, more elemental than – any definition of the group, as such, which can only ever encompass a portion of the relations that generate the forces felt there.

Most critically, Durkheim deployed his force-confirming electrical comparison in the face of rationalist reductions that devalued just such experiences of force or collective energy and reduced them to mechanical operations or mental projections. Unlike Robertson Smith, though inspired by his fine attention to ritual as a medium of power, Durkheim used an analogy between ritual forces and electricity in order to point up the *heightened* material reality, the different constitution, of a world that had moral and spiritual forces in it too.[4] He may have thus travelled beyond the terms of the materialistic and mechanistic discourse network of his day, but he seems to have got close to the real meaning of mana. Recent scholars of Oceanic mana have argued, indeed, that Durkheim's understanding is closest to the indigenous original. Mana may not be a 'spiritual electric' or a 'force' in any literal sense, but it is both materially efficacious and works across disparate bodies, serving as an 'ethical mediation' between otherwise disjunct levels of reality (Tomlinson and Tengan 2016, 19–20).

Reason and optimism

Our current thinking on electricity, energy and environment is of course challenged by forces that Durkheim and his contemporaries could not foresee and, perhaps most of all, by the large-scale ecological effects of energy production and distribution that seem to make nonsense of any claim that these have a distinct 'social' element, understanding of which could be primary. Encounters with novel forces and with both environmental and infrastructural decay and degradation have helped motivate turns away from 'human-centred' accounts of society and towards novel understandings of the *power of things* (Jensen, this volume). Despite the prevalence of the term 'Anthropocene', our contemporary energy ecologies are evidently neither subject to singular control nor encompassed by human will – even collective, concerted, political will (Blok, Nakazora and Winthereik 2016).

Unwinding ourselves from culturally bound illusions of human agency and Promethean control is not an easy task, howsoever urgent it may be, given how deeply these mythic dreams of power run in modern thought, let alone in the design and organization of our infrastructures (Berman 1982). In closing, I would like to suggest, however, that this task is aided not hindered by ongoing anthropological attention to collective registers of meaning and value – our own and others.

The depth of the challenge that we confront can be gauged by how *little* critical purchase is sometimes won even by sophisticated attempts to shift towards the viewpoints of things, or systems. As Casper Jensen has argued, these can be little more than redescriptions of the facts of a certain technological or natural history rather than enabling more decisive ontological reorientations in our relations with things and environments. This is acute and entirely fair. But I must respectfully disagree with Jensen when he says that such efforts fail because they replace the arduous effort to grasp systems and events from the perspective of 'things themselves' with merely human *knowledge of things* (Jensen 2015, 24). I would argue, instead, that no salvation is to be sought in things as such.

As Gretchen Bakke points out here, an electricity grid is not a thing in the first place; it is a network of energetic relations that actively ties together heterogeneous elements in ways that repeatedly, recursively orchestrate them with the rhythms of (human) social life. And as Jamie Cross shows, the material elements in these relations are discussed and debated in a vocabulary rich with polysemous terms like 'current', that are at once political metaphors and esoteric references to powers that, depending on the context, we may qualify as spiritual or social. Such 'energy talk' (to coin a phrase) conjures forth a collective, shared world of relevance, one that is animated not only by energetic relations but by judgements about the goods and evils these may bring to local environments (cf. Harvey and Knox 2012, 534).

A key part of what Durkheim claimed was that whatever knowledge may be in relation to the world, or the individual faculty it may rest upon, it is at least in part collective, which means never neutral in relation to its objects *or* its subjects. The collective aspect of knowledge enriches all its constituents and transforms them; moreover, it emerges more often as a feeling or a special *forcefulness* than a conceptual illumination. This enrichment of thought with feeling is the hallmark of the *conscience collective* and what I believe Durkheim meant by effervescence.

On these very terms, ongoing ethnographic experiments that attend to the power of things and infrastructures in our physical and lived-in worlds are necessary and fruitful, especially those that draw on poetry and embodied experience to enrich reflection, crafting new sites of attachment for emergent collectives (Winthereik, Maguire and Watts, forthcoming; Watts 2012). The collaborative nature of much of this work only underscores that it is collective concepts and shared understandings – collective representations with a social, historical or mythic, but still irreducibly human reference – that are at stake, and most demand our critical attention.

Such attention to collective representations returns us to the conceptual legacy of the *Année Sociologique* school, our disciplinary inheritance from Durkheim and Mauss' collaborative institutional and pedagogical efforts to make the values that are incessantly inscribed in bodies and persons, through the relations that they sustain, the basis of a comparative science of human being. In an appreciation of Marcel Mauss, Louis Dumont once wrote that this legacy is 'one of widened reason and deepened optimism' (Dumont 1986, 201). This widened reason is borne in anthropological, poetic, or embodied attention to other people's living sense of the forces that bind them in solidarity with other denizens of the earth. I have tried to show here that this reason was, in the early years of anthropological thought, further widened by the effort to translate such difficult-to-think bonds of solidarity, order and interdependence into a vocabulary which would make sense of *their* social thought in the terms of *our* science and technology, necessarily traducing both along the way.

The optimism of which Dumont spoke is the other side of this problem of comparison – recast as an opportunity for thought. However inadequate their figural terms, metaphorical and analogical comparisons produce the possibility that what is thinkable in one system may become the basis of a value transformation in the other. For this reason and optimism both to reach their potential, however, we cannot examine things as discrete entities, however vibrant, lively, or perspectival they may be (or even as assemblages of such entities), but must approach them as we find them, set in their social, relational and figural relations with humans and other things. Undertaking such an approach, we may even find that the analogies we invent to forge some tentative relations across different conceptual worlds – like that between spiritual power and electrical currents, or between political and physical energy – have a seemingly independent power of social explanation, turning up again and again on vastly different occasions (as we saw with the reappearance of an electrical analogy for spiritual power, in Singh's ethnography).

Bringing this Durkheimian legacy into the anthropology of infrastructures may ultimately require a rapprochement between, on the one hand, the political-economic and 'new materialist' approaches that so far have dominated in this field and, on the other, the moral anthropology which still deals with categories of person and collective standards of value (Robbins 2013). In one current formulation, the phenomenological study of morality is said to arise from ethnographic evidence of people's 'attuned concern for the relationality that constitutes [their] very existence' (Zigon and Throop 2014, 3). I can think of no better, no more Durkheimian, description than this of what is at stake when people talk about, think about, or work upon an infrastructure, and name the forces it distributes.

Notes

1 For similar presentist reasons, Dominic Boyer has recently invited anthropologists to 'rethink the evolution of anthropological theory through its changing electrical environments' (Boyer 2015, 537), or, as he has put it elsewhere, to 'link the truth regimes of expert knowledge to the experiential and material conditions of expert knowledge practices' (Boyer 2010, 92).

2 In addition to James's rather sympathetic but scholarly interest in spiritualism, Tylor explored these phenomena as a basis for understanding 'primitive' religions, while Morgan himself participated in spiritualist practices. See Stocking (1971) and Feeley-Harnik (2001).

3 The rendering (here, in Karen Smith's translation) of Durkheim's '*un choc que on l'a pu comparer*' as 'has been compared' may imply a too definite reference to earlier works of religious studies – other translations have simply 'can be compared' (Durkheim 2001, 142). Still, the parallel with Robertson Smith's formulation is striking. It is a task for further research to explore how the ethnographic sources

Durkheim cites here treat the power of mana and taboo; we shall see here that Codrington, at least, insists that mana is a purely moral phenomenon with no physical basis. In my reading, it is Durkheim's innovation to insist on the physical reality of these forces without reducing them to an effect of physical contiguity alone.

4 Indeed, it is essential to note, following Carol Greenhouse, that throughout Durkheim's thought, despite some traces of automatism in his account of the totem, 'social relations are not [ever] automatically moral relations'. When social relations are felt as moral relations, moreover, this not because of an external imposition on what are otherwise free or unforced relations but rather a result of special attention being given to their social form as such, the divisions and separations they create as much as the connections they enforce between people (Greenhouse 2011, 169). The 'symbols are imperfect', we might say with Durkheim, and yet that does not diminish the reality of the forces being symbolized.

References

Anand, Nikhil. 2017. *Hydraulic City: Water and Citizenship in Mumbai*. Durham, NC: Duke University Press.

Baciocchi, Stephane and Jean-Louis Fabiani. 2012. 'Durkheim's Lost Argument (1895–1955): Critical Moves on Method and Truth', *Durkheimian Studies*, 18: 19–40.

Barry, Andrew. 2015. 'Thermodynamics, Matter, Politics', *Distinktion: Journal of Social Theory*, 16(1): 110–25.

Berman, Marshall. 1982. *All That Is Solid Melts into Air: The Experience of Modernity*. New York: Simon & Schuster.

Blok, Anders, Moe Nakazora and Brit Ross Winthereik. 2016. 'Infrastructuring Environments', *Science as Culture*, 25(1): 1–22.

Boyer, Dominic. 2010. 'Digital Expertise in Online Journalism (and Anthropology)', *Anthropological Quarterly*, 83(1): 73–96.

Boyer, Dominic. 2015. 'Anthropology Electric', *Cultural Anthropology*, 30(4): 531–39.

Coleman, Leo. 2017. *A Moral Technology: Electrification as Political Ritual in New Delhi*. Ithaca, NY: Cornell University Press.

Dumont, Louis. 1986. 'Marcel Mauss: A Science in the Process of Becoming', in *Essays on Individualism: Modern Ideology in Anthropological Perspective*, 183–201. Chicago, IL: University of Chicago Press.

Durkheim, Émile. 1953. 'Value Judgments and Judgments of Reality', in trans. D. F. Pocock. *Sociology and Philosophy*, 80–97. Glencoe, IL: The Free Press.

Durkheim, Émile. 1968. *Les Formes élémentaires de la vie religieuse: Le système totémique en Australie*. 5ième ed. Paris: Presses Universitaires de France.

Durkheim, Émile. 1995. *The Elementary Forms of Religious Life*, trans. Karen E. Fields. New York: Free Press.

Durkheim, Émile. 2001. *The Elementary Forms of Religious Life*, trans. Carol Cosman. New York: Oxford University Press.

Feeley-Harnik, Gillian. 2001. 'The Anthropology of Creation: Lewis Henry Morgan and the American Beaver', in Sarah Franklin and Susan McKinnon (eds), *Relative Values: Reconfiguring Kinship Studies*, 54–84. Durham, NC: Duke University Press.

Greenhouse, Carol J. 2011. 'Durkheim and Law: Divided Readings over *Division of Labor*', *Annual Review of Law & Society*, 7: 165–85.

Harvey, Penny and Hannah Knox. 2012. 'The Enchantments of Infrastructure', *Mobilities*, 7(4): 521–36.

Harvey, Penny and Hannah Knox. 2015. *Roads: An Anthropology of Infrastructure and Expertise*. Ithaca, NY: Cornell University Press.

Harvey, Penny, Casper Bruun Jensen and Atsuro Morita. 2017. 'Introduction: Infrastructural Complications', in Penny Harvey, Casper Bruun Jensen and Atsuro Morita (eds), *Infrastructures and Social Complexity: A Companion*, 1–22. New York: Routledge.

Helmreich, Stefan. 2013. 'Potential Energy and the Body Electric: Cardiac Waves, Brain Waves, and the Making of Quantities into Qualities', *Current Anthropology*, 54(S7): S139–48.

James, William. 1917. *Varieties of Religious Experience: A Study in Human Nature*. New York: Longmans, Green & Co.

Jensen, Casper Bruun. 2015. 'Experimenting with Political Materials: Experimental Infrastructures and Ontological Transformations', *Distinktion: Journal of Social Theory*, 16(1): 17–30.

Jensen, Casper Bruun and Atsuro Morita. 2015. 'Infrastructures as Ontological Experiments', *Engaging Science, Technology, and Society*, 1: 81–7.

Jones, Robert Alun. 2005. *The Secret of the Totem: Religion and Society from McLennan to Freud*. New York: Columbia University Press.

Karsteni, Bruno. 2012. 'Durkheim and the Moral Fact', trans. Amy Jacobs, in Didier Fassin (ed.), *A Companion to Moral Anthropology*, 21–36. Malden, MA: Wiley-Blackwell.

Kittler, Friedrich A. 1990. *Discourse Networks 1800/1900*, trans. Michael Metteer with Chris Cullens. Stanford, CA: Stanford University Press.

Larkin, Brian. 2013. 'The Politics and Poetics of Infrastructure', *Annual Review of Anthropology*, 42: 327–43.

Lemert, Charles. 2006. *Durkheim's Ghosts: Cultural Logics and Social Things*. New York: Cambridge University Press.

Lévi-Strauss, Claude. [1954] 1992. *Tristes Tropiques*, trans. John and Doreen Weightman. New York: Penguin.

Mauss, Marcel. [1903] 2001. *A General Theory of Magic*, trans. Robert Brain. New York: Routledge Classics.

Needham, Rodney. 1976. 'Skulls and Causality', *Man*, N. S. 11(1): 71–88.

Redfield, Robert. 1948. 'Introduction', in Bronislaw Malinowski (ed.), *Magic, Science, and Religion and Other Essays*, vii–xi. Boston, MA: Beacon Press.

Robbins, Joel. 2013. 'Monism, Pluralism, and the Structure of Value Relations: A Dumontian Contribution to the Contemporary Study of Value', *Hau: Journal of Ethnographic Theory*, 3(1): 99–115.

Rogers, Douglas. 2015. *The Depths of Russia: Oil, Culture, and Power after Socialism*. Ithaca, NY: Cornell University Press.

Schmidgen, Henning. 2002. 'Of Frogs and Men: The Origins of Psychophysiological Time Experiments, 1850–1865', *Endeavour*, 26(4): 142–8.

Siegel, James. 2006. *Naming the Witch*. Stanford, CA: Stanford University Press.

Singh, Bhrigupati. 2014. 'How Concepts Make the World Look Different: Affirmative and Negative Genealogies of Thought', in Veena Das, Michael Jackson, Arthur Kleinman and Bhrigupati Singh (eds), *The Ground Between: Anthropologists Engage Philosophy*, 159–87. Durham, NC: Duke University Press.

Smith, W. Robertson. [1889] 1972. *The Religion of the Semites: The Fundamental Institutions*. New York: Schocken Books.

Sneath, David, Martin Holbraad and Morten Axel Petersen. 2009. 'Technologies of the Imagination: An Introduction', *Ethnos*, 74(1): 5–30.

Stocking, George W. 1971. 'Animism in Theory and Practice: E. B. Tylor's Unpublished "Notes on 'Spiritualism'"'. *Man*, N. S. 6(1): 88–104.

Tomlinson, Matt and Ty P. Kāwika Tengan. 2016. 'Introduction: Mana Anew', in Matt Tomlinson and Ty P. Kāwika Tengan (eds), *New Mana: Transformations of a Classic Concept in Pacific Languages and Cultures*, 1–36. Acton, ACT: ANU Press.

Watts, Laura. 2012. 'OrkneyLab: An Archipelago Experiment in Futures', in Tim Ingold and Monica Janowski (eds), *Imagining Landscapes: Past, Present and Future*, 59–76. Burlington, VT: Ashgate.

Winthereik, Brit Ross, James Maguire and Laura Watts. Forthcoming. 'The Energy Walk: Infrastructuring the Imagination', in David Ribes and Janet Vertesi (eds), *Handbook of Digital STS*. Princeton, NJ: Princeton University Press.

Young, Michael W. 2005. *Malinowski: Odyssey of an Anthropologist, 1884–1920*. New Haven, CT: Yale University Press.

Zigon, Jarrett and C. Jason Throop. 2014. 'Moral Experience: Introduction', *Ethos*, 42(1): 1–15.

4

No current: Electricity and disconnection in rural India

Jamie Cross

Nestled in the high plateaus of Koraput, in the highlands of Odisha, India, is the Gaudaguda Valley: a globally insignificant, locally inconspicuous cluster of villages, hamlets and settlements. The 4 kilometres walk into the valley from the nearest town takes you through eucalyptus plantations and fields of millets and rice and across two rivers.

On one side of the valley is a 500-metre-high escarpment that looms out of the fields. At 5.30 pm, as dusk falls, a line of spotlights appear motionless high on the ridge top. Four full moons of electric white; sentinels standing guard against the night. Owned and run by NALCO – the National Aluminium Corporation – the spotlights mark one of Asia's largest bauxite mines. The lights are so bright that they can be seen 50 kilometres away, making it possible to pick the ridge out from a five-story rooftop in Koraput town, the region's district capital.

In the Gaudaguda Valley, the NALCO lights occupy the night. The lights don't shimmer, they don't glow; they stare, asserting the mine's presence on the hilltop like a military base. From the ridge top, mine employees and government officials watch the valley floor, the night-time illuminations turning this into a place of darkness, backwardness and potential insecurity.

From an un-electrified housing colony or 'sahi' in the valley's largest village, people watch the ridge top. A man in his late thirties called Ballava follows the changing location and proliferation of the spotlights, tracking the mine's slow creep northwards, following the bauxite.

The people of the *Sahi* are Parojas, one of India's poorest and most marginalized indigenous or Adivasi communities, who supply the mine with informal day labour. The Parojas are the valley's majority population but live in socially segregated colonies or in small breakaway settlements, marginalized economically and politically by a settler community, the Goudas, who dominate the region's agricultural economy and local-level government to the degree that they once renamed the valley (and its largest village) after themselves.

The Gaudaguda Valley is not entirely un-electrified. At night, the darkness is not uniform. The valley's light-scape has an uneven geography – with homes, hamlets and colonies lying in degrees of pitch and shadow – that has much to tell us about local histories of electricity. Like elsewhere in Odisha, one of India's poorest states, access to electricity here maps directly onto income and caste. Over forty years ago, Ballava's father witnessed the extension of an electricity grid across the valley floor. The first electricity pylons were planted here in 1984, connecting the homes of Gouda families to a publicly owned regional power grid. Across the valley, the coming of the grid was a historic event, a moment of modernist rupture that marked the beginning of new exclusions.

Twenty-five years later, following the liberalization of Odisha's electricity sector, this network of substations, transformers and cables was no longer publicly managed but owned and operated by a private utility company. In 2014, the Government of India rolled out a new, nationwide village electrification scheme, the *Deendayal Upadhyaya Gram Jyoti Yojana*, which set out to catalyse the electrification of places like Gaudaguda by paying regional electricity companies to extend the grid to un-electrified villages. The rationale for grid electrification programmes in the highlands of Orissa are about governance and security as much as the extension of rights and entitlements to public goods, like energy. Under the terms of the scheme, however, the Paroja Sahi did not qualify. India's Ministry of Power defines an electrified village as a village in which 10 per cent of all households have an electricity connection, where there is an electricity transformer, and where public institutions (schools, local-level government offices, health centres) are electrified. According to this definition, Gaudaguda was already electrified.

In Gaudaguda, the Parojas set out to press a claim that the grid should be extended to their colony. Ballava led a delegation to a nearby market town where he petitioned the local government electricity officer, known colloquially as the 'electricity sarkar' or the 'lineman'.

'You're not on the list, just wait,' the lineman told them. 'After all if the government had to install new poles and wires in your village it wouldn't be able to install it elsewhere.'

In rural India, as the anthropologist Akhil Gupta (1995, 2012) has long argued, it is through interactions with local-level government officials like this lineman that villagers confront the Indian state and through the practices of such officials that the Indian state comes to be known, understood and imagined. As successive Indian governments have re-formatted the economy around what we might now call austerity, bureaucrats and state officials have been key mediators (Bear 2015). For Ballava, it was precisely the lineman's commitment to 'red tape', to official rules and procedures, that confirmed his suspicion that state resources were being unequally distributed and that the flow of electricity mapped directly onto patterns of caste power, influence and inequality.

From the perspective of people like Ballava, life off the grid in a place like the Gaudaguda Valley is also life on the periphery of the grid: life lived in proximity to big grids, to networked infrastructures for electricity distribution and centralized systems for the distribution of public goods, rights and entitlements. Here people use the English word *current* to talk about, refer to and describe the availability of and their access to electricity. *Current* is a social and political thing; its presence or absence is never just about electric power or a connection to the grid but also about rights and entitlements, about political recognition and connections to the state.

Globally, one-seventh of humanity – somewhere between 1.1 and 1.3 billion people, according to the statistics published by the World Bank and the International Energy Agency – live without any connection to the mains electricity grid – to wires, cables and pylons or planned, centralized networks for the transmission or distribution of electricity. India has some of the lowest rates of access to grid electricity in the world, with upwards of 300 million people in India living without any connection to a mains electricity grid at all. This chapter sets out to open up the material politics of electricity off the grid by exploring the salience of *current* in rural India. As anthropologists respond to changing social and economic demands for electricity across the rural world, I propose that thinking through *current* allows us to foreground questions of citizenship and justice.

No *current*

In electrical engineering, the English word 'current' is used to describe the flow or movement of an electrical charge, measured in amperes. Across much of India today, however, 'current' or 'karant' is a vernacular keyword for talking about the flow or movement of electricity from networks of pylons and wires into everyday life (Cross 2017). In Odisha – like elsewhere in India – 'current' has entered an everyday, non-English vernacular as a colloquial term for electricity. Just as a technical vocabulary for electricity has provided the English language with powerful metaphors, so too in India, where speakers of Hindi, Urdu, Telugu, or Odiya also find that 'current' is good to speak with: rich with allegorical or metaphorical possibilities for talking about modernity and development, life and death, kinship and fraternity, love and sexuality. From early nineteenth-century experiments with electricity in the princely state of Mysore to postcolonial investments in rural electrification, the flow of 'current' into the Indian body politic has been the lifeblood of modernization and development. As India's first prime minister, Jawaharlal Nehru, once put it, in an oblique reference to Lenin's famous statement (see Introduction): 'The moment you take electricity, all kinds of things begin to move' (Kale 2013).

Yet even as the word flows across communities of language, class and caste, in contemporary India, the passage of electric current into and through everyday life has been uneven and erratic. By comparison with other papers in this collection where electricity is taken for granted, people living in much of rural India have learned to live with an unpredictable and haphazard supply, so much so that the Hindi language expression '*Current nahin hai*' ('no current') is ubiquitous. In everyday conversation, current has a physical quality that makes it as material as wires and pylons, transformers and substations. Current, we might say, is infrastructure: a thing that creates the ground on which other things work, 'present to the senses' yet only 'visible in relationship to other things' (Larkin 2013).

In much of India, current is only visible in relation to bulbs, fans, fridges and pumps. Across North India, the word 'current' is synonymous with and used interchangeably with *bijli*, the Hindi and Urdu word for lightning and electricity. Similarly, in the south: ask the Telugu-speaking residents of a village in Andhra Pradesh how they know when there is 'no current' and your question will be ridiculed. 'If there is current there is light. If there is no current, there is dark', I was once told, with mocking laughter.

Just as current illuminates, so too it mediates. With current comes radio, television and the mobile phone; flows of information and media forms: news, film, music, the SMS, the MMS, weather updates, commodity prices and advertisements. While the word 'current' may be ubiquitous across North and South India, its use is shaped by patterns of access to the grid. In un-electrified India, the English word 'line' is sometimes a more prominent part of local vocabulary for talking about electricity. 'In town people say *current*', people told me around the Gaudaguda Valley, 'but here in the interior people say *line*'.

Both words make electricity visible in its absence. In the region's market towns and district capitals, there are lines, but no current to flow through them. In the village, there are few lines at all. When the power goes off in Gaudaguda, people say '*line nahin hai*' rather than '*current nahin hai*' and the local government electricity officer, known elsewhere as 'the electricity sarkar', is here known colloquially as the 'lineman'.

In town, blackouts are greeted with 'the current fell', a phrase that summons images of dangling wires and cables. Indeed, this is not an uncommon phenomenon. Illegally connected electricity cables and overloaded connections frequently burn out and trip local grids, leaving wires hanging overhead. Electrocutions make news, providing provincial stringers with guaranteed column inches, and India's regional newspapers carry regular reports of deaths or injuries from hanging wires.

The phrase '*Chhoona Mana Hai*' or 'Touching is Prohibited', for example, appears on electricity transformers across India, and just as it warns people of dangers, it is also suggestive. 'Who's that standing there like a pole?' sang Aamir Khan in the 1990 song *Khambe Jaisi Khadi Hai*, from the Bollywood film *Dil*. 'This body of mine is electric', sang his co-star Madhuri Dixit in reply. 'I've got 440 volts: touching is prohibited'.

The song's chorus line is so well-known that it can connect people across language, caste and class. One night in the highlands of Odisha, passing lines of high-voltage pylons that stood waiting for wires to be strung between them, I listened to a young energy-policy researcher from Hyderabad sing in sync with Mohan, the newly married taxi driver. Bound together for a moment by lascivious verse and male camaraderie, the current surged from one to the other and, through them, to me. 'If Madhuri Dixit came and fell on me like an electric pole', Mohan said, 'swear on God: it would be fun getting electrocuted.' In other times and places across these highlands, the same word associations have metaphorical power for women too. Sitting one night in the Poraja Sahi during the festival of *Ganesh Chauviti*, drinking *handia* or rice beer with a mixed, inter-generational group of men and women, around a small metal vessel burning kerosene, we talked about life lived off the grid. As the discussion became more lubricated and raucous, the discussion turned to private matters. 'Even the men around here don't have current', one of the women said, to uproarious laughter.

Elsewhere, people use the words reflexively, alert to their associations with colonial language and as a way of passing comment on the uneven distribution of electricity supply. 'Why do you speak of "current"?' I asked Mohan, as he drove his taxi between the towns of Kakariguma and Koraput, 'isn't that an English word?' 'The Britishers left their language behind', he said, 'but they didn't leave the lines'.

Yet contrary to Mohan's version of colonial history, the British made virtually no investment in the distribution of electricity outside of their new capital, Delhi. Instead, it was Nehru who married the expansion of a national electricity grid to a rationalizing, techno-scientific project. Reflecting on a project of rural electrification in Soviet Russia, he wrote of a scheme that could 'prepare the way for ... industrialisation' and 'produce an industrial mentality among the peasantry'; 'lighted up by electricity', he wrote, peasants 'began to get out of the old ruts and superstitions and to think on new lines' (Nehru 2003). Over the course of the twentieth century, however, some of India's most impoverished and marginalized communities have remained at the frontiers of rural electrification, even as their land has been acquired for hydroelectric dams and power plants.

To speak of 'current' in India today, then, is to speak of the political economy of energy. Current connects. For people without electricity, current holds out the promise of political recognition, of equal rights and entitlements as citizens. But current is also government. Programmes of rural electrification like those across the India–Pakistan border or spaces of Naxalite insurgency explicitly extend the presence of the state, just as politicians use the promise of free or subsidized electricity to extend their influence at election time. In much of rural India, the distribution of electricity maps onto historic patterns of caste and class inequality and exclusion. From villages in western Uttar Pradesh to southern Odisha, the homes of Dalits and Adivasis are less likely to have metered electricity connections than the homes of high-caste farming and trading families. Little surprise, then, that the disenfranchised experience the absence of current not as a blockage in the circuit but as an appropriation or re-direction.

The electric village

Electricity and fuel have remained almost entirely absent from the twentieth-century sociological and anthropological record of rural life in modern India. Take the Oxford-trained Indian scholar M. N. Srinivas who, today, is credited with establishing the sociological and social anthropological study of village India and making the study of caste hierarchy central to these disciplines. Yet by establishing the contours of what is of interest in the Indian village, Srinivas also excluded key aspects of postcolonial investments in infrastructure and rural development. Despite making repeated visits to the same village in Tamil Nadu between 1948 and 1964, Srinivas's published writings on life in rural India, including his most well-known monograph, *The Remembered Village* (Srinivas 1976), completely ignore the coming of electricity. As Srinivas explains in the introduction to this book, he had set out to live in a village that had remained un-electrified and, when he arrived there to begin fieldwork, he carried a kerosene lantern and a special permit permitting him one litre of kerosene per month, courtesy of a family connection to a local bureaucrat. Despite his own needs, like many other anthropologists who followed him into the villages of North and South India over the next half-century, he ignored the changing demands of rural people themselves for modern forms of energy or shifting patterns of fuel consumption.

Yet during the 1950s and 1960s, rural electrification had become a key tenet of India's development planning and green revolution agriculture. Meanwhile, the coming of electricity to India's villages was transforming relationships of caste. In the 1960s and 1970s, energy infrastructure projects had become central to government strategies for rural development. The installation of new electricity connections – alongside the construction of roads, canals and telephone connections as well as the establishment of schools, colleges, hospitals, police stations, credit cooperatives and banks, fertilizer and seed stores, grain and sugar-cane purchasing centres and ration shops – generated rural employment. As people with government jobs supported those without, rural infrastructure development projects helped to legitimate a changing socio-economic landscape and the emergence of new class of rural farmers (Srinivas 1976, 155). At the same time, the supply of electricity, the repair of electric lines and the payment of electricity bills become central to farming.

By the time another Indian anthropologist, Akhil Gupta, arrived in the village of Alipur, on the plain between the Ganges and Jamuna rivers in the north Indian state of Uttar Pradesh in the mid-1990s, the preoccupations and interests of social scientists in village India had been definitely refocused. Electricity and electrically powered technologies were now legitimate objects of enquiry that offered windows onto processes of social change and transformation.

In Alipur, where Gupta lived and carried out ethnographic fieldwork between 1984 and 1985, the installation of electricity lines had been quickly followed by the installation of electrically powered tube wells that pumped water for irrigation. As Gupta describes in his book *Postcolonial Developments* (Gupta 1998), in rural Uttar Pradesh, electrically powered agrarian technologies like the tube pump had symbolic power and material effects. To the farmers of Alipur, Gupta wrote, the electric tube well was never just a means of pumping groundwater. It was also a potent symbol of modernity and modernization, 'one that lay at the end of a chain of signifiers', (Gupta 1998, 275) and it was a machine that transformed relations between farmers and between farmers and the state.

In the mid-1980s, Alipur had had an erratic supply of electricity. The reason was not the fragility of the physical infrastructure or an excessive demand for power but the inability of the state government to charge people for the electricity they used. Attempts to introduce electricity metres had proven unviable. Indeed, Alipur's farmers saw the main achievement of their agricultural trade union, the Kisan Union, as their success in preventing electricity board officials from harassing farmers for failing to pay their bills (Gupta 1998, 89). When metering failed, the state electricity board began to bill farmers a fixed amount each month based on the size of their tube wells. As they sought to limit power consumption and increase revenues, the electricity board cut supply, leaving farmers with 6 instead of 24 hours' electricity a day.

As Gupta describes, the 'start and stop' rhythm of the grid had a material effect on local agriculture, shaping the use of water resources. Alipur's paddy fields were irrigated by pumping water into a network of small irrigation canals. If the electricity cut out before the field was irrigated, the water in the canals would have drained before the power came back on, and the process would have to be repeated. The process was extremely inefficient and time consuming. For many farmers, the only solution was to invest in more than one pump and run them simultaneously. As the number of tube wells multiplied, the costs of irrigating the same area of land also increased.

This ethnography of life in rural India invites anthropologists of energy to see fuel and electricity as important analytics for understanding caste power and control in the country's agrarian economy. Just as 'power over energy has been the "companion and collaborator" of biopolitics and biopower', as Dominic Boyer puts it (Boyer 2014), so too we might see how power over energy has been the companion and collaborator of the social and symbolic politics of caste that govern the Indian village.

More recently, anthropology reminds us that the continued absence of an electricity infrastructure – substations, transformers, poles and cables – can also have material effects. Even if by the end of the twentieth century, the 'chain of signifiers' for modernity or modernization had failed to reach closure in an electrical appliance or machine being operated in a village or rural home, it was very likely to end close by and certainly in the nearest market town. Writing about indigenous politics, environmentalism and Maoist insurgency in rural Jharkhand, for example, Alpa Shah (2010) has described how the lack of infrastructure drove the migration of middle and higher castes from forest villages into rural market towns. Thirty-five kilometres from the state capital, Ranchi, where Shah lived and conducted research over a decade between the 1990s and 2000s, she watched the population of the small market town of Bero double in size as the *Sadans*, descendants of rural landowners, abandoned their mud-brick homes in the forest in search of running water, better schools and 'sporadic electricity'.

To whom the current flows

When I moved to the Gaudaguda Valley with my wife and 6-month-old son during the monsoon of 2012, it did not take long for the antagonisms, mutual disparagement and inter-dependencies between the landed dairy farmers, the Gaudas and the Parojas to appear. Conflicts and animosities between the Goudas and the Adivasis protruded from the surface of village life like the granite rocks that disturbed the fields of rice and millet on the valley floor. One day I accompanied Ballava, a soft, bespectacled Paroja man in his late forties, to his paddy fields, where he wanted to put up scarecrows. 'Only when the Gaudas and their sons die will we prosper,' Ballava told me, matter-of-factly, as he looked back towards the village in which he had been born and the grove of mango trees opposite the colony where he had lived his whole life.

His comment seemed less like a hope that violence would actually be visited upon the members of this dominant caste than a straightforward description of their vice-like hold over the village economy. To one side of us, that day in the paddy fields, a line of seven or eight women were working on Gauda-owned land, labour for which they would receive a share of the harvest. To the other side was a half-kilometre section of tarmac road, the contract for which had been won by a Gouda family, who also determined who could be employed in its construction. Beneath us lay an old shed with a new padlock, from which the Goudas dispensed rations to those with state-issued ration cards.

In the early 2010s, the largest village in the Gaudaguda Valley had 386 households and a population of 1,470 people. According to that year's census records, the Paroja Adivasis made up just over half, or 51 per cent, of the village. Yet the Gaudas and other high-caste Hindu families perceived the demographics of their village quite differently. Most imagined themselves as a minority and frequently told me that Adivasis made up 80 per cent or more of the village's population. Such misperceptions were indicative of the unease and insecurity felt by upper-caste landowners and business families in a corner of Orissa that had become a violent hotspot of Maoist or Naxalite activity.

The highlands of Orissa first came to the attention of social anthropology through the work of Verrier Elwin – ethnologist, Ghandian activist and one-time deputy director of the anthropological survey of India – who produced controversial studies of tribal custom, myth art and folklore (Guha 1999). In the 1950s, this part of India gained notoriety through the work of Manchester School anthropologist Frederick Bailey. Bailey documented the historic expansion of Hindu dairy farmers onto indigenous tribal lands here and wrote about the mid-century transformations in the region's political economy as this rural elite kept the state at bay and became its chief mediator. In Bailey's classic phrase, this was an 'economic frontier' at the edge of postcolonial administration, where rural elites were transforming Adivasi land into a commodity that could be bought, sold and accumulated (Bailey 1957).

At the beginning of the twenty-first century, caste elites maintain their livelihoods and their dominance over indigenous communities in rural India by controlling local-level government and appropriating resources or extracting indirect benefits from the developmental machinery (Shah 2010). In Gaudaguda, the control of a dominant caste was articulated in the circulation of oil-based fuels, kerosene and diesel; and connections to wires, pylons and transformers. Fuel and electricity all expressed or articulated the social politics of rural life, offering an alternative lens through which to understand the reproduction of caste injustice and inequality. Material differences between fuels and the electricity infrastructure – their relative mobility or fixity – create different possibilities and temporalities for the exercise of control. In Gaudaguda, the higher-caste Gaudas could control the flow of subsidized fuels, like kerosene, to Adivasi households directly and immediately by controlling the supply, price and sale of rations to individual households. Their capacity to control the installation and transmission of electricity, meanwhile, was indirect and required them to retain influence with state bureaucrats and officials and to retain control of local-level political institutions like the *panchayat*.

Forty years after the coming of electricity to the Gaudaguda Valley, the majority of Adivasi homes remained entirely unconnected to the mains, while Gouda homes have fans, televisions and plugs to charge mobile phones. More than these electric appliances, however, it is the simple electric light bulb that makes energy inequality most visible. Walking around after dark, Gaudaguda, the valley's largest village, was unevenly illuminated, with households and colonies lying in varying degrees of pitch and shadow. This light-scape mapped directly onto caste, revealing both the spatial segregation and spatial investments of different communities.

In the Parana Adivasi colony, homes are built directly onto the earthen street. The doors remain open but the street remains dark. The light from candles or homemade kerosene lanterns is so weak that it barely illuminates a single room. Little or no surplus light leaks through the wooden door frame, out of the Paroja home into the street. At night in the colony, people sit or squat outside their homes in the dark.

In the quarter of the village occupied by a community of Kamars, electrified homes illuminate the street. The yellow halo from one or two incandescent bulbs or the white glow from a compact fluorescent tube light spills out over the threshold onto the narrow paved road. Three families here have opened kiosks, selling sweets and cigarettes from square windows built into the side of their homes, and as people gather here to talk or smoke, the light of commerce creates new public space.

By contrast, the homes of the village's wealthiest Gouda and Sodhi families can be made out from afar, marked out in the night by the excess of electric lighting. Many of these families have also installed external lights on the external walls of their homes. Although many people describe these as 'security lights', their prominent display also makes them conspicuous markers of status and wealth. While this high-caste lighting might be intended for public display, it is not intended for public consumption. The homes of most Gouda and Sodhi families are built back from the street. Shrubs, trees and fences or paving slabs and compound walls establish a physical barrier or distance from human or vehicular traffic. As a consequence, their domestic lights remain private, illuminating the facade of a home, a doorway or a yard while leaving the street in shadow.

The supply of electricity in places like Gaudaguda remains unreliable. While rural electricity systems are not *un-amenable* to the application of power by social and political groups, *neither* are the interests and resources of communities like the Gaudas sufficient to make them work. Electricity supply is erratic, shaped by patterns of consumption in towns and the demand of local industries. In the village, supply frequently collapses at the height of summer, when urban consumers turn on their fans. In the summertime, even those families with mains electricity connections keep batteries charged for night-time lighting or continue to keep a supply of kerosene, which remains the staple source of lighting for 75 per cent of the village. Even for the Gaudas, continued and sustained access to electricity is dependent on their complex relationships to subcontracted engineers, technicians and the 'lineman'. The same complex relationships that allow the Gaudas to sustain their own access to electricity are exactly the same that allow them to restrict access for others, in ways that are calculated not just to reassert their political and economic control over the Parojas but also to maintain the strength of their local sales of subsidized kerosene. As the Indian government and non-government entities harness solar photovoltaic technologies to projects of rural electrification in Odisha, the relationships and material politics that have shaped patterns of access to electricity over the past twenty-five years have come to shape transitions to a low-carbon economy.

The solar future

In India today, physical connection to the electricity grid is no longer seen as the only sustainable or achievable model for increasing the access of poor people to modern forms of energy, or 'current'. Instead, uneven patterns of access to the grid are being reframed by politicians, international financial institutions and entrepreneurs as an opportunity for the expansion of off-grid solar-energy systems, which will allow people to generate their own electricity.

Over the past five years, the Government of India has made solar energy central to visions of future energy security, poverty reduction and development. Against the backdrop of concerns about climate change, energy poverty and energy security, the possibility of expanding access to energy in a distributed or decentralized way, harnessing the power of the sun in ways that allow people to meet demands for electricity without a connection to the mains electricity grid, has become urgent and influential. The unique affordances of the silicon solar cell have made electric sunshine a critical part of global public and political futures. National politicians seek to establish India as a global leader in solar energy, making the solar economy an engine of growth, capable of attracting foreign investment, creating jobs and meeting rising demand for energy. Planners and policy makers, corporate executives and social entrepreneurs, journalists, environmental activists and energy-policy scholars present the rapid expansion of the country's solar photovoltaic economy as an unquestionable public good and a model for low or middle-income economies across 'the global south'.

Grand visions of a future in which people living on and off the grid have access to a clean, affordable, reliable source of electricity played an important role in political campaigning during India's 2014 national election. Campaigning on a solar platform helped the party to communicate a pro-development message to its voters, deflecting attention away from the party's relationship to the Hindu right and projecting an image of its leader, Narendra Modi, as a green-energy pioneer. A week after Narendra Modi became India's prime minister in 2015, leading his Bharatiya Janata Party (BJP) to a sweeping electoral victory, he pledged to the nation that every household in India would have at least one indoor light bulb powered by clean, renewable solar energy by 2019. If all goes well, the head of the BJP's energy division told journalists from around the world, household solar projects would allow every home to run two light bulbs, a solar cooker and a television. Modi expanded the new government's energy goals further with a promise of 'round the clock power for all by 2022'. But he also announced after winning the election, 'It is not enough to produce renewable energy. It is also important to produce it in a decentralized way'. 'My ultimate end', he said, 'is to produce solar power on roof tops and in farmers' fields'.

In India, like elsewhere, the promise of a life lived off the grid is mobilizing people, shaping politics and driving policies (Cross 2016). Yet there is nothing new about solar energy in rural India. In 1984, the same year that the mains electricity grid was extended to Gaudaguda village, solar-powered street lights were installed in five of the valley's Paroja villages under a district-level government development programme. These street lights represented the Government of India's first attempt to harness solar photovoltaics to projects of rural electrification, and they have been a mainstay of off-grid village electrification projects ever since.

Forty years later, these street lights play little part in local narratives about the coming of electricity. The street lights themselves are nowhere to be found, the poles long since dismantled and the panels sold on, and they rarely appear in oral histories of electrification. The same fate has befallen other experiments with renewable-energy technologies in the valley. A decade after an international non-governmental organization (NGO) installed a biomass gasifier in Gaudaguda, for example, the system and the organization had faded from local memories.

In the 2010s, the valley saw new attempts to extend access to energy through the distribution of domestic solar-powered lighting technologies. An Indian NGO installed a solar lantern charging station in one of the villages, and the NALCO mine distributed solar lanterns as part of a corporate social responsibility campaign. Meanwhile, the valley was also becoming a frontier market for solar-energy companies selling their brand-name solar lanterns as a cleaner, cheaper alternative to kerosene. When my family and I left the Gaudaguda Valley in 2012, we bought solar-powered lanterns for Ballava and others who had helped to look after us.

In January 2015, I made a return visit to the Gaudaguda Valley. Returning to the Paroja *sahi*, I was surprised to see a line of wooden poles running down the middle of the street. With no immediate prospect of electrification, people had taken matters into their own hands. Over the course of a month, Ballava and others, I learned, had dug up old wooden telegraph poles from across the valley, carried them home and planted them in a line down the middle of their colony. If they could only show the government that they had poles, Ballava explained, they hoped that the wires might follow.

The struggle by this Adivasi community for electricity despite the state's neglect – the story of the excavation of these heavy wooden poles and the sheer physical effort involved in carrying them several kilometres back to the *sahi* – was at once a scathing indictment of the indeterminacy or bureaucratic indifference of the Indian state and at the same time a powerful reminder of people's continued investment in and commitment to the electricity grid. Indeed, at the very moment that attempts to extend access to electricity in India have embraced decentralized or off-grid solar energy, people's material and symbolic investments in the grid appear stronger than ever.

Only disconnect

Off the grid, large-scale electricity infrastructures do not disappear into the background but become the object of heightened attention. Just like the hydraulic infrastructures built to distribute water in India's mega-cities (Anand 2017a), rural India's electric infrastructures do not just distribute 'current'; they also distribute difference and inequality. In inner-city Mumbai, however, the hydraulic infrastructures can give rise to heterogenous publics, mixed along class and religious lines, as the water network and water zones do not easily discriminate between different classes of resident who live alongside each other and are serviced by the same pipe (Anand 2017b; Björkman 2015). By contrast, in rural Odisha, electricity distribution networks map tightly onto the spatially segregation of caste and class. Here, programmes and plans for the expansion of the grid reproduce historic patterns of energy inequality between wealthy, land-owning farmers, Adivasis and Dalits. Village access to electricity is not always absolute; people do not simply live on or off the grid. Rather, most people live alongside the grid, with variegated patterns of access to electrified institutions (schools, clinics) and electric devices or technologies (pumps, mobile phones). For those whose homes and households remain un-electrified the promise of a grid connection is the promise of a social, political and technical connection to the state. In places like Gaudaguda, the network of transformers, pylons and wires that carry electricity from regional power stations into rural homes is the medium through which people imagine claims for state recognition, resources and entitlements. Here, 'current' is nothing if not a mode of citizenship: a form of political recognition, materialized and made possible by a material and technical connection to the grid, that affirms the capacity of people as equal members of a modern, Indian nation state.

Thinking with 'current' – or what the editors of this book might call 'current thinking' – presents an opportunity to extend these insights into recent debates about energy poverty, precariousness and vulnerability in the global south. For some scholars, notions of energy or fuel poverty – terms that continue to be deployed by researchers and policy makers to address problems of inadequate access to energy in developing countries – do not capture the ways that poverty might be an outcome of, or embedded in, wider institutional and spatial configurations (Bouzarovski and Petrova 2015). Attempts to address this in ways that capture the social, technical and environmental factors that prevent people from securing a materially and socially needed level of energy service in their homes has seen debate shift to broader understandings of 'energy precariousness' or 'energy vulnerability' (Bouzarovski et al. 2013, 2014). Such terms emphasize how the driving forces of energy deprivation extend beyond the home – to the structure of built environments, social practices and energy needs – while adding an important temporal dimension. These terms attempt to lift into focus the 'socio-technical' factors that lead people to become energy poor or prevent people from becoming 'energy secure'.

Yet in the context of rural Odisha, these notions of energy poverty, precariousness and vulnerability fail to grip the live wires of caste and class that have shaped and continue to shape the flow of current into everyday life. In a place like Gaudaguda, what we might call energy vulnerability is relational; it is an outcome of longstanding structural violence that has left some groups of people vulnerable to situated communities of interest, including dominant castes. To the extent that the villages Poraja Adivasis are seeking to address their vulnerability, they are not simply seeking stability or security but are also seeking equality and justice.

Against this backdrop, far from satisfying unmet needs for energy among the rural poor, India's off-grid solar revolution is making 'the grid' an ever more pressing matter of public concern, debate and struggle. Across rural India, expectations for grid-like standards of electricity are shaped by local histories of inequality and exclusion. A silicon solar photovoltaic panel might be able to convert sunlight into an electrical current, but the more important question for poor, rural adopters is whether it is capable of converting 'current', in its everyday, vernacular sense, into political recognition or connection.

India's solar engineers and renewable-energy policy makers are focused on the question of when the price of solar-powered electricity will reach price parity with on-grid electricity from conventional sources. Yet life off the grid in rural India will remain a second-class alternative until the lived experience of decentralized energy systems can realize the promise of the grid and readdress local histories of energy inequality and exclusion. As long as decentralized energy systems fail to address energy access as relational and fail to account for the socio-material politics that shape patterns of electrification, however, the off-grid future will continue to produce disconnection.

References

Anand, Nikhil. 2017a. *Hydraulic City: Water and the Infrastructures of Citizenship in Mumbai*. Durham, NC: Duke University Press.

Anand, Nikhil. 2017b. 'Hydraulic Publics', *Limn*. http://limn.it/hydraulic-publics/ (accessed 4 February 2019).

Bailey, F. G. 1957. *Caste and the Economic Frontier: A Village in Highland Orissa*. Manchester: Manchester University Press.

Bear, Laura. 2015. *Navigating Austerity: Currents of Debt along a South Asian River*. Stanford, CA: Stanford University Press.

Björkman, L. 2015. *Pipe Politics, Contested Waters: Embedded Infrastructures of Millennial Mumbai*. Durham, NC: Duke University Press.

Bouzarovski, S. and S. Petrova. 2015. 'A Global Perspective on Domestic Energy Deprivation: Overcoming the Energy Poverty–Fuel Poverty Binary', *Energy Research & Social Science*, 10: 31–40.

Bouzarovski, Stefan, Saska Petrova and Sergio Tirado-Herrero. 2014. 'From Fuel Poverty to Energy Vulnerability: The Importance of Services, Needs and Practices', *SWPS 2014-25*. https://ssrn.com/abstract=2743143.

Bouzarovski, S., S. Petrova, M. Kitching and J. Baldwick. 2013. 'Precarious Domesticities: Energy Vulnerability among Urban Young Adults', in K. Bickerstaff, G. Walker and H. Bulkeley (eds), *Energy Justice in a Changing Climate: Social Equity and Low-Carbon Energy*, 30–45. London: Zed Books.

Boyer, D. 2014. 'Energopower: An Introduction', *Anthropological Quarterly*, 87(2): 309–33.

Cross, J. 2016. 'Off the Grid', in Penelope Harvey, Casper Bruun Jensen and Atsuro Morita (eds), *Infrastructures and Social Complexity: A Companion*, 186–96. London: Taylor & Francis.

Cross, J. 2017. 'Current in South Asia', *Journal of South Asian Studies*, 40(2): 291–3.

Guha, R. 1999. *Savaging the Civilized: Verrier Elwin, His Tribals, and India*. Chicago, IL: University of Chicago Press.

Gupta, A. 1995. 'Blurred Boundaries: The Discourse of Corruption, the Culture of Politics, and the Imagined State', *American Ethnologist*, 22(2): 375–402.

Gupta, A. 1998. *Postcolonial Developments: Agriculture in the Making of Modern India*. Durham, NC: Duke University Press.

Gupta, A. 2012. *Red Tape: Bureaucracy, Structural Violence, and Poverty in India*. Durham, NC: Duke University Press.

Kale, Sunila. 2013. *Electrifying India: Regional Political Economies of Development*. Stanford, CA: Stanford University Press.

Larkin, Brian. 2013. 'The Politics and Poetics of Infrastructure', *Annual Review of Anthropology*, 42: 327–43.

Nehru, Jawaharlal. 2003. *Glimpses of World History*, 848. Delhi: Jawaharlal Nehru Memorial Fund/Oxford University Press.

Shah, A. 2010. *In the Shadows of the State: Indigenous Politics, Environmentalism, and Insurgency In Jharkhand, India*. Durham, NC: Duke University Press.

Srinivas, M. N. 1976. *The Remembered Village* (No. 26). Los Angeles: University of California Press.

5

What the e-bike tells us about the anthropology of energy

Nathalie Ortar

Every morning I get on my bike and climb the slope that goes up from my house. For a long time, I used to push my bike up this slope. I was usually sweating by the time I got to the flat part. The fact that most of my journeys around town were to go to my place of work or for professional meetings had influenced my choice of bicycle and made me opt for a city bike that was comfortable but not great on performance. However, ever since I have had my electrically assisted bicycle (e-bike), all that has changed: I turn it on at my house and after releasing maximum assistance, I savour the sensation of being pushed along every time I pedal. Of course, I still need to pedal, and that is why I opted for an e-bike rather than a different type of two-wheeled vehicle or a car, but this new type of bike has radically altered the effort made and therefore my way of cycling and its effects. It is not that I do not like traditional bicycles – I still go mountain biking at the weekend on a bike without electric assistance – but this bike has radically altered my way of moving around on a daily basis to such an extent that I could not do without it now.

I am a female researcher in anthropology and I am more than fifty years old. I have been cycling since my childhood, but I started cycling on a daily basis during my doctoral studies in Paris, mostly to avoid taking the bus and to get some physical exercise. I stopped for a few years when I moved to the south of France and started again when I got a position in Lyon thirteen years ago. I have an easy 9-kilometre ride of mostly flat terrain, except for the hill at the very beginning of my journey in the morning and at the end of it in the evening. Lyon is at the confluence of two rivers, the Saône and the Rhône, which have shaped the landscape, creating a flat part to the east of the city gained on marches and a western part agglomerated to steep hills. The metropolis of Lyon is trying to lower its CO_2 emissions through a climate plan that includes reducing car use. As part of this political initiative, for almost fifteen years now the metropolis has made efforts to develop cycling and has created new bike lanes and a bike sharing system, the success of which has increased dramatically since the arrival of e-bikes on the market. Indeed, the specificity of the landscape is a major factor for the success of the e-bike. Despite their cost, shops selling e-bikes have flourished, and as the city has been registering a regular increase in ridership from 10 per cent to more than 20 per cent every year since 2010,[1] e-bikes are increasingly noticeable. A seller with whom I spoke told me that the average mileage per year for an e-bike was 7,000 kilometres. He concluded that obviously those who buy e-bikes use them on a regular basis and to cover longer distances than the average city cyclist. And I, with my 9 km journey to work, correspond to the average e-bike user (Verloes, Louvet and Jacquemain 2015).

Within the frame of this chapter, I propose a reflective exercise on my own practice and to use physical movement as a medium for better understanding the qualities of lived experience (Sanders-Bustle and Oliver 2001). This narrative is personal but also reflects the many conversations I have had over time with other e-cyclists, both before and after I got my e-bike.

The principle of the e-bike is that it is still a bicycle, so electric assistance produced by a motor does not kick in until the cyclist pedals. It can be plugged in anywhere electricity is available, and unlike e-cars, it does not need any specific infrastructure. The increased capacity from the energy produced by the bike seems to have little effect on the way the bike is used, but it makes going up slopes easier where the land is hilly, which is the case in Lyon. It is also easier to get going again after stopping, and it can even assist cycling on the flat. Indeed, the first fans of the e-bike were already cyclists, and whereas it is possible to use any other motorized two-wheeler without knowing how to cycle, this is not possible in the case of the e-bike. From this point of view, the e-bike is still a bike like any other. Using it requires cycling skills already in existence but it makes daily or occasional use of the bike easier by reducing the effort necessary to get around.

The e-bike is more than a bicycle, however, as it involves a motorized element and the use of energy in the form of electricity. Contemporary research highlights the invisibility of energy and of electricity in particular: its daily importance to Western societies only becomes apparent when there is a lack of it, either because of a blackout (Rupp 2016) or for economic reasons (Knight and Argenti 2015; Knight and Bell 2013). This invisibility is linked partly to remoteness from the sources of electricity production and partly to the steady flow of that production to the user through the grid (Raineau, 2018; see also Bakke and Özden-Schilling, this volume). The invisibility of use and the quantity of materials necessary for its production make understanding of the unmediated relationship between human beings and energy difficult to explore, and we need to refocus 'our attention at the periphery of the power network' (Shin, this volume).

Indeed, as shown by the work of both historians and anthropologists, the use of a new source of energy transforms our understanding of daily life. The historian Christophe Granger (2018), for example, has revealed how the introduction of electric light led to a change in perceptions and bodily movements at nightfall. Electric lighting naturalized new ways of seeing and appreciating the visible world, ways which wrought changes in the intimacy of homes but also in relationships with others outside the home. In this volume, Hiroki Shin observes the complex process of electrification in Japan and how consumers circumvented the regulation of electrical outlet use to fulfil their growing need for electricity (Shin, this volume). Where the contemporary period is concerned, this subject has been illustrated in the work of Tanja Winther and Harold Wilhite (2015) dealing with the transformation of social relationships and of the relationship to internal and external spaces caused by the establishment of electricity use in Zanzibar. But how does this work when the analysis involves a pre-existing object where the sole change is the addition of a motor that does not even render all effort redundant?

The e-bike can be seen as an innovation whose effects on daily life I shall attempt to define. 'Positive innovation does not derive only … from borrowings, adaptations or creative localisations. On the one hand, it is affected by the evolution of the technical system leading, among other things, to the miniaturisation of objects of consumption. … On the other hand, social and symbolic representations are powerful activators of the object's metamorphoses' (Segalen and Bromberger 1996, 10–11). Innovation therefore proceeds from an encounter between humans who combine know-how with knowing how to communicate (Bromberger and Chevallier 1999). What are these mechanisms in the case of the e-bike, what are they based on and what can the use of this two-wheeled transport tell us about the effect produced by energy on human society? In this chapter, I propose to explore the modalities of an anthropology of energy, firstly through exploring how it fits into everyday routines, secondly by questioning the effects produced by materiality and thirdly through the social interpretation of these changes.

Cycling routines

Using the e-bike falls within a continuum of other experiences I have in my life as a cyclist that is made up of learning and feeling. Routines synthesize the idea of continuous learning. Routines belong to a network of tacit agreements and deep-rooted reflexes around which daily life, both domestic and professional, is structured (Ehn and Löfgren 2010), and they act as a memory for the body (Kaufmann 1997). Routines help to make actions automatic. They are regular sequences that are seen as physical techniques which make ordinary activities efficient, including the use of objects of whatever kind (Juan 2015). Routines are based on materiality inasmuch as they act upon and are performed within a material environment which may affect them (Mauss 1936). Thanks to repetition, routines gradually come to be performed without thinking, to rephrase the words of Albert Piette (Piette 2009). They fall within a 'cognitive economy' (Piette 2013, 70) corresponding to the deployment of sequences of actions which make the work of social interaction easier. They are at the core of an anthropology of the everyday but also of techniques. Indeed, the use of a technical object also proceeds by means of understanding how it fits into a set of practices relating to skills which call upon a variety of learning experiences.

As with any two-wheeled mode of transport, using an e-bike requires an ability to control balance, as well as the use of brakes and speed. I learned these skills as a child on my first bike, an orange bike that my parents gave me for Christmas when I was seven. Riding a bike also means learning how to behave in traffic and therefore knowing the social and legal rules of the road, which are initially taught by parents and then by institutions when one takes the test (at eleven years old in France) to acquire a cycling permit, possibly followed later on by the driving test. Riding a bike is therefore a physical act, because the body is set in motion. It is also technical, since this action is mediated by an object; and it is social too, since the cyclist moves within a socialized environment. How does using an electric bike modify these routines? Although the basic skills, that is, learning to keep one's balance on two wheels while pedalling, are the same as with a bike without electric assistance, using an electric bike requires additional skills. The first and most important was not to let myself be surprised by the way the bike reacted to being pedalled when it was stationary. I was used to playing with the pedals and I could no longer do this. This is particularly important at the beginning when you are crossing roads that are somewhat dangerous and you wrongly estimate the speed of the vehicle crossing. The way the bike behaved therefore forced me to learn this procedure all over again with this new vehicle. The use of a two-wheeled vehicle with a motor is not new to me. I used a moped when I was young, but I found that the e-bike does not have the problems I associated with the moped: noise, smell and passivity, except when going uphill, when you had to pedal to help the motor. The electric bike has none of these disadvantages because it is silent and has no smell. The noise is the same as on a bike: the slight swish of the chain rubbing against the derailleur when you change gear. The particular skills needed for the electric bike do not really amount to much. Using my bike, however, required a fairly high level of cycling skills; it was made to cover long distances and hills, and it had a ten-speed derailleur to optimize journeys. On most bikes, the gears change themselves, thus releasing the user from the need to do this. Using an electric bike may, in this case, even be considered to involve unlearning one's technical knowledge of the possibilities of a bike. A friend told me that since she had been using an electric bike, she found it difficult to use a normal bike because she had lost the habit of thinking about changing gears. This is not a direct effect of the energy but of the extra technicality that provides energy by allowing more automation which, because the bike is motorized, may be linked to the motor.

Most of the skills used and made part of a routine through my daily practice of riding a bike therefore come from my initial socialization. Without them, it would not be possible to use my bike. The adaptation demanded by the use of a motorized bike specifically involved becoming accustomed to the power of the motor so as not to expose myself to danger and to be able to use it to the best of my ability. What has changed is the speed of my body, which demands that I reassess its spatial position and its relation to other objects. It is therefore my cognitive abilities that have been tested through using this means of transport.

Materiality

For anthropologists, materiality is at the heart of their questioning when they are dealing with the use of technical objects. This is because, as Daniel Miller has noted, it is by studying what 'people do with objects' (Miller 1998, 19) that we can best understand how they create practical worlds. To continue my example of the e-bike, the bike becomes an extension of the body, which allows it to multiply the capacity of the body and, by the same token, leads it to modify its perceptual schema. I like walking better than cycling, but it would take me too long to walk to work. I therefore opted for the bike because I do not like public transport very much and I find driving in town irritating. So the increased capacity given me by a bike without assistance was the reason I initially opted for this means of transport. Going to work and coming back by bike enabled me to shorten my commutes and gave me some breathing space, literally as well as figuratively.

The body is subjective just as much as thought is (Warnier 1999, 21), because 'each subject is the product of a sensory and material environment' (Diaso 2009, 62) which needs to be analysed. A bike, to rephrase the terminology of Jean-Pierre Warnier (1999), offers increased capacity. Warnier uses the idea of the body map, which takes 'account of the fact that the perceptions and movements of the subject are coordinated, and that this coordination is the result of a sensorial and motor training' (Warnier 1999, 26). The 'body synthesis' which results from this 'is the synthesised and dynamic perception that a subject has of himself, of his motor behaviours and of his position in space and time. It mobilises all the senses in their relationship to the body itself and to the material culture. Elements of material culture therefore integrate with motor behaviours with their qualities of sensitivity, dynamism and individuality' (Warnier 1999, 27). This synthesis is the result of continuous learning which is maintained throughout one's whole existence. It therefore has great individual, cultural and social variability but guarantees the continuous nature of the subject's relationship to the environment. It alternately swells and retracts to include multiple objects (cars, domestic utensils, clothes, sports equipment, etc.) in the motor behaviours of the subject. Objects join forces with the subject to mitigate 'the constituent incompleteness of the human subject' (Warnier 1999, 12).

The world of cycling is a world of technique. Cycling can be considered as a tool that extends the whole person, delivering intentional action rather than body force (Ingold 2000, 319), and, as Spinney states, 'the cycling anatomy – of both bike and driver – does not come ready made; it is crafted through the cultural practice of cycling' (Spinney 2006, 717). The body learns to feel rhythm and, as Perry points out, 'riding a bike is a cyclical exercise that activates the body's circulatory systems' (Perry 1995, 3). Technique matters, as to ride the bike effortlessly, the user needs to know how to work gears. For those who practice the most, culturally mediated technologies then come to shape the rhythms and habits of the body-subject, which become one with the bike when clipped to the pedal (Spinney 2006, 719). The rider becomes part of the machine, a cyborg

(Haraway 1991) as, according to Spinney, the rider and the machine develop a symbiosis.

Using the e-bike on a day-to-day basis is also about technique. Gears matters too, but not as much as the feeling given by the presence of the motor and the impulse it gives while pedalling. It does not give the feeling of becoming one with the machine but rather of a friendly presence that is ready to help. What the motor gives is the same experience as when someone pushes you while climbing, and what the biker does is to play with the amount of help he or she is ready to receive according to the length and the difficulty of the journey. The e-bike is felt as a separate entity whose strength is felt at each pedal revolution. It is not therefore so much a matter of feeling one with the machine than of feeling the help given by the machine and measuring the amount of help one wishes to receive to ease the journey. The incompleteness of the human subject cannot be here transcended by an embodiment of the machine but is exceeded by the presence of the motor. Thus, it is not a matter of feeling one with the machine but rather of feeling the help given, of adjusting it. The incompleteness of the human subject is here temporized by his or her ability to accept help to increase the capacity of an already existing tool, a help that is felt while pedalling. The energy provides here a feeling distinct from the one provided by the machine without added motorization.

Sensory stimuli

The great change I experienced by owning an e-bike concerned the possibility of no longer having to go to work by car, meaning no longer being stuck in traffic jams in the morning and evening, no longer switching to automatic pilot in the midst of irritable motorists. The extra energy provided by the bike translated into less car use and the possibility of travelling around more often by my favourite means of transport. In a way, it was a simple transfer of energy from one means of transport to another, but this transfer involved using different routes and having access to journeys that gave me a feeling of riding for pleasure in order to get to work or go home in the evening. The extra energy provided by the bike certainly led to a lower total consumption compared to the car, but above all it gave me the possibility of travelling freely through places of my own choosing, a common practice adopted also by the e-cyclers I met. This choice of journeys according to their aesthetic qualities had already been the case to some extent.

I let myself make such choices in the morning but never at the end of the day, as the extra ten minutes at that time were essential. Having more time and energy means I can always take my preferred route, which enables me to ride on a cycle track totally removed from the traffic along the banks of the Rhône and then along a canal, which is more pleasant both visually and in terms of its scent.

I also chose the bike for the feelings it offers. This was the primary reason I chose to cycle, and it has been reinforced since I have an e-bike. I like to feel what the weather is like: the biting of the cold, the damp of the rain, the softness of the spring or the heat of summer. I also like to feel the air sweeping over me. I like the feeling of speed going downhill, even though it always frightens me a bit. I like to be able to take the time to stop in the morning when there is a beautiful sunrise, to watch the Rhône flowing by, to watch the rabbits running around, to experience the passers-by, to greet them and maybe stop for a chat without worrying about whether I am badly parked or not. I like not having any interference from external noises, overtaking cars that are stuck in traffic jams and being able to ride where they cannot go. The bike lets you use your sense of smell – the sense that is relatively little engaged in normal everyday life. To smell is to have access to the rhythm of the seasons in a different way than by sight: the changing fragrance of the flowers in spring and summer, the smell of wet earth and slightly rotting leaves in autumn and of wood fires in winter. There are unpleasant smells from car exhausts, which remind me how much cars pollute, and from the water treatment plant alongside my route when it is not working properly. These effluvia accompany me and make these journeys particularly distinctive compared to using the car or public transport. So I like travelling by bike because of the possibility of choosing my itinerary according to its aesthetic quality. I like cycling because I like feeling my body living and my muscles working. In *L'éloge de la bicyclette (In Praise of the Bicycle)*, Marc Augé (Augé 2010) endeavours to describe the multiple sensations and relationships arising from the practice of cycling in town. For him, this practice thus forms part 'of a gradual knowledge of oneself' and of time. Cycling is indeed also a means of measuring the time that has elapsed. Because of the way sensations stored up from childhood are telescoped alongside current sensations, the cyclist becomes aware of his or her ageing assessed in the light of his or her physical abilities. The bike favours 'a writing, often a free, even wild writing – an experience of automatic writing, surrealism in the act, or, on the contrary, a more constructed meditation, more formulated and systematic, almost experimental, through places previously selected by the refined taste of the erudite' (Augé 2010, 55–6).

The use of the e-bike brought out other feelings which added to the previous ones. The e-bike altered the effort I had to expend every day to move around and thus it allowed to feel more. The push it gives me in the morning was not a real push because it was my pedalling that caused it, but it feels like that, and it is my first pleasure of the morning and a source of amusement when people in the street see me go uphill apparently without effort.

Gregory Bateson noted that 'the mental world is not limited by the skin' (Bateson [1972] 2008, 250) but interacts with the environment through a multitude of sensory pathways. *Because*, as Marie-Pierre Julien, Céline Rosselin and Jean-Pierre Warnier point out, 'sensory experience, in a given situation, cannot be reduced to the sum of the sensations' (Julien, Rosselin and Warnier 2006), sensory anthropology helps us think from an empirical point of view about the articulation of scales of observation between the anthropology of the singular proposed by Julien et al. (2003) and Julien and Rosselin (2009) and that of Tim Ingold (2011) and the microsocial.

> Anthropology of the senses is based on the idea that sensory perceptions are not (or not only) a matter of physiology or psychology, but primarily the product of a cultural orientation which leaves a margin for individual sensibility. Sense impressions form a prism of meanings of the world; they are shaped by education and put into play according to the personal history of each individual. It is an individual's sensory resources which divide his world up into schemata of understanding and action. In the same community, they vary between one individual and another but they more or less agree on the essential. (Le Breton 2008)

The sensory approach is not specific to the study of the electric bike, but it affects the choice of the mode of transport and, in so doing, it affects the use which is made of that mode of transport (Ortar 2016b). Indeed, the space incorporated is the place where human awareness and experience take material and spatial form (Turner [1984] 2008). Its creation is the syncretism of space, movement and language. The space occupied by the body, its perception and experience, contracts and expands according to the individual's emotions and state of mind, their sense of self, their social and cultural relationships and predispositions. This self is perceived by Western culture as being 'naturally' located in the body (Scheper-Hughes and Lock 1987). Sensorial anthropology includes the body, not as a metaphor of social and cultural conceptualization but as an organism upon which culture exerts an influence. The study of the electric bike cannot ignore this approach. The experience is both shared because of its cultural background and unique because individuals not only structure space differently from one another, but also experience it differently and live in distinct sensory worlds (Hall 1968).

Dealing with the question of energy use in the domestic sphere, Sarah Pink has relied on her own thinking about the way a home is constructed as well as on auto-ethnography, because 'the ways we use air, water, gas and electricity cannot be dissociated from our sensory and emotional experiences regarding the home. They are contingent upon the infrastructures of the home and share in the formation of the sensory home' (Pink 2011, 117). The fact that energy is invisible for the user (Shove et al. 2008), as it is for the ethnographer, and is not consumed *per se* but in the form of the goods and services it procures (Wilhite 2005, 2) is, however, as she rightly remarks, not such an unusual situation for the ethnographer. In order to submit the uses of domestic energy to ethnographical study, it is necessary to capture the qualities of the experience, whether this is sensory, emotional or related to memory. This is what Alan Warde (2005) has called the internal benefit of practice. To carry out research into energy, it is therefore important to engage in ethnographic practice using visible and material methods, technical processes and people who consume energy, extending these to other spheres beyond the purely domestic.

Dependency

Pedalling on this new bike, controlling it in order to move about on it, were not, however, the greatest transformations brought about by motorization: this came from the use of battery power. Using an electric bike means learning to move about while taking account of the limits of the means of transport chosen, of the mysterious charge held by the battery, which I never fully conceptualize (see Bakke, this volume). There is something of a contradiction here between the freedom of movement provided by two wheels and the limits of its battery. In fact, when you have an electric bike, you have to think in a very organized way about charging the battery. Within the context of daily life, having become dependent on objects which themselves depend on battery capacity, such a requirement may seem obvious, but in the context of the bike this nevertheless demands an ability to think ahead that might not necessarily be as important for other daily activities. In fact, when you think battery, you must think charging, either from an electric current directly accessible where the bike is kept or by removing the battery and taking it to a place where charging is possible. Charging means access to the grid or to some kind of device providing electricity. Having an e-bike implies, therefore, access to some sort of infrastructure, and it implies the need not just for trails and roads to get around but also electricity. In this respect, the e-bike is a step into a form of dependence, a dependence to the charge itself. Having a bike with a battery means that you must not forget to put it on charge, and this must therefore become part of your daily routine. The development of routines around the battery requires a routine to be set up where none has been required before. Thinking of charging one's battery is a simple, trivial action but it has important consequences; that is, the user avoids running out of power during journeys.

Apart from the need to acquire this daily routine, management of the battery also represents a constraint when there are unusual journeys, and this requires learning how to use the technology. On the e-bikes, the battery is held in by a lock to prevent it being stolen – a lock that therefore needs a key that must be neither lost nor forgotten when the battery is being charged. This does not normally cause me any problem because my battery has sufficient autonomy for my everyday comings and goings. It becomes more of an issue when I make an exceptional journey that requires the battery to be charged during one of the stops on the journey. Using the e-bike then involves anticipating the charges and therefore not forgetting the key and the charger. In addition to these practical aspects, the use of the e-bike makes it necessary to anticipate one's movements and plan them according to the limits of the battery capacity, an approach that is fundamentally different from that of using a normal bike. Battery use also makes it necessary to anticipate the consequences of the weather forecast in winter. In fact, cold reduces battery capacity. So it is a matter of also anticipating machine failure and planning one's movements. The increased capacity provided by the battery entails a loss of autonomy in organizing one's journeys, and a need for planning, which is not necessary when using a 'traditional' bike.

The use of the battery requires new routines to be created and some loss of autonomy to be accepted in order to gain capacity. The use of the e-bike is therefore not a neutral process and involves accepting an increased dependency on the socio-technical system and less freedom of movement to gain increased capacity.

The need to recharge the battery also implies that the places I go to are connected to a local or national means of producing electrical energy. As independent electricity production is still rare in France, this therefore implies that I need to go somewhere that is dependent on the national distribution network. Alain Gras (1997) has pointed out that one of the transformations brought about by electricity use is the dependence on what he calls 'macro-structures'. By 'macro-structure', he means the infrastructures which channel energy: oil and gas pipelines and, of course, high-voltage electrical power lines. This dependency is apparent in car usage, which depends on supply points. This is even truer where the electric bike is concerned because of the time that it takes to charge the battery as well as its more limited running time. Using the electric bike beyond urban areas therefore means putting myself at the mercy of infrastructures and carrying out calculations for my journeys that are dependent not only on the distance to be travelled but also on the electricity distribution network. This additional constraint tells us something about the limitations on movement implied by energy dependency. Use of the bicycle is in fact only possible within the limits of the energy distribution network: the low range, between 30 and 45 km according to use, does not permit journeys that extend far from supply points. This therefore restricts freedom of action to an area lying within a socio-technical network. To repeat a metaphor used by Tim Ingold (2007), the lines along which I move have become contingent upon the high-tension lines, the nodes of possible access to energy.

Temporality

Dependency was always something present when I began to use my e-bike; however, I justified its use by its practical usefulness and the increased dependency on the grid by the time both saved and given. The e-bike saves me a considerable amount of time on my journeys. Speed is not the main advantage of the e-bike. In fact, it is limited to 25 km/h, which means that beyond that, the assistance is deactivated. The cyclist then finds himself- or herself on a very heavy bike with no appropriate gearing system to brake with, unless he or she pedals very fast. The time gain occurs when starting again from stationary. One of the irritations of urban cycling is the need to stop frequently. It takes effort to set off again and time to regain one's cruising speed. The real gain lies in being able to set off again without any effort and being able to get back to one's cruising speed very quickly. The decreased effort I need to make to start off again increases the pleasure I get from cycling, as it makes my journey more fluid. It has therefore altered my experience of my journeys around town.

Time saved and decreased effort are two crucial aspects in the choice of an e-bike. Before I had my e-bike, I used to go to work on an ordinary bike. However, I only went by bike three days out of five because it was too physically tiring. Although it took me the same time by car in the morning as by bike, around forty minutes, in the evening the car journey was quicker, which enabled me to collect my children without leaving work too early. Indeed, one of the great pleasures of the city bike, whether electric or not, is to no longer be a slave to congestion and to be able to overtake stationary cars and then slip onto the tracks along the banks of the Rhône, going under the ring-road, which is always congested in the mornings.

Sarah Pink (2004) notes that the domestic organization of daily life necessarily takes place in multiple situations, because interactions within the home only acquire meaning when account is taken of all the places which influence the supplying and organization of the domestic unit (Ortar 2014, 2016a). To be able to acquire a new source of mediated energy, it is necessary to understand how this links up on a day-to-day basis with all the various activities. If this approach is more sociological in inspiration, it is nevertheless essential for understanding the context in which the innovation is received, its effect upon daily life and the part it plays in reconfiguring this, as well as the way it changes the user's relationship to time over a day, a month or a year. The increased capacity procured by the bike alters the individual's social time and, by extension, that of the entire family.

Discussion

This presentation of the various elements around the use of the e-bike, whether these involve a change in the experience, the necessary learning process, the increased capacity provided by motorization or the limits and constraints imposed by the use of the battery, informs what could be an anthropology of energy. Energy directly affects the activities of people through the increased capacity it provides; it enables people to act differently or to extend an activity they have already begun. Thus, it modifies their relation to time and their daily routines. However, energy also creates situations of dependency; it modifies the relationship with autonomy on a daily basis. Energy enables capacity to be increased but it limits action and constrains it, enclosing it in pre-existing processes which are largely outside the actor's control.

Adoption of the technical object also depends on subjective elements like the feelings engendered by its use. These feelings are important because they affect the use that will be made of the technical object that is mediating energy. An anthropology of energy therefore requires that various different daily experiences be investigated, from the innermost to the most external, in order to be able to grasp what energy does to humans. We should examine what energy provides in terms of increased capacity to undertake activities and also in terms of well-being in the pursuit of those activities; and we should also explore the feelings experienced without the use of energy, but to which energy grants us greater access. The anthropology of energy therefore needs to combine contributions from different fields: studies in materiality and technology and from the sensory sphere, as well as studies of time and of day-to-day existence, with the aim of understanding the relationship to the technical object, the advantages it brings, how learning to use it takes place and also how the use of this object becomes part of everyday life.

More broadly speaking, any energy switch is accompanied by profound social changes (Melosi 2010). According to Laura Nader, Cesarino and Hebson (2010), moving from essentially carbon-based energy to other energy sources fundamentally reconfigures societies; such a transformation is accelerated by environmental and economic crises which are already causing behavioural changes. The current energy transition not only reflects technical and scientific choices but also has a profound effect on our ways of being together, our relationships with our environment and our daily routines, for reasons that are as much practical and ecological as financial. These are the factors that an anthropology of energy must get to grips with by accounting for the complexity which underlies every adoption of a new technical process, even one as trivial as the electric bike.

Note

1 *À Lyon le trafic vélo a augmenté*, http://www.rue89lyon.fr/2017/01/27/a-lyon-trafic-velo-a-augmente-de-26-2016 (consulted 22 March 2017).

References

Augé, Marc. 2010. *Éloge de la bicyclette*. Paris: Rivages poche/Petite bibliothèque.
Bateson, Gregory. [1972] 2008. *Steps to an Ecology of Mind*. Chicago, IL: Chicago University Press.

Bromberger, Christian and Denis Chevallier (eds). 1999. *Carrières d'objets, Ethnologie de la France*. Paris: Éditions de la Maison des sciences de l'homme.

Diaso, Nicoletta. 2009. 'La liaison tumultueuse des choses et des corps: un positionnement théorique', in Marie-Pierre Julien and Céline Rosselin (eds), *Le sujet contre les objets... tout contre. Ethnographies de cultures matérielles*, 21–83. Paris: CTHS.

Ehn, Billy and Orvar Löfgren. 2010. *The Secret World of Doing Nothing*. Berkeley: University of California Press.

Granger, Christophe. 2018. 'Une révolution de l'œil. Lumière électrique et gouvernement du visible, 1870–1914', in Nathalie Ortar and Hélène Subrémon (eds), *L'énergie et ses usages domestiques: Anthropologie d'une transition en cours*, 37–60. Paris: Pétra.

Gras, Alain. 1997. *Les macro-systèmes techniques, Que Sais-Je*. Paris: PUF.

Hall, Edward. 1968. 'Proxemics', *Current Anthropology*, 9(2): 83–95.

Haraway, D. J. 1991. *Simians, Cyborgs, and Women: The Reinvention of Nature*. London: Routledge.

Ingold, Tim. 2000. *The Perception of the Environment: Essays on Livelihood, Dwelling and Skill*. Londres: Routledge.

Ingold, Tim. 2007. *Lines: A Brief History*. London: Routledge.

Ingold, Tim. 2011. *Being Alive: Essays on Movement, Knowledge and Description*. Londres: Routledge.

Juan, Salvador. 2015. 'Le concept de routine dans la socio-anthropologie de la vie quotidienne', *Espace populations sociétés* (1–2).

Julien, Marie-Pierre and Céline Rosselin (eds). 2009. *Le sujet contre les objets... tout contre. Ethnographies de cultures matérielles*. Paris: Éditions du CTHS.

Julien, Marie-Pierre, Julie Poirée, Céline Rosselin, Mélanie Roustan and Jean-Pierre Warnier. 2003. 'Chantier ouvert au public', *Techniques & Culture* [online], (40). http://tc.revues.org/1559 (accessed 7 February 2019).

Julien, Marie-Pierre, Céline Rosselin and Jean-Pierre Warnier. 2006. 'Le corps : matière à décrire', *Corps*, 1(1): 45–52.

Kaufmann, Jean-Claude. 1997. *Le coeur à l'ouvrage : théorie de l'action ménagère*. Paris: Nathan.

Knight, Daniel and N. Argenti. 2015. 'Sun, Wind and the Rebirth of Extractive Economies: Renewable Energy Investment and Metanarratives of the Crisis in Greece', *Journal of the Royal Anthropological Institute*, 21: 781–802.

Knight, Daniel and Sandra Bell. 2013. 'Pandora's Box: Photovoltaic Energy and Economic Crisis in Greece', *Journal of Renewable and Sustainable Energy*, 5(3): 1–16.

Le Breton, David. 2008. *Anthropologie du corps et modernité, Quadrige Essais Débats*. Paris: Presses Universitaires de France.

Mauss, Marcel. 1936. 'Les techniques du corps', *Journal de Psychologie*, 32(3–4). http://classiques.uqac.ca/classiques/mauss_marcel/socio_et_anthropo/6_Techniques_corps/Techniques_corps.html (accessed 21 November 2015).

Melosi, Martin. 2010. 'Energy Transitions in Historic Perspective', in Laura Nader (ed.), *The Energy Reader*, 45–60. Oxford: Wiley-Blackwell.

Miller, Daniel (ed.). 1998. *Material Cultures: Why Some Things Matter*. Chicago, IL: University of Chicago Press.

Nader, Laura, Leticia Cesarino and Chris Hebson. 2010. 'Introduction', in Laura Nader (ed.), *The Energy Reader*, 1–16. Chichester: Wiley-Blackwell.

Ortar, Nathalie. 2014. 'Le quotidien peut-il être durable? Routines dans la baie de San Francisco', *Norois* (231): 13–25.

Ortar, Nathalie. 2016a. 'Dealing with Energy Crises: Working and Living Arrangements in Peri-Urban France', *Transport Policy*. doi: 10.1016/j.tranpol.2016.09.008.

Ortar, Nathalie. 2016b. 'Domesticating Transport: The Sensory Experience of Work-related Travel', *The Senses and Society*, 11(3): 275–85.

Perry, David. 1995. *Bike Cult: The Ultimate Guide to Human-Powered Vehicles, Four Walls Eight Windows*. New York: Da Capo Press.

Piette, Albert. 2009. *Anthropologie Existentiale*. Paris: Petra.

Piette, Albert. 2013. 'Au coeur de l'activité, au plus près de la présence', *Réseaux* (182): 57–88.

Pink, Sarah. 2004. *Home Truths: Gender, Domestic Objects and Everyday Life*. Oxford: Berg.

Pink, Sarah. 2011. 'Multimodality, Multisensoriality and Ethnographic Knowing: Social Semiotics and the Phenomenology of Perception', *Qualitative Research*, 11(3): 261–76. doi: 10.1177/1468794111399835.

Raineau, Laurence. 2018. 'Chapitre 4 : Les contradictions d'une transition énergétique morcelée', in Nathalie Ortar and Hélène Subrémon (eds), *L'énergie et ses usages domestiques: Anthropologie d'une transition en cours*, 101–13. Paris: Pétra.

Rupp, Stephanie. 2016. 'Dynamics of Disruption in New York City Blackouts', *Economic Anthropology*, 3: 106–18.

Sanders-Bustle, Lynn and Kimberly L. Oliver. 2001. 'The Role of Physical Activity in the Lives of Researchers: A Body-Narrative', *Studies in Philosophy and Education*, 20: 507–20.

Scheper-Hughes, Nancy and Margaret Lock. 1987. 'The Mindful Body', *Medical Anthropology Quarterly*, 1(1): 6–41.

Segalen, Martine and Christian Bromberger. 1996. 'L'objet moderne : de la production sérielle à la diversité des usages', *Ethnologie française*, 26(1): 5–16.

Shove, Elizabeth, Heather Chappells, Loren Lutzenhiser and Bruce Hackett. 2008. 'Comfort in a Lower Carbon Society', *Building Research & Information*, 36(4): 307–11. doi:10.1080/09613210802079322.

Spinney, Justin. 2006. 'A Place of Sense: A Kinaesthetic Ethnography of Cyclists on Mont Ventoux', *Environment and Planning D: Society and Space*, 24: 709–32.

Turner, Bryan. [1984] 2008. *The Body and Society: Explorations in Social Theory*. London: Sage.

Verloes, Alia, Nicolas Louvet and Gautier Jacquemain. 2015. *Le vélo à assistance électrique: un nouveau mode de transport métropolitain.* 6-t: Paris.

Warde, Alan. 2005. 'Consumption and Theories of Practice', *Journal of Consumer Culture*, 5(2): 131–53. doi:10.1177/1469540505053090.

Warnier, Jean-Pierre. 1999. *Construire la culture matérielle. L'homme qui pensait avec ses doigts.* Paris: Presses Universitaires de France.

Wilhite, Harold. 2005. 'Why Energy Needs Anthropology', *Anthropology Today*, 21(3): 1–2. doi:10.1111/j.0268-540X.2005.00350.x.

Winther, Tanja and Harold Wilhite. 2015. 'Tentacles of Modernity: Why Electricity Needs Anthropology', *Cultural Anthropology*, 30(4): 569–77.

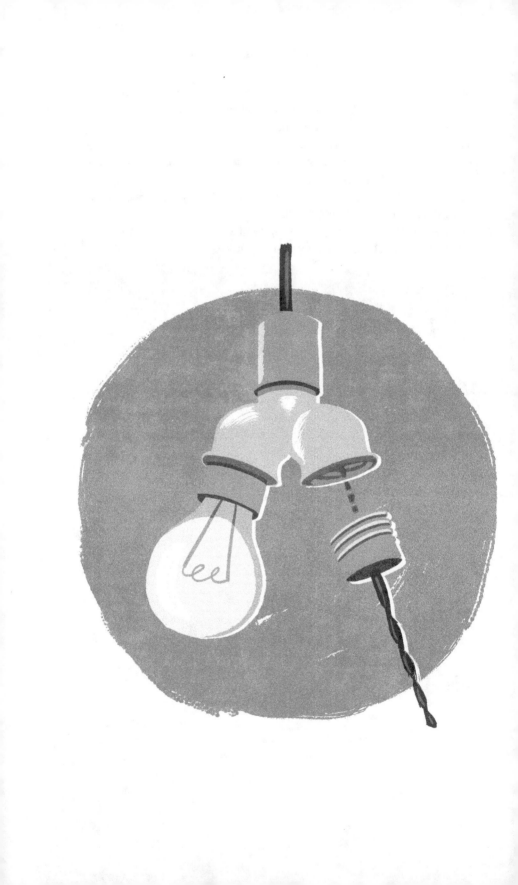

6

At the edge of the network of power in Japan, c. 1910s–1960s[1]

Hiroki Shin

In February 1951, a service member of an electric utility company visited a newly built house in the suburbs of Tokyo. When he entered the house to inspect the main switch, he discovered that the lady of the house was cooking stew on an electric cooker which, under the terms of her supply contract, she was not allowed to use. She was duly reprimanded and fined for breaching the contract. After he left, she took her husband's Smith & Wesson handgun from the drawer – she was a police officer's wife – and shot her two children and herself. One of the children survived the injury, but the wife and the other child died the next day (*Yomiuri Shimbun*, 15 February 1951). This violent episode had little to do with the economic situation of the family, as they could undoubtedly afford electricity. It related more closely to the wider issue of domestic infrastructure, the socially constructed idea of 'legitimate' electricity use and users' everyday practices. To explore these issues, this chapter focuses on the role of 'small things' in the development of electrification in Japan: wires, metres, sockets and wall outlets and how they were used and modified by consumers. The connective devices – located at the junction between electricity supply and consumption – were not only essential components that enabled electricity use but also defined the ways in which electricity was consumed.

Fred Schroeder's 1986 article opened up the topic of connective devices – previously considered to be minor forms of technical equipment – to a wider question of domestic electrification. In the article, Schroeder explored how domestic electrical plugs and receptacles constituted a 'technological roadblock' for the expansion of electricity use (Schroeder 1986). While Schroeder examined connective devices largely within the context of their technological development, Graeme Gooday discussed electricity and gas metres as objects whose development has been shaped by both providers' and users' interests. By correctly quantifying and visualizing consumption, the metres helped consolidate the sense of trust in the energy supply market by ensuring that users were not overcharged and that providers were sufficiently remunerated for their service (Gooday 2004).

More generally, theoretical and empirical works in science and technology studies (STS) and anthropology offer important insights into how technology use is mediated by objects and users. Moving beyond the functionalist approach to technical objects, STS have directed attention to the agency of technical objects that operates through their design, including assumptions about by whom and in what context they are used. As Madeleine Akrich argued, 'technical scripts' embedded in the design of technical objects bind users' actions. At the same time, technical devices operate within wider, heterogeneous networks of social relations, legal systems and economic power structures. The complex and contingent nature of human–object relationships means the original intention of the designers is not always dominant in practical scenes of object use, leaving spaces for negotiation and resistance (Akrich 1992; Oudshoorn and Pinch 2003, 205–24). An electricity metre can be used to control consumption, but users sometimes find ways to bypass it by mobilizing the knowledge and skills of informal networks of, for example, corrupt members of utilities, local technicians or amateur engineers. Anthropological studies show such forms of resistance. In Michael Degani's study (2013), street technicians in Tanzania often help indebted customers to surreptitiously reconnect to the supply grid. Lamia Zaki described how electricity theft by shantytown dwellers in Casablanca, which often took the form of violent attacks on officials, was grounded in the inhabitants' sense of rights and their anti-authoritarian sentiment (Zaki 2008). The border between licit and illicit connection can be negotiable, such as in Zanzibar, where utilities often overlook unauthorized connections on ceremonial occasions like weddings and funerals (Winther 2008, 107–8). These studies demonstrate that technical scripts are as open and fluid as they are binding and restrictive. The openness and fluidity of technical scripts allow consumers to actively take part in technological development. As Oldenziel and Hård argued in their recent book (2013), Europe's technological development owed much to tinkering and rebelling consumers, who modified, co-designed and selectively adopted technology. The same is true of Japan which, by the 1980s, came to be known as a technology-obsessed, gadget-loving nation.

Not so much of a bright life: Electricity comes home

First introduced in 1886, the use of electricity in Japanese households spread rapidly from the 1910s onward, when nationwide hydropower development began. The proportion of wired households – that is, the electrification rate – grew rapidly between 1920 and 1933, from 50 per cent to more than 80 per cent, ahead of the United States' 69 per cent and Britain's 44 per cent (Kurihara 1964, 180; Makino 1992, 55–6). The electrification rate, however, is an imperfect measure of electricity use, as it only shows the population's access to electricity and does not address how or how much electricity they consumed. In fact, per capita electricity consumption in Japan remained much smaller than other countries with lower electrification rates. A Japanese user in 1938 consumed 60 per cent less electricity than an American user. The reason was simple: the large majority of electrified households only used electricity for illumination. Diffusion of electrical appliances, such as the vacuum cleaner and washing machine, was much faster in the United States and Britain than in Japan (Makino 1992, 58; Bowden and Offer 1994, 731).

With the exception of urban cities like Tokyo, only a small minority of domestic users were on a metered tariff, while the majority were on 'night-time-only' fixed-tariff contracts, calculated not by the amount of electricity consumed but by the number of electricity lamps. In 1928, fixed-tariff customers in Tokyo paid 0.4 yen a month for a 5-candlepower lamp, 0.55 yen for a 16-candlepower lamp, 0.65 yen for a 24-candlepower lamp and so forth (Tokyo Chamber of Commerce 1928, 6). Without the need for metre installation costs, the fixed tariffs also helped to smooth the way for electrification. In contrast, a metered contract was expensive because users needed to pay for the lease of the single-phase metre, an additional expense of 0.1 to 0.2 yen per month.[2] Many utilities only allowed metered contracts for consumers that owned more than five lamps, though in Tokyo, some companies installed the metre for houses with only one or two lamps. In the 1930s, around 80 per cent of electricity consumers paid a fixed tariff and had electricity only during the night (Kajima 2013) (Figure 6.1).

The utilities' promotion of electrification generally focused on widening the customer base rather than boosting each user's consumption. Although some companies that operated in urban competitive areas and were interested in cultivating off-peak demand did promote appliances beyond illumination, users needed to pay a higher tariff for non-illumination purposes. The Kyoto Electric

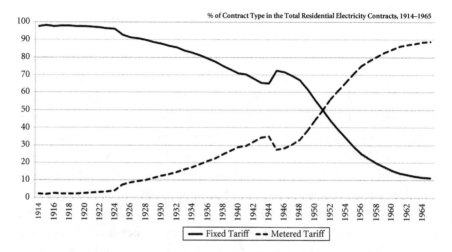

Figure 6.1 Fixed tariff and metered tariff, 1914–1965.

Source: *Denkijigyō Yōran*, various years. Courtesy of Atsushi Kajima and the Electric Power Historical Museum, Tokyo, Japan.

Lighting Co.'s electric heating tariff in 1915 included the use of electricity (0.038 yen per kwh), the stove (3.30–6.75 yen per month) and the metre (0.3–0.8 yen per month) (Kyōto Dentō 1939, 153–4). When the starting monthly salary of a bank employee was around 40 yen, electricity was not cheap. Consequently, even in Tokyo, those who had electric heaters for cooking or space heating comprised only 1.2 per cent of the total domestic electricity users (Tokyo Chamber of Commerce 1928, 10).

Historians tend to privilege the stories of early electricity adopters, but there was a substantial gap between the image of modern electrical life, circulated by electrification advocates and appliance manufacturers, and the reality of average consumers' lives. A model room exhibited in a Transport and Electricity Exhibition (1928) was filled with various electrical appliances, such as electric lamps, heaters, dryers and an electric hair iron, and it was also equipped with seventeen electric outlets (Murase 2009, 52). Such electrical life was well beyond the means of the large majority of consumers. On average, an electrified household at the time only had a few lamps of little more than 20 watts that were usually dim (Tamura 1942, 22). The large majority of houses at the time had a few lamp sockets dangling from the ceiling. As frequently shown in contemporary advertisements, users connected additional devices, such as an electric iron or a foot warmer, to the lamp socket (Figure 6.2).[3] When the only lamp socket in a room was occupied by an additional device, the users could not use electric lighting – they needed to choose between light or, say, an iron.

To solve such a problem, an entrepreneur in the 1920s started to market 'two-way' sockets that enabled the use of multiple devices from a single socket. The device became extremely popular: in the 1930s, between two and three million were sold annually. However, it was not a fundamental solution to the problem of domestic electrical infrastructure.

The slow diffusion of electrical appliances in pre-Second World War Japan thus had multiple causes. The technical scripts of lamp socket and home wiring with a limited number of electricity outlets reflected the early utilities' idea that the sole use of electricity in the home was for illumination,

Figure 6.2 Matsushita Electric Company's advertisement for an 'electric foot-warmer', 1928.

Source: Courtesy of the Panasonic Museum, Osaka, Japan.

an idea that constrained diversifying electricity use. The popular contract type also restricted the use of electricity beyond illumination and night-time use. The use of lamp sockets for additional devices and the popularity of two-way sockets show that consumers negotiated the prescribed use of electric lamp sockets. The following section will show how electricity connection was also a matter of resistance and conflict.

'Consumers cheat companies': Electricity theft and misappropriation

The dynamic nature of the issue of electricity connection is represented by the steady increase in illicit use of electricity. The most obvious form of illicit use, electricity theft, already existed in the 1890s (Okamoto 2013). Even after the inclusion of electricity theft in the criminal code in 1907, utilities preferred not to prosecute offenders. This did not mean that utilities overlooked malefactors; rather, they established a broader definition of theft and contract breach under the category of 'misappropriation' of electricity to regulate users' behaviour. In addition to the simple form of electricity theft, fixed-tariff users' consumption of electricity beyond contracted hours and purposes was considered a breach of contract. Connecting additional devices without the providing company's authorization and tinkering with wiring, sockets and metres constituted misappropriation, as did the use of two-way sockets in most supply areas.

As the number of wired houses increased, utilities faced a significant number of misappropriation cases. For instance, in an eight-month period between 1925 and 1926, an electric provider discovered 53,436 cases of electricity misappropriation – 11 per cent of the houses inspected (Hōrai 1927, 102). As metered users were a minority, tampering with the electricity metre was relatively rare. More common methods were the use of unauthorized appliances (including light bulbs not supplied by the provider), rewiring the home to increase electricity outlets or tapping electricity from a nearby supply cable to circumvent night-time-only supply. Many offences were motivated by the wish to dodge the cost of the official rewiring service, contract change and payment for metres; however, just as many misappropriation cases were committed by users frustrated by the slow and tedious processing of contract change or rewiring work by utilities. A customer in Tokyo lamented that installing an additional light bulb often took more than a week and, for electric heating and other appliances, 'we need to spend many days for cumbersome consultation with utilities' (Matsushita Denki 1933, 141). As utilities recognized, electricity misappropriation was not necessarily committed by those who could not afford electricity. Middle-class households were frequently found illicitly using electricity even when they could afford it.

Electricity theft was a complex problem. As a contemporary American scholar has pointed out, the growth in electricity distribution and per capita electricity consumption worked as an incentive for consumers, because the expanding use of electricity increased the share of the utility bills in their household expenditures. The greater the costs of electricity in a household, the more consumers were enticed to dodge the burden. Moreover, when electricity use was normalized in society and people's dependence on electricity deepened, reducing consumption became harder even in the face of a significant economic changes such as an economic depression, which forced some households to choose to use electricity illicitly rather than cut down on their electricity use (Yopp 1935, 3–4).

Advocates of domestic electrification generally believed that electricity use could be promoted by raising the level of knowledge about electricity among consumers. The growth of electricity misappropriation showed that educating electricity consumers had an unexpected consequence. On one hand, utilities hoped that consumers would become competent users of electricity who could fix minor problems like a blown fuse (Okuda 1947, 56). On the other hand, with the circulation of electricity knowledge through the public media and school education, the temptation to tinker with equipment and try new appliances increased. Electricity experts saw a direct link between electricity knowledge and misappropriation. One utility company learned that the worst offenders were found among its employees (*Denki Keizai Jiron*, 15 July 1933). At any rate, what Akrich called the 'distribution of competence' was fluid and changeable. The absence of connective devices in the home, contractual constraints and the broad definition of electricity misappropriation tended to limit the number of those competent enough to modify the household infrastructure. Notwithstanding, equipped with electricity knowledge, consumers started to find ways to bypass various constraints imposed on their use of electricity.

The misappropriation problem worsened during the immediate post-Second World War period. Against the background of general fuel shortages, domestic electricity consumption was on the rise because electricity was cheaper and more readily available than other fuels. The post-war boost in electricity consumption was accompanied by a significant increase in illicit use. In 1946, for example, 25 per cent of electricity consumption was attributed to illicit use. The misappropriation was persistent and continued until the early 1950s, when an electricity expert, Susumu Kajita, reported that 'consumers cheat the companies by using more electricity than what they contract for and overload the lines' (Kajita 1950). A nationwide survey on the situation of the eight supply regions in 1948 found 603,074 cases of misappropriation, indicating that, in some regions, more than 20 per cent of users committed illicit electricity use (*Denki Shimbun*, 30 August 1948). The supply companies responded by rigorously patrolling customers' houses. In 1949, the Kansai Electric Distribution Company organized a 'Fair Use' campaign, and its Inasawa branch, for instance, enlisted all branch employees, except for female clerks, to patrol 15,800 of their customers.

The inspectors invaded customers' domestic space, examining light bulbs and wiring and carefully checking every room to find hidden appliances. They found customers using electric cookers, heaters and other items without the company's authorization. Some perpetrators tapped into nearby supply cables using a detachable connector that could be quickly removed and hidden away during the inspectors' visit. Some rewired their homes, concealing the extended wiring behind walls or inside beams, pillars and pipes. Unauthorized items were also hidden in cupboards, cabinets, closets and larders. Metered customers had ways to tamper with the metre. It was common knowledge that one could purchase devices at backstreet shops that reversed the electricity metre (Chubu Haiden 1954, 317). Canny users obstructed the working of the induction disc in the metre with metal wires, and some users put spiders inside the metre, thinking that spider nests might stop the disc from rotating. Users were inventing intricate ways to use electricity behind the utilities' backs; one inspector reported that, as far as the company was aware, there were 118 different methods of illicit use (*Denki Shimbun*, 13 February 1950).

Users were often helped by neighbourhood engineers, electricians and carpenters, who advised and provided services to hide cables and extra outlets. As pointed out in studies on illicit use in today's developing countries, electricity theft often mobilizes informal social networks and family connections (Zaki 2008, 120; Degani 2013, 185–6). The collective nature of illicit use is also shown by the fact that 'stolen' electricity is often shared within a household and among relatives and neighbours (Winther 2012, 111–19). Nevertheless, utility companies in post-war Japan portrayed the offences as being committed by selfish and immoral individuals. Just as in the pre-Second World War period, the utilities steered away from economic explanations of illicit use, claiming that offenders could afford to pay the bills but were trying to avoid doing so (Nihon Denki Kyōkai 1950, 50). According to the supply companies' logic, illicit use was not caused by poverty but by the lack of moral sense. The illicit users were also selfish, the utilities stressed, because their excessive electricity use overloaded the local supply network, creating frequent local blackouts that inconvenienced their neighbours. The utilities relied heavily on neighbourhood informants to detect offenders, encouraging mutual surveillance. The moral argument went further, as it was claimed that electricity misappropriation impaired the moral sense of family members, especially when 'innocent children saw their parents committing an ill-natured act of stealing others' property' (Tanahashi 1948, 5–6). Thus the utilities' moral campaign, propagated through posters, handbills and radio broadcasts, attempted to isolate offenders from their neighbours and even within the family.

The suicide of the policeman's wife in Tokyo in 1951 mentioned at the beginning of this chapter encapsulates the cultural construction of electricity misappropriation at the time. In a subsequent report, the bereaved husband was quoted as saying that 'he had no grudge against the electricity company' (*Yomiuri Shimbun*, 17 February 1951). Accepting the utilities' moral argument, the husband admitted that his wife committed an immoral and selfish act. The wife, on the other hand, killed herself and her child, believing that the discovery of illicit electricity use tarnished the reputation of her family. The construction of misappropriation as a crime of selfish individuals was at odds with the collective nature of energy use. In Japan, up until the mid-twentieth century, personal use of electricity was the exception rather than the rule. Electric lighting entered first into the household's working or communal space – the kitchen and living room – and it took a while before private rooms such as the bedroom and children's rooms came to be equipped with electric lamps (Shibusawa 1979, 343; Tokyo Dento 1932, 7). Other electrical appliances which saw relatively early diffusion – such as electric irons, cookers and washing machines – were generally for the benefit of the entire household. Even radio and TV, in the early stages of their penetration, were enjoyed by the family as a whole rather than by a single member of the household. In the case of the policeman's wife, her illicit electricity use enabled her to cook dinner for her family, and therefore her family was the collective beneficiary of the electricity use.[4] However, the individualist formulation of illicit use tended to single out housewives, who had traditionally been regarded as the managers of household fuel use, as being solely responsible for restraining the household from what was labelled as the selfish misuse of electricity.

The hunt for illicit users created tension between providers and users; in fact, metre readers tended to face a violent response from customers on discovery of misappropriation. In 1948, the electricity industry's trade union demanded that companies take precautions against potential violence triggered by the discovery of illicit use (*Denki Shimbun*, 10 December 1948). In the same year, a metre reader had been brutally murdered by a Buddhist monk found using an electric cooker without authorization (*Yomiuri Shimbun*, 7 December 1948). In part to avoid such violent conflicts, utilities turned to technical means, investing substantially in electricity metres, breakers and limiters. The number of installed metres more than doubled between 1945 and 1952 from around four million to nearly ten million (Figure 6.3). This also meant that, by the mid-1950s, the majority of users had been transferred to metered tariffs, and their electricity consumption was now captured by the measuring device. For the most part, contract change was compulsory, especially for those whose illicit use was discovered by the supply company.

The installation of metres and other user-restraint devices reduced the risk of direct conflict between utilities' employees and customers. Simultaneously, the utilities gradually withdrew from users' domestic space, as metres replaced the restriction on the types and numbers of appliances in users' homes. By the mid-1950s, providers largely stopped prohibiting additional appliances and outlets and began concentrating on the amount of electricity consumed, as shown on the electricity metre. Unauthorized rewiring remained a contract breach, but as long as users paid their bills, it was treated as a minor incident. The restrictive regime of electricity consumption came to an end.

As Kirshner and Power argue in this volume, the everyday spaces of electrical power are contested domains in which the state and energy suppliers' attempt

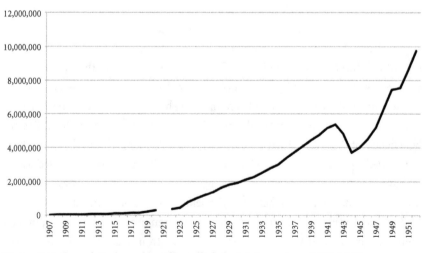

Figure 6.3 Cumulative number of installed electricity metres, 1907–1952.
Source: *Denki Jigyō Yōran*, various years.

to discipline consumers can be subverted by users' resistance and practices (Kirshner and Power 2018). To a significant extent, post-war Japan's landscape of electricity use was shaped by the micro-politics of everyday life.

Culture of safety and energy governmentality

The withdrawal of providers from electricity users' domestic space continued in the late 1950s, when it became a common practice to install the metre outside the house. The separation between the domestic space of the home, in which users enjoyed the freedom to use electricity as they saw fit, and monitoring of their consumption from outside was established. With the relaxation of the contractual ban on additional appliances and outlets, consumers gained control of their electrical lives. The utilities' definition of misappropriation was simplified to include only metre tampering and straightforward electricity theft. As a result, the number of misappropriation cases significantly declined.

In the conventional chronology of Japan's electrification, the mid-1950s is chiefly understood as the beginning of the post-war electrification boom. The so-called 'three sacred treasures' – TV, the washing machine and the fridge – became the objects of desire for Japanese consumers. Along with these consumer durables, sales of smaller appliances, such as the iron, sewing machine, toaster, mixer and rice cooker, increased. The introduction of new appliances to Japanese homes required infrastructural upgrades, as the diverse range of appliances increased each household's electricity consumption.

The process of infrastructural renewal was by no means easily achieved. With the extension of electricity networks to millions of houses, a sweeping infrastructural upgrade was beyond the power of utility companies. Unlike investment decisions regarding large networks, home wiring upgrades required the willingness of individual households with different priorities, interests and economic resources. Even in relatively new housing stocks, such as the post-war apartment blocks (*danchi*), the rapid pace of electrification far exceeded the expectations of architects. Led by the Japan Housing Corporation (JHC), construction projects started in the mid-1950s in order to provide housing for the increasing population of urban white-collar families. Equipped with the dining kitchen, city gas supply and family bath, *danchi* life represented the aspirational lifestyle of young nuclear families. As soon as the new flats were populated with aspirational consumers, however, the technical script of the *danchi*'s room design proved to be a constraint to expanding electricity use. For instance, in 1957, a young couple moved into a *danchi* flat, bringing with them a desk lamp, toaster, coffee maker, iron and radio. Four years later, they had a *kotatsu* heater, record player, vacuum cleaner, fridge, sewing machine, electric rice cooker and TV (Tomita 1962, 328–9). They bought these new appliances only to realize that their houses were not equipped for using the increasing number of appliances – the first standard JHC flat design had only one electricity outlet in the kitchen and one in the living room – which became a perennial source of residents' complaints (Nihon Jūtaku Kōdan 1975, 139; Jūtaku Kenkyūjyo Iinkai 1954). As a researcher commented, the JHC architects' projection of the electricity demand increase represented a gross underestimation (Tomita 1962, 340–1). Not surprisingly, residents were found modifying the wiring, often in breach of the tenant agreement (Izawa 1965, 223). The situation was far worse in old housing stocks and traditional-style houses. Even as late as 1967, more than a quarter of houses in Tokyo had fewer than two electricity outlets, 28 per cent had three or four outlets and 4.2 per cent had none (Nihon Denki Kōgyū Kai 1967, 39).

It was clear that neither the JHC nor utilities were able to keep up with the frenetic pace of electrification by assuming the burden of rewiring customers' houses. Instead, energy providers and appliance manufacturers began to stress that consumers had to take care of their own wiring upgrades by planning for their current and future needs. Utilities finally realized that tinkerers of home wiring could be turned into their allies. In 1958, the Adequate Wiring Programme was initiated by the energy providers, manufacturers and the semi-governmental Electricity Safety Committee. The programme set in motion a nationwide publicity campaign, exhorting consumers to upgrade their home wiring and other equipment. The campaign extensively employed advertising films, posters, magazine articles, radio broadcasts and TV commercials, and a number of wiring advice bureaus were established in various parts of the country (Horii 1960).

The Adequate Wiring Programme stressed the safety hazards of inadequate or obsolete wiring. Before the Second World War, safety issues were occasionally raised, especially to intimidate tinkering users; however, in the early stage of electrification, the utilities usually presented safety as a minor issue to reassure their consumers of electricity's safety (Hōrai 1927, 105–6). The issue of safety emerged strongly during the post-war electrification boom, when the increase in domestic electricity consumption strained home wiring with insufficient capacity, creating the danger of overloading, which could result in home fires. By then, electricity had become a major cause of home fires, surpassing the number of fires caused by the kitchen stove, chimney and arson (Figure 6.4). The hazard of home fires became the recurrent theme in the Adequate Wiring Programme's publicity campaign. For example, the Shikoku Electric Power Company's 1959 film *Mama no Otegara* [*Mom's Great Feat*] depicted vivid scenes of a home fire caused by overloading the obsolete wiring in an apartment. Another film, *Naraga Shi Harikiru* [*Mr Nagara Tries Hard*] (1964), reminded users that simply retrofitting electricity outlets to old home wiring was as dangerous as the early practice of connecting multiple devices to a lamp socket (Figure 6.5).

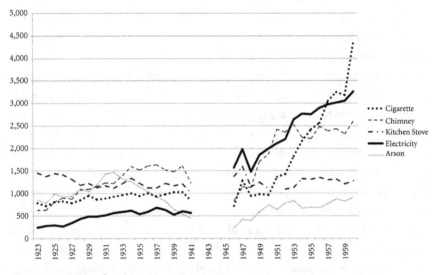

Figure 6.4 Home fires by cause, 1923–1960.
Source: Japan Ministry of Internal Affairs and Communications, Statistics Bureau http://www.stat.go.jp/data/chouki/29.htm.

Figure 6.5 *Nagara Shi Harikiru*, Tokyo Electric Power Company, 1964.
Source: Courtesy of the Electric Power Historical Museum, Tokyo, Japan.

The programme targeted a single member of households: the housewife. A 1957 film, *Michiko no Yume* [*Michiko's Dream*], shows a housewife, despite her husband's indifference to home wiring, eventually achieving the electrical life of her dreams by getting rid of 'octopus wiring' (several electrical cords dangling from a ceiling lamp socket) to install wall outlets and switches in the kitchen, living room and bedroom. As Joel Tarr and Mark Tebeau (1996) argued, the early household safety movement in the United States firmly targeted housewives, putting them in charge of safety in the domestic environment and of protecting their children and family. The same construction of the role of the housewife in domestic electricity use can be observed in Japan during the electrification boom. The Adequate Wiring Programme sought to propagate the image of housewives as 'home safety managers' and to make wiring upgrades an important responsibility of homemakers. In the gendered construction of safety culture, consumerist language is the distinctive characteristic. In 1957, a popular lifestyle magazine featured a 'shopping guide for connective devices' ('Shopping Guide' 1957). Reviewing a variety of plugs and switches on the market, the article encouraged consumers to develop a sharper eye for the quality of connective devices so as to avoid home fires: 'Don't leave it to contractors and electricians. You must choose the best product.' Similarly, a Matsushita Electric Company's publicity booklet advised consumers to 'equip your home with more wall outlets than you think are necessary' for safety and convenience. In a later issue of the same booklet, a housewife in Hiroshima proudly announced that her new kitchen had 'plenty of power outlets, as I will be using more electrical appliances in the future' (Matsushita Denki, *Kurashi no Izumi*, n.d., Vols 18 and 25).

The utilities' withdrawal from domestic space gave electricity users freedom to choose which and how many appliances they used in their homes. This liberal regime was accompanied by the large-scale campaign that sought to instil a culture of safety in consumers' minds. The Foucauldian theory of liberal governmentality can explain the social and cultural configuration that intimately connected safety and consumer freedom (Defert 1991). In the late 1950s, what emerged in Japan was a form of governmentality that regulated electricity users' conduct through self-discipline and technical provisions in the liberal market. The installation of electricity metres on the exterior of the home shows how the withdrawal of direct intervention and control of individual users' electricity use was accompanied by the everyday technology of monitoring and self-regulation. Electricity metres outside homes rendered electricity consumption inside the house visible to utilities from outside. As far as the amount of electricity consumption was concerned, consumers were more closely monitored by utilities than they were during the period of fixed tariffs. Inside the home, users were expected to regulate their conduct themselves by checking the level of electricity consumption and number of appliances according to their economic resources and home infrastructure. Consumer freedom in electrical life came in tandem with the everyday technology and technique of self-discipline.

The liberal state clearly played a part. The standardization of domestic electricity plugs and receptacles in 1950 was followed by an Indoor Wiring Regulation (1954) and the Electrical Appliance and Material Safety Law (1961). Most consumers did not keep up with the intricate regulations and laws concerning their home wiring, but as home decision makers, they were caught in the complex web of home wiring and outlet regulations, and their decisions were influenced as much by their pursuit of convenience as by the internalized sense of safety. The safety-oriented governmentality by no means emerged in a vacuum. One can see a link between the early moral campaign against electricity misappropriation and the later safety campaign, as both campaigns shared an individualist construction of electricity use. In the former period, individual users were cautioned against the selfish and immoral act of misappropriating electricity; in the latter period, the same individual users – which increasingly meant housewives – were told to take responsibility for home safety by equipping their houses with adequate wiring. The continuation of the individualist framework meant that the safety-oriented energy governmentality was built upon the legacy of the early restrictive regime.

Conclusion

To some extent, consumer self-discipline oriented around the notion of safety still operates today, though the infrastructural upgrades made over the last several decades have made its operation inconspicuous. What, then, is the relation between the energy governmentality, carried over from the previous period, and new technology, such as the smart metre? Some scholars argue that the widespread introduction of the smart metre will create an opportunity for implementing an environment-focused governmentality (Stripple and Bulkeley 2014). Such a process would require a good understanding of the pre-existing culture of energy. As Tom Hargreaves (2014) points out, multiple forms of governmentality operate in everyday life, to which a new form of governmentality is supplanted or inserted. In order to anticipate how the new energy governance will work, it would be useful to know about older or existing forms of energy governmentality (Boyer 2011).[5] Here, historical and anthropological investigations of electricity use can play an important role by helping us understand the complex process of electrification, including its experience and implications (Winther and Wilhite 2015). For instance, we can start thinking about the collective responsibility for controlling household energy consumption within a family or community by looking back on the past social construction of individualized energy use.

Illicit use of electricity has never disappeared. It is a fact of life in today's India, Pakistan, Jamaica and Tanzania, and it also exists in developed countries like the United States, the United Kingdom, Italy and Japan (Kassakian and Schmalensee 2011, 9; Smith 2004, 2073). Across the world, researchers have begun to look for explanations for persistent electricity theft beyond issues of economy or technology.[6] Kirshner and Power argue, for instance, that electricity theft in developing countries has often resulted from political neglect of the affordability issue for low-income electricity consumers in favour of concentrating on expanding the supply network (Kirshner and Power 2018). Similarly, the continued reliance on the civic and moral discourse in the Indian utilities' battle against the illicit use of electricity demonstrates that the issue is enmeshed in a wider socio-cultural context (Criqui 2016). When examined closely, energy users' illicit practices often show the operation of technical scripts, tinkering consumers and politico-economic regimes.

For both licit and illicit use of electricity, today's consumers are the children of early tinkering electricity users. Many of us inhabit houses and offices with multiple taps, adapters, USB hubs and multiple chargers, hardly noticing the continuing warnings against octopus wiring. Consumers are still modifying the landscape of everyday energy use. At any rate, in order to understand electrification of the home over the last hundred years or so, we need to redirect our attention to the edges of the electricity network. Although policy makers, utilities and network engineers have tended to focus on the core and main arteries of electricity distribution, for energy users, the centre stage of modern electrical life has been firmly located at the edge of the power network.

Notes

1 This chapter draws on research findings from the 'Material Cultures of Energy: Transitions, Disruption and Everyday Life in the Twentieth Century' project (UK AHRC, AH/K006088/1). The author would like to thank Frank Trentmann,

Heather Chappells, Vanessa Taylor, Rebecca Wright and Takuji Okamoto for their comments and suggestions.
2 Until the mid-1930s, most electricity metres were imported from Britain, Germany, the United States and Switzerland. For example, *Denki Jigyō Yōran*, 20 (1929), 1040–1.
3 For a similar situation in the United States (Schroeder 1986, 530).
4 On Japanese women's traditional role as managers of domestic fuels (Yanagita 1998, 395).
5 However, it must be noted that there are certain limitations to the governmentality perspective for studying energy consumption in everyday life. See Trentmann (2012, 541–2).
6 There is a growing body of literature on the contemporary challenge of energy theft. See Smith (2004), Never (2015) and Winther (2012).

References

Akrich, M. 1992. 'The De-Scription of Technical Objects', in W. Bijker and J. Law (eds), *Shaping Technology/Building Society: Studies in Sociotechnical Change*, 205–24. Cambridge, MA: MIT Press.
Bowden, S. and Offer, A. 1994. 'Household Appliances and the Use of Time: The United States and Britain since the 1920s', *Economic History Review*, 47(4): 725–48.
Boyer, D. 2011. 'Energopolitics and the Anthropology of Energy', *Anthropolicy News*, 52(5): 5–7.
Chubu Haiden. 1954. *Chubu Haiden Syashi*. Chubu Haiden, Nagoya.
Criqui, L. 2016. 'Delhi: Questioning Urban Planning in the Electrification of Irregular Settlements', in A. Luque-Ayala and J. Silver (eds), *Energy, Power and Protest on the Urban Grid*, 86–111. London: Routledge.
Defert, D. 1991. '"Popular Life" and Insurance Technology', in G. Burchell, C. Gordon and P. Miller (eds), *The Foucault Effect: Studies in Governmentality*, 211–33. Chicago, IL: University of Chicago Press.
Degani, M. 2013. 'Emergency Power: Time, Ethics, and Electricity in Postsocialist Tanzania', in S. Strauss, S. Rupp and T. Love (eds), *Cultures of Energy: Power, Practices, Technologies*, 177–92. Walnut Creek, CA: Left Coast Press.
Denki Jigyō Yōran, Teishin Shō Denki Kyoku/Nihon Denki Kyōkai, Tokyo, various years.
'Denki Senyō Bōshi to Dōtokuteki Syakaishūsei no Zesei', *Denki Keizai Jiron*, 15 July 1933.
Denki *Shimbun*, Tokyo, 30 August 1948; 10 December 1948; 13 February 1950.
Gooday, G. 2004. *The Morals of Measurement: Accuracy, Irony, and Trust in Late Victorian Electrical Practice*. Cambridge: Cambridge University Press.

Hargreaves, T. 2014. 'Smart Meters and the Governance of Energy Use in the Household', in J. Stripple and H. Bulkeley (eds), *Governing the Climate*, 127–43. New York: Cambridge University Press.

Hōrai, Y. 1927. *Denki Jyōshiki*. Tokyo: Hakubunkan.

Horii, T. 1960. 'Tekisei Haisen Undō', *Shōmei Gakkai Shi*, 44(7): 100–1.

Izawa, T. 1965. 'Denka Seikatsu no Genjyō to Kōdan Jyūtaku ni okeru Denka Seikatsu no Shōrai', in Nihon Jūtaku Kōdan, *Syokuin Kenkyū Ronbunshū*, 203–34. Tokyo: Nihon Jūtaku Kōdan.

Jūtaku Kenkyūjyo Iinkai. 1954. 'Tokyo Toka Konkurīto Apāto Jyūkyo ni Kansuru Chōsa Hōkoku 1', *Jūtaku Kenkyū*, 4: 1–36.

Kajima, A. 2013. 'Nihon ni okeru Teigaku Dentō Sei to Denkyū Kasitsuke no Hensen', *Kitakyūshū Kōgyō Kōtō Senmon Gakko Kenkyū Hōkoku*, 46: 9–26.

Kajita, S. 1950. 'Losses in Electricity', report to Van Swearingen, 13 June, GHQ/SCAP Records RG331, Box 8251, Folder 35, National Diet Library Japan.

Kassakian, J. and R. Schmalensee. 2011. *The Future of Electric Grid: An Interdisciplinary MIT Study*, Technical Report, Massachusetts Institute of Technology.

Kirshner, J. and M. Power. 2018. 'Electrification and the Consolidation of State Power in Mozambique' in this volume.

Kurihara, T. 1964. *Denryoku*. Tokyo: Kōjyunsha.

Kyōto Dentō. 1939. *Kyōto Dentō Kabushikigaisya 50 Nen Shi*. Kyoto: Kyōto Dentō.

Makino, F. 1992. 'Katei Enerugī no Syakai Keizaishi [Residential Energy Use in Pre-War Japan]', *Tokyō Gakugei Daigaku Kiyō* III, 43: 37–79.

Matsushita Denki Sangyo. n.d., late 1950s. *Kurashi no Izumi*, vols. 18 and 25.

Matsushita Denki Seisakusho. 1933. *Denki Juyōsya wa Nani wo Nozonde iruka*. Tokyo: Matsushita Denki.

Murase, K. 2009. '"Katei Denka" no Dispurei', in Y. Fukuma, K. Namba and N. Tanimoto (eds), *Hakuran no Seiki*, 37–71. Matsudo: Azusa Shuppan.

Never, B. 2015. 'Social Norms, Trust and Control of Power Theft in Uganda: Does Bulk Metering Work for MSEs?', *Energy Policy*, 82: 197–206.

Nihon Denki Kōgyōkai. 1967. *Taikyū Shōhizai no Jyuyō Dōko Chōsa*. Nihon Denki Kōgyōkai, Tokyo.

Nihon Denki Kyokai. 1950. *Denki no Senyō wo Dōshite Fuseguka*. Nihon Denki Kyokai, Tokyo.

Nihon Jūtaku Kōdan. 1975. *Nihon Jūtaku Kōdan 20 Nen Shi*. Nihon Jūtaku Kōdan, Tokyo.

Okamoto, T. 2013. 'Tōden no Hōri, Hozumi Nobushige no Shunjun', *Sūri Kagaku*, 51(3): 70–7.

Okuda, T. 1947. *Nenryō to Seikatsu*. Tokyo: Kōdansha.

Oldenziel, R. and M. Hård. 2013. *Consumers, Tinkerers, Rebels: The People Who Shaped Europe*. Basingstoke: Palgrave Macmillan.

Oudshoorn, N. and T. Pinch. 2003. 'Introduction: How Users and Non-Users Matter', in N. Oudshoorn and T. Pinch (eds), *How Users Matter: The Co-Construction of Users and Technology*, 1–28. Cambridge, MA: MIT Press.

Schroeder, F. 1986. 'More "Small Things Forgotten": Domestic Electrical Plugs and Receptacles, 1881–1931', *Technology and Culture*, 27(3): 525–43.

Shibusawa, K. (ed.). 1979. *Meiji Bunkashi 12, Seikatsu Hen*. Tokyo: Hara Shobō.

'Shopping Guide'. 1957. *Kurashi no Techō*, 40: 128–35.

Smith, T. 2004. 'Electricity Theft: A Comparative Analysis', *Energy Policy*, 32: 2067–76.

Stripple, J. and H. Bulkeley (eds). 2014. *Governing the Climate: New Approaches to Rationality, Power and Politics*. New York: Cambridge University Press.

Tamura, K. 1942. *Senjikeizai to Denryokukokusaku*. Tokyo: Tōa Seikei Sha.

Tanahashi, M. 1948. *Denki Senyō Bōshiho Yōtei*. Funabashi: Denki Bunka Sha.

Tarr, J. and M. Tebeau. 1996. 'Managing Danger in the Home Environment, 1900–1940', *Journal of Social History*, 29(4): 797–816.

Tokyo Chamber of Commerce. 1928. *Tokyo Chihō Denkiryōkin ni kansuru Chōsa*. Tokyo.

Tokyo Dento. 1932. *Denka Shiryō*, vol. 55, Dentō Juyōka Survey.

Tomita, K. 1962. 'Kodan Jūtaku no Denka Seikatsu to Haisen Sekkei ni Tsuite', in Nihon Jūtaku Kōdan, *Syokuin Kenkyū Ronbunshū*, 328–48. Tokyo.

Trentmann, F. 2012. 'The Politics of Everyday Life', in F. Trentmann (ed.), *The Oxford Handbook of the History of Consumption*, 521–47. Oxford: Oxford University Press.

Winther, T. 2008. *The Impact of Electricity: Development, Desires and Dilemmas*. New York and Oxford: Berghahn Books.

Winther, T. 2012. 'Electricity Theft as a Relational Issue: A Comparative Look at Zanzibar, Tanzania, and the Sunderban Islands, India', *Energy for Sustainable Development*, 16: 111–19.

Winther, T. and H. Wilhite. 2015. 'Tentacles of Modernity: Why Electricity Needs Anthropology', *Cultural Anthropology*, 30(4): 569–77.

Yanagita, K. 1998. 'Hi no Mukashi', in Yanagita Kunio, *Yanagita Kunio Zenshū*, vol. 14. Tokyo: Chikuma Shobō.

Yomiuri Shimbun, 7 December 1948; 15 February 1951; 17 February 1951.

Yopp, H. T. 1935. 'The Growth and Prevention of Electricity Energy Diversion', master's thesis, Georgia School of Technology. https://smartech.gatech.edu/handle/1853/17622 (accessed 13 March 2017).

Zaki, L. 2008. 'Transforming the City from Below: Shantytown Dwellers and the Fight for Electricity in Casablanca', in Stephanie Cronin (ed.), *Subalterns and Social Protest: History from Below in the Middle East and North Africa*, 116–37. London: Routledge.

7

Can the Mekong speak? On hydropower, models and 'thing-power'

Casper Bruun Jensen

According to the Consultative Group for International Agricultural Research (CGIAR)'s research programme on water, land and ecosystems, there are 241 completed dams in the Mekong basin, 29 are presently under construction and 91 more are being planned.[1] The majority will be located in Laos, a country that envisions a future as the 'battery of South-east Asia'.[2] However, many dams are also planned in Cambodia, since a cheap, steady supply of electricity is a prerequisite for luring foreign companies into the country's special economic zones (Jensen 2019). Along the Mekong, electrified futures are everywhere on the agenda.

Shrouded in secrecy, Chinese hydropower investments flow into Cambodia as part of bundled economic packages. As development ensues, people living close to dams are threatened with displacement or denied access to land and means of livelihood. Ecologies suffer, too, as development proceeds without environmental mitigation measures and water flows are altered, diverted or stopped. Yet, despite promises of electrification, rural people have yet to see many or, in some cases, any, benefits. International and local non-governmental organizations (NGOs) join protests against the dams.

Meanwhile, colluding foreign and local businessmen and politicians engage in various forms of resource extraction, from illegal dredging of sand and gravel for export to Singapore[3] to the destruction of forests in search of valuable timber for the upscale Chinese market. On top of this, the Mekong region is estimated to be one of the areas in the world most vulnerable to climate change. The spring of 2016 saw an unprecedented heat wave, and threats of both droughts and floods are increasing as river flows and rain patterns transform.

The push to hydropower occurs in a landscape overflowing with events and initiatives, saturated with promises and threats, political manoeuvring and forms of knowledge. Yet, this does not mean that the setting is comprised only of people, their dreams and their struggles. Made of, and populated by, rivers and streams, animals and an array of infrastructures, this is a landscape of more than humans. Inspired by new materialism and object-oriented philosophy, recent anthropology of energy argues forcefully for the need to deal with these non-humans, with materiality, with things. And in the Mekong basin, too, such powers can hardly be overestimated. Yet, how to deal anthropologically with the forces of things remains elusive.

My vantage point for engaging this issue is an ongoing exploration of how the present and future Mekong basin is turned into an object of knowledge and action by diverse forms of hydrological, ecological and climate modelling. Starting from the question of how and why the river is modelled and by whom, this project aims to understand the practical and policy uses, but more often lack of use, of the many models circulating in the Mekong.

Perhaps the link between electrification and hydrological modelling seems tenuous. However, since the effects of Mekong hydropower development are not amenable to direct verification, being ambiguous, distributed over thousands of kilometres and unfolding gradually over long time spans, they must be modelled. Hydrological models, in combination with other kinds of models, are used to estimate the consequences dam cascades, built to produce electricity, are likely to have for water flows, sedimentation flows and the habitats of fish and other animals.

In the following, I examine how the powers of dams and electricity are elicited, mediated and made visible through models that thereby exhibit their own powers. At one level, this chapter thus aims to add nuance to discussions about how the power of things, or non-things (Bakke, this volume), like electricity, can be anthropologically elicited. At another, an examination of the complicated relations between dams, rivers and models opens a discussion about the kinds of subject positions available to those in search of less destructive paths to an electrified Mekong.

Alternating currents: Electricity and climate change in anthropology

As exemplified by the present volume, electricity and energy are topics of increasing social scientific interest (see also Agustoni and Maretti 2012; Boyer 2014; Strauss, Rupp and Love 2013; Urry 2014).

Painting broadly, one might point to two ways in which the anthropology of energy deals with its phenomena. The first engages in ethnographic study of local practices, for which a broader story of political economy often forms the general context. In this vein, the editors of *Cultures of Energy* (Strauss, Rupp and Love 2013, 10) note that since the 'human use of energy is understood and experienced through cultural frameworks,' the key question is how energy plays a role in the making of socially meaningful worlds. Accordingly, 'the enormous energy challenges facing us all are fundamentally cultural and political *rather than* technological' (Strauss, Rupp and Love 2013, 10, my emphasis). As indicated by the phrase 'rather than,' the cultural and political here *replaces* energy and its infrastructures as the topic of concern.

Other approaches are more closely connected with the anthropology of infrastructure (Harvey, Jensen and Morita 2016; Jensen and Morita 2017) prefigured by research in science and technology studies (STS) (e.g. Bowker 1994; Summerton 1994). For one thing, electricity networks *are* infrastructures, and Thomas Hughes' (1983) path-breaking *Networks of Power* was concerned with how they were shaped. For another, the analytics of these approaches often relies on a core insight from the STS corpus: that technological systems tend to fade from view, becoming invisible in front of our eyes or under our feet. Thus, Timothy Mitchell (2013) has analysed the historical process whereby oil became the spinal fluid of modern societies, and Dominic Boyer (2015, 532) has recently written that 'electricity is a fascinating subject of inquiry because it is in many respects the foundational apparatus upon which the experience of modernity has been constituted since the late nineteenth century'. This emphasis on non-human agency resonates strongly with STS analyses including actor–network theory and Andrew Pickering's *The Mangle of Practice* (1995). Increasingly, however, anthropologists also turn to new materialism and object-oriented ontology for guidance on how to deal with the force of things.

Contrary to socio-cultural analyses of energy, the second line of inquiry aims to find ways of taking non-human agency into account. At issue is the attempt to grapple with electricity and its infrastructures not as an underlying support system for cultural practice and meaning making, but rather as a set of material assemblages that generates heterogeneous effects beyond human perception and volition (Jensen and Morita 2017). Referencing Jane Bennett and Timothy Morton, Dominic Boyer (2015, 532), for example, finds inspiration in 'recent pushes to bring the material and nonhuman more securely into political theory'. He goes on to describe electric grids as grooving 'political efficacy, subjectivity, and affiliation' (2015, 533), ascribing to them the capacity to shape societies or even modernity as such.

Stopping one flow to start another

In Cambodia, dam development is conducted mostly by Chinese companies under BOT (build, operate, transfer) contracts. These contracts stipulate a timeframe for construction and confer upon the building company the right to operate the dam for a period, say 40 years, after which it will be transferred to the Cambodian government. According to recent national environmental impact assessment legislation, environmental and social safeguard and mitigation measures have to be in place, yet there is little accountability, transparency or enforcement of these rules (Siciliano et al. 2016). Accordingly, local people and environments suffer from the impacts of development, and resistance from national and international NGOs is vigorous, though largely ineffective.

In order to generate electricity, companies build dams that allow for the storage and controlled release of water. Stopping the natural flows of rivers like the Sesan, Sambor and Srepok in north-eastern Cambodia, dams start flows of electricity. Stopping the flows of fish and sedimentation that sustain local livelihoods, the dams instead propel flows of capital. Clearly, an understanding of this situation requires attention not only to people but also to things. But what exactly does this entail?

Jane Bennett's analyses of 'thing-power' offer an influential answer. For Bennett, 'thing-power' opens up to an 'adventurous ontological imaginary' in which matter is 'active, intricate, and awesome' (2004, 364; see also Scott 2013). She describes coming across a stick of wood, a plastic glove and a dead rat by a storm drain, feeling suddenly 'struck' by their singularity. In a flash, Bennett realized that these were not inert objects but rather lively parts of an assemblage,[4] which she defines as 'ad hoc groupings of diverse elements, of vibrant materials of all sorts … living throbbing confederations that are able to function despite the persistent presence of energies that confound them from within'. Using the massive American blackout of August 2003 as an illustration (see also Nye 2010), Bennett characterizes the electric grid as 'a volatile mix of coal, sweat, electromagnetic fields, computer programs, electron streams, profit motives, heat, lifestyles, nuclear fuel, plastic, fantasies of mastery, static, legislation, water, economic theory, wire, and wood – to name just some of the actants' (Bennett 2010, 25).

Bennett offers a lively narrative of interactions between generators, transmission lines and brush fire. Even so, her analyses leave the reader with little concrete sense of the processes that shaped these assemblages and conferred particular kinds of power on things within them. This mode of exposition cannot be detached from her aim to grasp non-human agencies in their singularity, *as such*. What is left out of this equation is the STS insight that things and people are *all* internally heterogeneous since all are shaped by emergent relations, entanglements and arrangements (e.g. Cussins 1998; Latour 1996a, b; Pickering 1995).

In a recent programmatic statement, Dominic Boyer and Timothy Morton (2016) propose a way of combining attentiveness to thing-power with the agency of people. Arguing that climate change requires the fabrication of another future, they suggest that it will bring forth a correspondingly new kind of 'hypo-subject'. Set in motion by a modern 'hyper-subject' obsessed with 'command and control' and wielding 'reason and technology to get things done', climate change will be made liveable by 'hypo-subjects', characterized, among other things, as caring and playful squatters and *bricoleuses* who 'work miracles with scraps and remains ... unplug from carbon gridlife [and] hack and redistribute its stored energies for their own purposes'. There are resonances between these ideas and Bennett's (2004, 349) suggestion that the recognition of thing-power may 'foster greater ethical' awareness or even a more 'enlightened self-interest' (2004, 361). The formulations also bear affinity with Isabelle Stengers' (1999, 193–4) argument that different assemblages hold potential for creating varied 'appetites that can act as 'lure[s] for feelings' for different futures. Yet, while Stengers, as does Bennett, highlights that things, like electrons, can create 'lures for feeling', she also insists that the question of what these powers are and do can only be posed concretely in terms of the 'cultural milieu' they enter into (1999, 202). This demand for specificity connects with her plea for 'slowing down' reasoning.

For Stengers (1999, 196), 'slowing down' means that one should not aim to 'purify the whole field in order to grasp a more general truth'. On the one hand, this means that social scientists should refrain searching for the truth of the power of things in themselves. On the other hand, it also entails the refusal of 'any temptation to *judge* [the] experience' (1999, 196) of those working with things like dams and rivers on the basis of any 'more general truth', such as the clean distinction between bad hyper-subjects and good hypo-subjects.

In the following, I take Stengers' refusal to purify either the force of things or the actions of people as a starting point for analysing entanglements of water flows, dam cascades and models, and the possibilities for imagining an electrified Mekong.

Knowing the Mekong

There are, of course, innumerable ways of experiencing the 'thing-power' of the Mekong (Jensen 2017). Correlatively, this 'thing-power' itself can be decomposed and reconstituted in a thousand ways. The casual visitor may encounter scenic sunsets, river dolphins, dredging boats or garbage accumulated where the river passes urban areas. Such fleeting scenes might well testify to 'thing-power' in Bennett's sense of an unexpected experience giving rise to a flash of intuition. For people living by or on the river, the experiences of 'thing-power' are differently embodied, more long lasting and more consequential. They have to do with such things as knowing fish migrations and water flows, understanding the seasonal patterns of rain and flooding and their consequences for growing crops and how to safely navigate the river as a storm approaches. For entrepreneurs or politicians who are interested in large-scale economic potentials, the power of the river may be apprehended in the form of sand that can be dredged for export or as water flows that can be captured by dams and turned into electricity.

As for these dams, their building and operation on the Lao and Cambodian Mekong is subject to fierce criticism from NGOs like the World Wildlife Fund (WWF) and International Rivers. The objections are similar to those raised elsewhere against dam development (Whitington 2019). Obligatory environmental assessments are lacking or fatally flawed. Fish migration will be threatened. Underwater explosions may lead to the extinction of the remaining Irrawaddy dolphins. And there are significant threats to a great many ecological niches. Criticism further highlights the forced eviction of local populations, threats to food security and the fact that dam development is carried out on the back of wildly exaggerated promises about how much electricity will be generated. Even if all the planned dams of Laos are built, for example, the country will probably never become the 'battery of South-East Asia', since the electricity production is unlikely to add up to more than a few per cent of regional demand.

Because the pre-studies, reports and models that inform Chinese decisions to push particular hydropower projects are not publicly available, it is impossible to know how, precisely, they inform concrete policies. Yet, it seems safe to assume that various economic projections and engineering expertise is sitting in the background of decisions to commit to infrastructure projects of this order. Sooner or later, information about such projects reaches the public sphere. To critical observers, like environmental NGOs, it looks patchy and generally dubious. In response, they produce counter-knowledges, often in collaboration with university researchers from abroad; as we shall see, however, foreign governments may also commission critical analyses. Such reports will usually highlight a range of technical issues and environmental and/or social problems. Often, these counter-knowledges take the form of, or are significantly based on, models. And thus, hydrological models become part of the terrain on which contests over dams, and electricity, are played out.

The 'thing-power' of models

In 2015, the Vietnamese Ministry of Natural Resources and Environment commissioned the Danish Hydraulic Institute (DHI), which specializes in hydrological modelling, to conduct a 'Study on the Impacts of Mainstream Hydropower on the Mekong'. The report concluded that the cascade of planned dams would lead to a loss of capture fishery of up to 50 per cent and an overall loss of 10 per cent of fish species. Moreover, the entrapment of sedimentation by dams is predicted to lead to heightened vulnerability to sea-level rise and increased saline intrusion in the Vietnamese delta. All in all, 'the planned hydropower cascade would substantially and permanently alter the productivity of the natural system leading to degradation of all the delta's related value' (Executive summary, 3).

On (yet another) scorching hot day in May 2016, I had lunch with Mr Pélissier, a fisheries expert and well-published researcher with long experience working as a consultant in Cambodia. In his view, the main problem with Mekong dam development is the threat it poses to food security. Scientific studies predict that fish populations may decline by more than 40 per cent over the next several decades, a huge concern in the Cambodian context, where fish is the main source of protein for most of the population.

Having just read the DHI report, which drew similar conclusions, I asked about Mr Pélissier's view of its analyses. As far as the picture of fish decline was concerned, he thought the report got it more or less right. Indeed, he stated, bringing attention to this problem was probably a key reason why the Vietnamese government had commissioned the report in the first place.

This may sound strange, since the expected problems in the Vietnamese Mekong delta are less to do with fish decline than with coastal erosion, sea-level rise and saline intrusion. These are huge problems, since the delta grows 90 per cent of Vietnam's rice. As the delta diminishes, Vietnamese food security is therefore jeopardized. In contrast, Cambodia is pursuing rapid dam development as a solution to national security issues. Presently, the country is importing most of its energy from its old enemies Thailand and Vietnam, leaving the country in a weak position. Yet, Cambodia's food security is also vulnerable. As most of the population gets most of its scarce protein from river fish, a 40 per cent decline in fisheries would likely entail malnutrition or worse for many rural people. The gambit of the Vietnamese is thus to convince Cambodia that both countries are threatened by dam cascades and for similar reasons. And thus Mr Pélissier surmised that it was not at all random that the results of the DHI report were made public in Phnom Penh rather than in Vietnam. Moreover, he thought that it was a good idea. Since the Cambodian ruling party depends on votes from the rural poor, he thought that making visible the threat of food security to politicians might be one of the few viable possibilities for problematizing the strategy of building as many dams as possible. In contrast, a purely environmental concern would be likely to sway nobody.

By articulating the link between the building of dams, the decline of fish populations and accelerated delta erosion, the DHI report and Mr Pélissier's commentary illuminate the empirical entwinement of electricity generation, the gradual effects of climate change and national and regional politics in the Mekong basin. They also allow us to probe further the question of the varied articulations and mediations of 'thing-power'.

In the report and in Mr. Pélissier's interpretation, thing-power is everywhere evident. The difficulty, however, is ascertaining to which 'thing' the 'power' refers. Since the report is about the flow of the Mekong and its tributaries, we might argue that it is testimony to the power of the river. However, it might as well be said that what it really speaks about is the power of sedimentation, or fish, or dams or Vietnamese rice. Since the reports bears witness to the conjugation of all these powers in a complex relational assemblage, none of them can be singularized. Further, it is quite impossible to clearly separate which powers should be attributed to people and which to things. In reality, the agency of dam builders and politicians is as involved in changing the river as the forces of climate change and coastal erosion. The power of any particular thing *as such* is nowhere in view.[5]

Indeed, the difficulty of separating thing-power from people-power extends further. For in order to know certain things about the present and future of the Mekong river basin – the flow of sedimentation, changes in fish population or erosion in the delta, for example – it is necessary *to go through* hydrological models. Rather than a story about the thing-power of the delta or the river or of dams, we might thus say that this is in effect a story of how the thing-power of models come to 'give voice' to the power of other 'things', like dams, fish or the Mekong as a whole.

But if the impact of dams is known only through models, and the models differ, the question of how to model thing-power is subject to a series of complications. Rather than allowing us to glimpse any *unmediated* power of things, the multiple mediations of hydrological models thus oblige us to further decelerate reasoning. Mr Pélissier will continue to serve as a guide.

Whereas he basically agreed with the DHI report's estimations about food security, he found some parts of the *hydrology* quite dubious. It showed signs, he said, of downplaying the negative impact of the dams.

How to minimize the thing-power of dams

While the Mekong can be known in multiple ways, for some important purposes, the river and basin can basically only be known through models. If one wants to estimate fish populations, sedimentation flows or temperature rises, embodied experience is of limited help. Further, since baseline data about most environmental and social issues is either non-existent or hidden in ministerial cabinets, for foreign organizations and researchers, modelling offers an indispensable means of making Mekong futures visible and discussable.

Modelling, in turn, depends both on the data sets fed into them and on the presuppositions and relations built into their equations. Whereas an important dimension of the thing-power of models is to speak in the name of other things like water flows and sedimentation, their capacity for doing so is neither direct nor oracular. This is no secret to modellers, who are very sensitive to the fact that models are no better than their inputs and parameters (e.g. Beven 2009). They are also well aware that both of these can be subtly or bluntly manipulated.

Policy makers and the general public, however, are usually less knowledgeable. They typically encounter models as a series of results – graphs and visualizations or written explications, predictions and scenarios – rather than in the form of equations and datasets. Moreover, if they were presented with these equations and datasets, they would not have the scientific literacy to interpret them. Accordingly, there is good reason to use written language and colourful graphs as 'front stage' explanations. Yet, this means that the backstage of the models basically remain invisible.

Although modellers and other insiders are fully aware that no model is neutral, this does not typically lead them to reject their overall, or potential, explanatory power. Even though Mr Pélissier was sceptical of the assumptions underlying the model used to estimate the effects of dams on biodiversity and water flows in the DHI report, for example, he still accepted the estimate of fish reductions. So why did he think the effect of dams had been underestimated?

When asked, Mr Pélissier retracted somewhat. He made it clear that he had not looked into the final modelling parameters used by the DHI consultants, so he was actually unable to offer a definite opinion on the particular case. The scepticism he had expressed was a consequence of having joined an early consultation meeting with the DHI experts before the modelling had been conducted. However, he said, it is by no means unusual for hydrological models to minimize the effects of dams.

Dams generate electricity by storing water and releasing it. However, this can be done in many different ways. For example, it is possible to generate electricity at a steady rate, in which case the water level around the dam does not fluctuate very much. Since dams tend to be operated in accordance with peak demands, however, usually there will be fluctuations. To exemplify, if demand is highest in the evening, water will be dammed during daytime and the turbines switched on later in the day. The consequence is wildly changing water levels with ecologically devastating consequences. This modulation maximizes the dam's power to destroy ecologies and biodiversity. Because there is no reliable information on dam operations, however, these fluctuations are unknown, and the way they enter models depend on choices made by the modellers.[6] All that is needed to minimize the thing-power of a dam or a cascade is to assume a steady rate of electricity production or more subtly tweak or finesse the assumed operation rules.

It is quite unlikely that the DHI consultants deliberately wanted to minimize flow variations (or even that they had actually done so, as Mr Pélissier acknowledged). For one thing, their international reputation depends on maintaining an image of neutral expertise, making it unlikely they would compromise their models for reasons of regional politicking. For another, if they had done so, they would presumably have maximized the power of dams, as they had been hired by a Vietnamese ministry worried about the impact of dam cascades downstream in the Mekong delta.

But regardless, neither university researchers nor consultants commissioned to model the Mekong can avoid entering the territory of conjecture. Dealing with complex interactions of water, weather, sand and animals under significant time and resource constraints, they trade in necessary simplifications. Taking the path of least resistance by assuming a steady flow through all the dams merely exemplifies a trade-off with particularly clear implications. Invariably, therefore, the question of which powers should be assigned to modellers, which to models and which to the entities or processes they model can only lead to fuzzy answers.

Nor is this all. For whichever way the dams are modelled, Mr Pélissier insisted, *the curve of electricity* operates as an unquestioned assumption operating behind the models. What this means is that the unquestioned premise of dam development is the necessity of always *producing more and more electricity*.

The curve of electricity

Listening to Mr Pélissier, it dawned upon me that it is possible to speak of the *subject* of hydrological models in two ways. On the one hand, models have explicit subject matters, such as water and sedimentation flows. But they also contain an implicit human subject in demand of more electricity. Complementarily, it is also possible to understand the modelling of the subject in two senses. For alongside dams, water and sedimentation flows and fish populations, the expected, normal behaviour of people and societies are implicitly modelled too.

When Mr Pélissier observes that the curve of electricity operates as a background assumption of dam development, he is making a critical argument. Similar to many NGOs, he thinks dam development should be halted or at least substantially changed. However, he is critical not only of dams but also of the strategies of the many environmental NGOs that oppose them. Their modes of argumentation, he said, tends to focus on things like unique butterfly habitats, the threat to a particular rare fish or the loss of dolphin populations. 'It is a hopeless battle', he said; 'there used to be wild animals in Phnom Penh, too, but where do you see them now?'

This was not meant to express fatalism. Instead, Mr Pélissier argued that the problem with appeals to butterflies and snails is that their aesthetic form is incommensurable with the logic and modus operandi of bureaucrats and planners. Based on his own experience, he asserted that hard-headed Cambodian bureaucrats backed with Chinese money would simply not be swayed by appeals to biodiversity. Until NGOs learn to engage dam development on the terrain of the curve of electricity, he insisted, they will fail to generate any effective counter-position. To succeed, they will have to 'learn to speak the language of megawatts'.

These arguments open up to contrasting images of what kinds of subject positions may facilitate alternative electrified Mekong futures. Recall Boyer and Morton's broad contrast between hyper-subjects who seek to command and control the environment and hypo-subjects who unplug 'from carbon gridlife' to 'hack and redistribute its stored energies for their own purposes'. On the basis of this argument, they might well applaud NGOs that resist Mekong dams in the name of environmental protection and redistributive justice. Yet, although Mr Pélissier is not looking to unplug, he is also pursuing the question of how to 'redistribute stored energies'.

Here, we might return to Boyer's (2015, 533) argument that electric grids provide 'grooves' for 'political efficacy' and 'subjectivity'. Isabelle Stengers, too, has pointed to the danger of producing minds 'in a groove' (1999, 194, cited in Whitehead 1926, 196–7). And indeed, as we have seen, according to Mr Pélissier, the groove along which dam development on the Mekong runs is the curve of electricity. Recognizing the existence of this groove, he argues, is a precondition for imagining any viable Mekong energy future.

In his view, however, this transformation is unlikely to be brought about by environmental activists, because they, too, operate *in a groove of their own*. Unable or unwilling to compromise with their biodiversity aesthetics and normativity, these activists have no effective weapons with which to defeat the curve of electricity. Accordingly, they fail to make a dent in the calculating minds of Cambodian bureaucrats and Chinese investors.

'Do you know the Siam Paragon Shopping Mall in Bangkok?' he asks me. 'That mall uses as much energy as one of the North-eastern Thai provinces'. NGOs should examine cases like this shopping mall and press the question of whether its 'excessive electricity consumption is warranted', sustainable or even possible. Effective opposition to the dams thus entails challenging the image of a future where Siam Paragons spread everywhere.

Can the Mekong speak?

Posing the question 'Can the Subaltern Speak?' Gayatri Spivak (1988, 295) famously answered in the negative: as a product of 'imperialist subject-constitution', the subaltern could have neither history nor voice. In contrast, new materialists and object-oriented ontologists answer the question of whether 'things' can speak with a resounding 'yes'.

From an anthropological point of view, this affirmation requires careful scrutiny. Examining Mekong hydropower development, I have tried to slow down reasoning in order to grapple with the *entangled* powers of dams, river flows, fish population, rice growth, models and politics. Here I echo Timothy Mitchell (2002, 52), who replied to his own query as to whether the mosquito breeding by the Egyptian Aswan dam could 'speak' by pointing to the permeability of agency: 'What is called nature or the material world moves ... in and out of human forms'.

New materialists and object-oriented ontologists tend to view the recognition of such permeability as a denial of thing-power. Just as Spivak's subaltern was deemed unable to speak since she is always produced and represented by others, acknowledgement that the powers of dams, water or sediment is mediated by many relations is conflated with the complete effacement or silencing of these things. Aside from being empirically unsupportable, one consequence of this speeding up of reasoning on behalf of things is a disregard for the complex arrangements that articulate the varied voices of the Mekong.

Ethnographic attunement to such complicated entanglements creates a position from which to nuance arguments about thing-power. Far from silent, dams and rivers speak cacophonously in *a thousand tongues*. But these voices cannot be disentangled from those of other actors, including dam construction workers, fishermen, dying dolphins, environmental activists, Chinese economists, Cambodian policy makers and, not least, models. DHI's hydrological model itself is but one effort to confer upon the river the capacity to allow others to speak in its name. And, as we have seen, this model, too, speaks of many other things: sediment flows, fish populations, future consumers and the consequences of planned damming.

Here is a first lesson from slowing down reasoning. Even if one aims to articulate, capture or protect the thing-power(s) of the Mekong, one will have to make detours through the powers of other things. The general admonition to heed the force of things makes no difference unless one is able elicit that force through other means, like models. Further, even *within the model*, we encounter a chorus composed of many things and people. Recognizing this internal multiplicity opens up a space for inquiring about the kinds of subject positions available to those who wish to oppose current forms of Mekong electrification.

As noted, Jane Bennett (2004, 348) argues that increased attentiveness to thing-power might induce a stronger ecological sense. Boyer and Morton (2016) suggests that the fabrication of sustainable futures in the age of climate change will be in hands of 'hypo-subjects'. Activists fighting Mekong dam development in the name of environmental protection and sustainable livelihoods would seem to exemplify this kind of subject position, and it is difficult not to sympathize with their aims.

Yet such sympathy can also blind one to the limitations of their strategies. Pointing to the unlikelihood of politicians and entrepreneurs suddenly converting to environmentalism or becoming human-rights advocates, Mr Pélissier thus offers a second lesson in slowing down reasoning: possibly, the only viable way of pursuing environmental or social justice is by translating these concerns to the language of mega-watts, moving advocacy onto the terrain of modelling. The picture he paints is far more complicated and ambiguous than the clear distinction between coldly calculating hyper-objects and eco-friendly, experimental hypo-subjects.

Of course, we might also query the extent to which Mr Pélissier's diagnosis is right. In view of the difficulties environmental NGOs have in getting their agendas heard or implemented in Cambodia, his criticism clearly has a point. Yet it overlooks the extent to which these organizations are already committed to modelling such things as fresh water quality, relations between economic development and the natural resource base or the consequences of dams for biodiversity. While what is modelled varies, what is held steady in this imagination is the assumption that models are effective means for speaking truths about electricity to Cambodian powers. In reality, however, I have yet to come across any case in which *any* model has significantly changed political decisions.[7]

While the Mekong and its models both can and do speak in multiple voices – about fish, sand and electricity – this does not mean that anyone is there to listen.

Notes

1   See the overview provided by CGIAR's research programme on water, land and ecosystems at https://wle-mekong.cgiar.org/wp-content/uploads/unnamed-11.jpg. Accessed 11 July 2016.

2 Jared Ferrie. 2010. 'Laos Turns to Hydropower to Be "Asia's Battery"'. *The Christian Science Monitor*, 2 July. http://www.csmonitor.com/World/Asia-Pacific/2010/0702/Laos-turns-to-hydropower-to-be-Asia-s-battery/. Accessed 24 March 2015.

3 Lindsay Murdoch. 2016. 'Sand Wars: Singapore's Growth Comes at the Environmental Expense of its Neighbours'. *The Sydney Morning Herald*, 26 February. http://www.smh.com.au/world/sand-wars-singapores-growth-comes-at-the-environmental-expense-of-its-neighbours-20160225-gn3uum.html. Accessed 11 July 2016.

4 For a critique of Bennett's thing-power, see Abrahamsson, Bertoni and Mol (2015). For a clarification of the relation between Bennett's position and that of object-oriented ontology, which makes clear that the former is more resonant with STS and anthropological approaches than the latter, see Bennett (2012).

5 See Bakke (this volume) for a discussion of the ways in which electricity is not a thing but a relation. The same can be said for water flows and, arguably, for most or all other 'things' as well.

6 The problem has long been recognized, but it has not been solved. In a 2001 study, we are informed that 'assumed regulation rules were used for those dams included in the model. When the true operating rules for these dams are available, they should be incorporated into the model' (Kite 2001, 11). More recently, a study of the 3S river basin 'was limited to daily flow simulations because of current constraints in the availability of detailed operation rules of the proposed hydropower projects and actual flow measurements' (Piman et al. 2013, 731), and a study of sedimentation and hydropower notes that 'many reservoir operating policies are simply unknown at this time. Given the largely uncoordinated nature of basin development, operators are likely to be adapting their strategies in real time as the unknown policies of upstream reservoirs become available' (Wild and Loucks 2014, 5146–7).

7 It appears that the conventional idea of speaking truth to power is so deeply embedded in advocacy work that NGOs find it impossible to imagine an alternative in spite of continued failure. The question of what 'scientific facts' become in the political realm of 'theatre states' like Cambodia is worth pursuing further.

References

Abrahamsson, Sebastian, Filippo Bertoni and Annemarie Mol. 2015. 'Living with Omega-3: New Materialisms and Enduring Concerns', *Environment and Planning D*, 32: 4–19.

Agustoni, Alfredo and Mara Maretti. 2012. 'Energy and Social Change: An Introduction', *International Review of Sociology*, 22(3): 391–404.

Bennett, Jane. 2004. 'The Force of Things: Steps toward an Ecology of Matter', *Political Theory*, 32(3): 347–72.

Bennett, Jane. 2010. *Vibrant Matter: A Political Ecology of Things*. Durham, NC and London: Duke University Press.

Bennett, Jane. 2012. 'Systems and Things: A Response to Graham Harman and Timothy Morton', *New Literary Theory*, 43(2): 225–33.

Beven, Keith. 2009. *Environmental Modelling: An Uncertain Future*. London and New York: Routledge.

Bowker, Geoffrey C. 1994. *Science on the Run: Information Management and Industrial Geophysics at Schlumberger, 1920–1940*. Cambridge, MA: MIT Press.

Boyer, Dominic. 2014. 'Energopower: An Introduction', *Anthropological Quarterly*, 87(2): 309–34.

Boyer, Dominic. 2015. 'Anthropology Electric', *Cultural Anthropology*, 30(4): 531–59.

Boyer, Dominic and Timothy Morton. 2016. '"Hyposubjects". Theorizing the Contemporary', *Cultural Anthropology*, website, https://culanth.org/fieldsights/798-hyposubjects (accessed 21 January 2016).

Cussins, Charis. 1998. 'Ontological Choreography: Agency for Women Patients in an Infertility Clinic', in Marc Berg and Annemarie Mol (eds), *Differences in Medicine: Unraveling Practices, Techniques, and Bodies*, 166–202. Durham, NC: Duke University Press.

Harvey, Penny, Casper Bruun Jensen and Atsuro Morita (eds). 2016. *Infrastructures and Social Complexity: A Reader*. London and New York: Routledge.

Hughes, Thomas P. 1983. *Networks of Power: Electric Supply Systems in the US, England and Germany, 1880–1930*. Baltimore, MD: Johns Hopkins University Press.

Jensen, Casper Bruun. 2017. 'Mekong Scales: Domains, Test-Sites and the Micro-Uncommons', *Anthropologica*, 59: 204–15.

Jensen, Casper Bruun. 2019. 'Here Comes the Sun: Experimenting with Cambodian Energy Infrastructures', in Kregg Hetherington (ed.), *Infrastructure, Environment and Life in the Anthropocene*, 216–36. Durham, NC and London: Duke University Press.

Jensen, Casper and Atsuro Morita. 2017. 'Introduction: Infrastructures as Ontological Experiments', *Ethnos*, 82(4): 615–26. Online first. doi:10.1080/00141844.2015. 1107607.

Kite, Geoff. 2001. 'Modelling the Mekong: Hydrological Simulation for Environmental Impact Studies', *Journal of Hydrology*, 253: 1–13.

Latour, Bruno. 1996a. 'Do Scientific Objects Have a History? Pasteur and Whitehead in a Bath of Lactic Acid Yeast', *Common Knowledge*, 5(1): 76–91.

Latour, Bruno. 1996b. 'On Interobjectivity', *Mind, Culture and Activity: An International Journal*, 3(4): 228–45.

Mitchell, Timothy. 2002. *Rule of Experts: Egypt, Techno-Politics, Modernity*. Berkeley, Los Angeles, CA and London: University of California Press.

Mitchell, Timothy. 2013. *Carbon Democracy: Political Power in the Age of Oil*. New York: Verso.

Nye, David. 2010. *When the Lights Went Out: A History of Blackouts in America*. Cambridge, MA and London: MIT Press.

Pickering, Andrew. 1995. *The Mangle of Practice: Time, Agency and Science*. Chicago, IL and London: University of Chicago Press.

Piman, T., T. A. Cochrane, M. E. Arias, A. Green and N. D. Dat. 2013. 'Assessment of Flow Changes from Hydropower Development and Operations in Sekong, Sesan, and Srepok Rivers of the Mekong Basin', *Journal of Water Resources Planning and Management*, 139(6): 723–32.

Scott, Michael. 2013. 'The Anthropology of Ontology (Religious Science?)', *Journal of the Royal Anthropological Institute*, 19(4): 859–72.

Siciliano, Giuseppina, Frauke Urban, May Tan-Mullins, Lonn Pichdara and Sour Kim. 2016. 'The Political Ecology of Chinese Large Dams in Cambodia: Implications, Challenges and Lessons Learnt from the Kamchay Dam', *Water*, 8: 405.

Spivak, Gayatri Chakravorty. 1988. 'Can the Subaltern Speak?' in Cary Nelson and Lawrence Grossberg (eds), *Marxism and the Interpretation of Culture*, 271–313. Urbana: University of Illinois Press.

Stengers, Isabelle. 1999. 'Whitehead and the Laws of Nature', *Salzburger Theologische Zeitschrift*, 3: 193–206. https://www.sbg.ac.at/sathz/1999_2/stengers.pdf (accessed 22 September 2017).

Strauss, Sarah, Stephanie Rupp and Thomas Love. 2013. 'Powerlines: Cultures of Energy in the Twenty-first Century', in Sarah Strauss, Stephanie Rupp and Thomas Love (eds), *Cultures of Energy*, 10–41. Walnut Creek, CA: Left Coast Press.

Summerton, Jane (ed.). 1994. *Changing Large Technical Systems*. Boulder, CO, San Francisco, CA, and Oxford: Westview Press.

Urry, John. 2014. 'The Problem of Energy', *Theory, Culture & Society*, 31(5): 3–20.

Whitehead, Alfred North. 1926. *Science and the Modern World*. Cambridge: Cambridge University Press.

Whitington, Jerome. 2019. *Anthropogenic Rivers: The Production of Uncertainty in Lao Hydropower Development*. Ithaca: Cornell University Press.

Wild, Thomas B. and Daniel P. Loucks. 2014. 'Managing Flow, Sediment, and Hydropower Regimes in the Sre Pok, Se San, and Se Kong Rivers of the Mekong Basin', *Water Resources Research*, 50: 5141–57.

8

Electrification and the everyday spaces of state power in postcolonial Mozambique

Joshua Kirshner and Marcus Power

Sustainable energy provision is often framed as a matter for technical experts, a challenge of increasing connections and 'plugging' consumers into a grid infrastructure. Accordingly, improving access to energy is a process dependent on achieving economies of scale and one that can be managed in a socially neutral manner. Critical geographers studying energy have questioned this view, pointing to the political dimensions of energy provision and energy infrastructures as key sites of contestation (Calvert 2016; Huber 2015). From this perspective, energy production and use translates into control over space, and energy and its supporting infrastructure becomes a means for states to express their authority, extend their reach and consolidate territorial control. In this chapter, we draw on these insights into energy production, transmission and use as 'an important physical medium through which to tilt the balance of power and exert social control' (Calvert 2016, 7). Through examining processes of electrification in Mozambique, we suggest that the country's electricity infrastructures are used by the state to gain consent and legitimacy while doing the material and symbolic work to garner support for its project of modernity.

Despite the widely recognized importance of energy access for socio-economic development (Brew-Hammond 2010; Ockwell and Byrne 2016; Practical Action 2016), most investments in the energy sector in sub-Saharan Africa are disconnected from the energy needs of poor majorities. Fully two thirds of the continent's energy investment is dedicated to producing energy for export, while roughly half of current electricity consumption is used for industry – primarily mining and refining (IEA 2014). Moreover, users' needs and priorities, particularly those of the poor, have been frequently overlooked in national energy planning, as the focus is on locating strategic resources for global markets rather than providing energy services tailored to local conditions or offering a meaningful voice to users (Practical Action 2016; Castán Broto 2017).

Regardless of these limitations, electricity comes to symbolize what the state can do for citizens, in return serving as a valuable tool in supporting state legitimacy. The arrival of electricity affects state–citizen relationships in important ways. In rolling out thousands of kilometres of transmission lines, African officials highlight forms of state reach, renewing claims of modernity, even though these projects may affect relatively few people. Scott (1998) famously described state power as the capacity of infrastructures to order, arrange and make legible, such as through a cadastral map or a grid network. Building on these insights, Gandy (2004) has observed how the development of infrastructures (e.g. those around water) have been integrally connected with the enactment of new forms of urban governmentality, along with a wider transformation in the scope and rationale of state activity. In what follows, we argue that a similar argument can be made about electricity infrastructures – that they enact particular forms of governmentality and can be used to enhance the scope and rationale of the state. Electricity thus figures prominently in state formation and in geopolitical imaginaries of territory, nationhood and international relations (Huber 2015). From the wires, cables, poles and generators to the entrepreneurs, engineers, politicians and advisers who shape the process of electrification, electric grids create political power – just as they transmit it (Shamir 2013).

Drawing on field research[1] conducted in Maputo and Beira, Mozambique in 2013 and 2014, this chapter argues that energy provision is linked to efforts by the state to extend and centralize its political power. Yet the process of increasing energy access has been socially and spatially uneven, and many of the poorest have not benefited. Further, monopolization of the political and economic system by the ruling party, Frelimo (*Frente de Libertação de Moçambique*), in conjunction with domestic and transnational business elites, has marginalized large segments of the population, particularly the poor, from energy provision and planning.

The chapter aims to contribute to debates on energy and governance in arguing that political economy offers a set of tools to examine energy infrastructures and uses in specific locations, since they foster analysis of structural conditions and the changing relations between energy policies and energy industries (Büscher 2009), posing critical questions about who wins, who loses and why (Newell and Mulvaney 2013). Before examining institutional approaches to the state's development of energy policy, we begin by outlining the multiple connections between energy infrastructures and the state. We then consider the ways in which the state has extended its reach through off-grid rural electrification, which is often regarded by state actors as an alternative to the costly expansion of the centralized grid. Paradoxically however, off-grid solutions are typically implemented by centralized state agencies, often with little local input.

Electricity and the state

Despite calls to rethink the state 'as a social relation' state–civil society divisions have persisted in academic and policy debates (Painter 2006). Feminist, anthropological and post-structural approaches have reoriented attention away from formal state institutions and towards socially embedded processes through which ideas of the state are reproduced. States do not simply exist; rather, they are constantly evolving through everyday activities. Painter (2006, 754) argues that understanding states in terms of mundane practices reveals their 'heterogeneous, constructed, porous, uneven, processual and relational character'.

Recent work on postcolonial African statehood similarly views the state not as a finite entity – a fixed apparatus of borders, personnel, budgets and bureaucracies – but rather as 'an always-emergent form of power and control identifiable at multiple societal levels' (Bertelsen 2016, 3). The focus in much of this work is on state formation and state ordering, along with the various forces outside of and uncontrolled by the state. In the case of Mozambique, the national government received substantial amounts of aid in the wake of a severe sixteen-year civil war that followed independence from Portuguese colonial rule. Since the war, the Mozambican economic 'miracle' has been widely celebrated as a model for post-conflict development and macroeconomic growth, especially in donor circles (Castel-Branco 2015). Yet, scholars have also noted widening inequalities and class stratification, monopolization of capital and resources by Frelimo-affiliated elites and the concentration of economic and political power around the capital, Maputo, in the extreme south of the country (Bertelsen 2016; Sumich 2016).

This emergent and experiential quality of the state is useful for examining the connections between energy provision, infrastructures and broader social and political structures. Mozambique's electricity infrastructures – and the energy resources on which they are based – underpin national sovereignty while being increasingly embroiled within regional and global trade circulations. Concomitantly, they shape the lives of local people and livelihoods, despite ongoing deficiencies and inequalities in energy-services provision (Cipriano, Waugh and Matos 2015).

Electricity has been central to high modernist discourses and ideologies across the global South, given its associations with scientific and technological progress, expanding production, the mastery of nature and the rational design of social order. Electrification is closely associated with the Western notion of progress, so that extending electricity services to households means spreading 'progress' through the range of appliances and household items that claim to improve quality of life and allow people to participate in 'what is considered a modern lifestyle' (Labban 2012, 389). Electrification is also a process that guarantees 'dual access': people's access to electricity and thus to modernity, but also the access of the market to more people 'expanding quite literally with the extension of the electric grid' (Labban 2012, 389). Beyond this, the materiality of its infrastructure gives electricity a centralizing effect (Gupta, 2015). Power plants that generate electricity and distribute it through a broad network centralize command over the network, the flow of electricity through it and 'the accumulation of money flowing in the opposite direction' (Labban 2012, 390).

It is this dual access that the Mozambican government seeks to secure and expand. To support this goal, some 90 per cent of grid-connected electricity consumption in Mozambique is currently through prepaid systems (Baptista 2015). Some have suggested that prepayment facilitates access to urban services, including electricity, in low-income areas, empowering customers and generating new revenue for service providers. Others argue that prepayment imposes neoliberal-style reforms under the guise of an empowerment narrative, seeking to discipline consumers and benefiting only service providers (see McDonald 2009). In South Africa, where prepayment systems are also widespread, von Schnitzler (2013) writes of a low-intensity battle between residents tinkering with the prepaid electricity metering technology and utility officials trying to secure it. Consequently, von Schnitzler argues, it is important to track this 'technical micro-politics' involving residents, engineers and utility officials in a perennial struggle over the enforcement and evasion of payment.

Similarly, writing on water infrastructure in Mexico, Meehan (2014, 217) finds that technologies do not always perform as expected, enabling 'creative exploitation' by residents in ways which 'often transform the power geometries in which they are embedded'. In Mozambique, the World Bank (2015) has estimated 'non-technical losses', or electricity that is not metered or billed (in other words, pilfered) at some 10 per cent of total consumption. Such a figure indicates that electricity technologies do not always perform as expected by state planners and donors. This 'technical micro-politics' suggests the ways in which everyday spaces of state power centred on electricity should be understood as contested domains, and how state-led infrastructures and flows of electrical power can be subverted, transgressed, shaping wider geometries of social power.

The idea that objects – tools, beings and things – are pivots for sociopolitical inquiry is prominent in science and technology studies (Winner 1980; Star 1999), with burgeoning studies in geography. Along with energy and electricity, there is growing geographical interest in infrastructure (Luque-Ayala and Silver 2016). Infrastructure 'helps create, destroy, expand or limit the contours of what we call the state' (Meehan 2014, 216) and is also constitutive of difference, in effect limiting the jurisdiction of the state through varied modes of electricity provision, which are not fixed but are in flux and generative of new technologies, alternatives and improvised modes of power. The electric grid is thus 'a maker of groups and a generator of political and economic difference among groups and individuals' (Shamir 2013, 6). Energy infrastructures create fragmented spaces of inclusion and exclusion while also engendering inequalities, political claims and spaces for resistance (Luque-Ayala and Silver 2016). Ultimately, electricity (and its infrastructures) is important for sustaining modern societies as well as understanding modern forms of subjectivity, politics and economics (see Jensen, this volume; Boyer 2014).

In a more pragmatic sense, challenges around energy infrastructure and supply are often approached from top-down perspectives (Brew-Hammond 2010; Büscher 2009). Here, concerns with national energy security and sovereignty compete with the demands of export markets and the need to facilitate global trade and resource flows, concerns that often take precedence over household and community perspectives on energy and local energy geographies. Further, we still need to know much more about energy provision at the household level in Mozambique, and research on this theme is still scarce. An exception is Castán Broto's research on climate-compatible planning in peri-urban areas of Maputo, Mozambique's capital (Castán Broto, Salazar and Adams 2014). This study found that residents have limited expectations of municipal or national intervention in the provision of urban infrastructure, including roads, sanitation, waste collection and electricity. Maputo has the highest electrification rates in the country, but the peripheral *bairros* (neighbourhoods) are characterized by the ubiquitous presence of charcoal. More recently, Castán Broto (2017) has observed that charcoal use in Maputo's periphery is highly embedded in an economic system that enables some local control over energy resources in the absence of formal provision. This research dovetails with Nielsen's (2010) observation that neighbourhood-based organizations called *grupos dinamizadores*, dating to the early post-independence period, enrol citizens in service provision. In many Maputo neighbourhoods, these citizen groups 'stand for the state' in providing services that would otherwise be lacking. For Nielsen (2010, 164), this is a form of 'inverse governmentality', in which people appropriate or imitate certain functions of the state in the absence of government-supplied infrastructure and organization.

Baptista (2016) offers a place-specific account of the recent shift to prepaid electricity metres in Maputo. Examining everyday life practices, she suggests that the prepaid system has given households control over their own electricity consumption and allows urban dwellers to understand what they consume.[2] Prepayment has also extended access to energy-vulnerable populations, despite the structural inequalities in Maputo's provision of services and its broader patterns of urbanization. As in Castán Broto's (2017) account, Baptista (2016) notes that many households combine the use of charcoal with limited use of electricity, adjusting their electricity consumption to the financial resources available.

Mozambique's evolving energy provision system

In recent years, concerns about persistent low rates of energy access in Mozambique have entered public debates. From state policy makers to environmental activists and donor agencies, there is wide agreement on the need to secure clean, affordable and equitable energy access to meet basic needs, in keeping with the United Nations Sustainable Development Goals, ratified in 2015. This aspiration is often viewed within a wider low-carbon transition unfolding in various places in Africa (Ockwell and Byrne 2016; Ulsrud et al. 2015). Mozambique is increasingly looking to decentralized and renewable-energy systems for rural provision. It is also the site of struggles over extractive fossil-fuel interests, including export-oriented coal and gas mega-projects. These newly exploited resources hold the prospect of enhancing domestic energy access but with heightened carbon emissions.

Although estimates vary, Mozambique has among the lowest electrification rates in Africa, with the national grid currently reaching about one-fifth of its twenty-three million inhabitants, while some 80 per cent of the population continues to rely on wood, charcoal or animal waste for cooking and heating (World Bank 2015). The Energy Strategy developed by the Ministry for Energy and Mineral Resources aims to reach 50 per cent grid connectivity for the population by 2023 (Ministério da Energia 2014), yet there is a significant gap in the infrastructural investments needed to meet this goal, and the challenge is massive.

Mozambique's ruling Frelimo Party, founded during the anti-colonial struggle against Portugal in the 1960s, was inaugurated following independence in 1975 and came to power with a strong belief in centralization and state intervention. Frelimo's adoption of Marxism–Leninism rapidly evolved into a centralization of economic and political control so that the state could lead the task of modernizing the nation. During the Civil War (1976–1992), the promise of electrification figured strongly in Frelimo's campaign to persuade reluctant peasants to join the communal villages, a centrepiece of its socialist ideology (Geffray 1991), while the counter-revolutionary militia Renamo (*Resistência Nacional Moçambicana*) specifically targeted electricity transmission lines for attack. These infrastructures were central to postcolonial state formation, helping to extend the contours of the state and proclaim the benefits of socialist modernity.

Examining the historical development of Mozambique's electricity infrastructures enables consideration of the path dependencies that shape its contemporary energy system, or the ways in which past investments in grids and power plants limit the options available today and the scope for energy transition. Tracing the history of electricity networks also offers insights into the political contexts in which they emerged and the uneven geographies they helped to produce, as well as their possible futures.

Mozambique's development is shaped by centuries of colonialism and extractive mercantilist capitalism, and its electricity infrastructure remains rooted in and geared towards export to neighbouring countries. Anchoring Mozambique's electricity provision system is the Cahora Bassa hydroelectric dam. Completed in 1974, at a cost of US$515 million, on the Zambezi in the landlocked province of Tete with 2,075 MW of capacity, it was hailed as a testimony to Portugal's 'civilizing mission' and framed in the discourse of high modernism. The dam was proclaimed as an affirmation of Portugal's commitment to remain in Africa and a means of extending its colonial territorial reach and authority. Construction began in 1969, with the project financed by the sale of cheap electrical power to South Africa in exchange for support in the colonial war (Isaacman and Isaacman 2013).

During the 1960s, Frelimo waged a guerrilla campaign to block the dam's construction, arguing that it reinforced the military and economic alliance between Portugal and South Africa designed to perpetuate white rule in the region. Completed just 6 months before Mozambican independence, the newly installed Frelimo government had little alternative but to discard its long-term opposition to the dam and turn an exploitative colonial project into a national asset. Following independence, Frelimo hailed Cahora Bassa as a symbol of liberation which would, according to its Marxist-Leninist ideology, be instrumental in the 'socialization of the countryside'.

As Mozambique's Civil War became a proxy for wider Cold War divisions, South African-backed Renamo guerrillas sought to destabilize Frelimo's nascent socialist scheme. Renamo repeatedly sabotaged the hydroelectric dam's power lines, effectively paralysing the project. Electricity infrastructure thus became a key site of struggle during the conflict and in the wider battle for hearts and minds. By 1981, Renamo forces had dynamited pylons near Espungabera on the Zimbabwean border, reducing electricity exports by 50 per cent (AIM 1981).

Hidroeléctrica Cahora Bassa (HCB), the company that has managed the dam since 1977, supplies power to the Mozambican, Zimbabwean and South African grids through power-purchase agreements. HCB essentially remained under Portuguese colonial rule even after independence, as the Mozambican state lacked funds to repay loans for the dam's construction, and Portugal retained 82 per cent ownership. It was not until 2007 that HCB passed from Portuguese to majority Mozambican ownership of 85 per cent. Subsequently, expectations rose that Mozambique would prioritize national energy needs and reverse the dam's enclave nature, yet a high proportion of exports continue (Nhamire and Mosca 2014).

Mozambique produces a vast surplus of hydroelectricity at Cahora Bassa, yet it must observe pre-independence agreements between Portugal and South Africa, which guaranteed that most its electricity would be exported to South Africa at below market price. Around 65 per cent of HCB's production, or 1,500 MW of electricity, is currently exported to South Africa, connecting directly to the grid outside Pretoria (Baptista 2016). Electricity is then reimported into southern Mozambique via a substation in the South African border town of Komatipoort. Through such arrangements, Mozambique is drawn into the orbit of South Africa and its mineral-energy complex (Fine and Rustomjee

1996), a system that secured cheap energy to fuel industrialization during apartheid and continues to shape the country's energy system (Baker, Newell and Phillips 2014).

Electricity in Mozambique has thus been closely shaped by wider political and economic geographies. As Isaacman and Isaacman (2013) observed, Cahora Bassa was the largest dam in the world constructed for the specific purpose of exporting energy. This internationalization of electricity – the transfer across national borders of electric power and the capital and ownership required to generate it – makes it vulnerable to some of the strategic concerns linked to oil, including disruption of supply, volatile prices and struggles over control of revenues and infrastructures (Bridge and LeBillon 2013).

At independence in 1975, electricity access was confined to the capital, Lourenço Marques (the colonial designation of Maputo), and provincial centres, with generation from a series of municipal diesel generators, a coal-fired power station and small hydropower plants alongside Cahora Bassa. Mozambique now has a relatively small electricity system that emerged through regional projects such as Cahora Bassa, the Mozal aluminium smelter near Maputo and the Pande/Temane gas processing and pipeline project, managed by South African energy conglomerate Sasol. The grid network has developed as three distinct systems that lack interconnection. Electricidade de Moçambique (EDM), the state-owned electricity utility, had however connected all 128 district centres nationwide to the grid by 2014.

Most facilities owned and operated by EDM were inherited from the colonial period. Many are obsolete or needing urgent rehabilitation, further constraining access and efficiency. The northern provinces, for instance, depend largely on a single transmission line, such that one failure on the line is enough to cut electricity to vast regions of the country. To date, the state has prioritized grid extension to provincial and district centres, an effort that has left the country with an under-maintained network with scant back-up provisions and a heavy reliance on hydropower. According to state energy planners, average growth of 12.5 per cent is expected in the coming years, requiring an extra 100 MW in generation capacity every year (Cipriano, Waugh and Matos 2015).

Electricity, contested territory and state power

Liberal transition following the end of the Civil War in 1992, and the country's first multiparty elections in 1994, allowed the Frelimo Party to consolidate its hold and the party's effective monopolization of access to donors and international networks. Its influential role in the privatization process enabled it to 'centralize wealth and power in ways that were impossible under socialism' (Sumich 2010, 681). For Söderbaum and Taylor (2010), Mozambican state elites have prioritized relationships of patronage and rent-seeking over providing services to citizens.

The state uses material infrastructure – ranging from Cahora Bassa to the Mozal smelter – to narrate its presence; to counter fears of ethnic, regional or ideological fragmentation; and to gain legitimacy in the eyes of its citizens. Frelimo seeks to galvanize a territorial identity around a unitary state, yet its dominance of the political and economic system has provoked organized resistance. Much of this has been led by the former militia-turned opposition party, Renamo, which has created a sporadic insurgency in Mozambique's central region since 2013 as a means to demand provincial autonomy and a greater stake in newly exploited resource rents.

Alongside the extension of the centralized electricity network, the Mozambican state has been planning the construction of several large-scale hydropower projects to boost generation capacity. These are in part a statement of Mozambique's impending modernity and are intended to support export-oriented industry, but they are also in part about expanding the party-state's territorial influence and countering the wider discontent with Frelimo that Renamo has sought to tap into. Along with Mozambique's wider energy-policy environment, plans for these new hydro facilities are shaped by the Ministry of Mineral Resources and Energy (MIREME). The largest of the proposed projects is the 1,500 MW Mphanda Nkuwa dam, sited 60 km downstream from Cahora Bassa in Tete province, estimated at US$3 billion; the 'backbone' transmission system needed to transfer power to the Maputo region is costed at a further US$1 billion (World Bank 2015). The project was tendered to a consortium comprised of EDM, Insitec (a Mozambican private firm with links to former president Guebuza) and the Brazilian construction conglomerate Camargo Corrêa. The project has World Bank support and a mix of South African, Brazilian and Chinese investors.

The construction of Mphanda Nkuwa also depends on the South African utility Eskom's commitment to buy most of its electricity. Projected to displace 1,400 households and indirectly affect the livelihoods of a further 200,000 Mozambicans, the project represents a form of 'post-colonial amnesia', in which 'the consequences of producing power, measured in lost livelihoods and deteriorated ecosystems, are shunted out of sight' (Isaacman and Sneddon 2003, 38). It also potentially exacerbates colonial patterns of extraction, with a narrow focus on export-based growth.

The Mozambican state seeks foreign investment to catalyse these projects to attract energy-intensive industries and strengthen its role as an energy exporter country. Yet, it also prizes sovereignty over its energy system. Favoured by former president Guebuza, the slogan '*Cahora Bassa é nossa!*' (Cahora Bassa is ours) appears on a billboard in Maputo's main coastal thoroughfare, aiming to inspire national pride. In July 2015, opposition speakers in the Mozambican Parliament publicly rejected the slogan given the ongoing sale of electricity to South Africa. The speakers warned of a 'general crisis in the supply of electricity', suggesting that HCB's operations were outside of national control (Club of Mozambique, 2015). Pedro Couto, then energy minister, responded that engaging in a wider regional market would attract investors and would be less risky than relying on the limited domestic market while increasing state revenues.

The World Bank (2015, 12) has also advocated a focus on large-scale hydropower, arguing that electricity trade through the regional power pool might spark wider development and 'provide the critical mass needed to develop large energy projects within the country'. The state's ability to enact a vision of an energy future, and to balance its role in energy trade with enhancing provision for citizens, is thus shaped by the discretionary influence of a key multilateral donor and what Ferguson and Gupta (2002) have conceptualized as 'transnational governmentality'.

Founded in 1977, EDM is responsible for electricity transmission, distribution and some generation. A state-owned utility, EDM acts as an extension of the Frelimo state. Like MIREME, it has partnered with multinational companies in pursuit of opportunities emerging in the extractive industries and fossil-fuel power generation. EDM has been subject to political influence, with critics accusing it of outsourcing its duties to companies linked to Frelimo elites. This fits a broader pattern in which senior government officials have set up private companies to service the electricity sector, or the emerging oil and gas industry, as they enjoy privileged access to information, engaging with foreign capital to make private gains (interview with Ana Pinheiro, European Commission Delegation in Mozambique, 17 September 2013). EDM officials have also created start-ups to provide services supporting grid expansion, while petty corruption involving company technicians allegedly proliferates at the local level (Nhamire and Mosca 2014).

While increasingly strained by rising demand, EDM is also understaffed, with insufficient technical personnel to cope with regular grid operations and maintenance while simultaneously working on the new connections programme. From 2011 to 2014, EDM connected roughly 120,000 households per year, but it would need to link an additional 57,000 households above its current rate annually if it is to meet the government's 50 per cent access target[3] by 2023 (World Bank 2015). The utility also faces administrative constraints. In urban areas, it has limited information about new planned neighbourhoods that require power connections given a lack of coordination with the municipal authorities responsible for authorizing the construction of housing and urban infrastructures (Baptista 2015).

In recent years, investment in power generation and transmission infrastructure has not kept pace with industrial development. As a result, EDM's capacity surplus in 2008 quickly became a deficit, forcing it to contract out for energy provision during peak hours and begin load shedding in the central and northern regions. This arrangement takes the form of licensing and divestment of generation operations to third-party independent power producers (IPPs), regarded by the state as crucial for enhancing supply in the time frame needed to attract new investments. This in turn has meant a deregulation of tariffs to a degree sufficient to induce IPPs to enter the market. Through EDM and MIREME as mediators, the state has joined with multinational corporations involved in coal extraction, while the electricity generated will likely cost more than that generated at Cahora Bassa.

A proliferation of non-transparent activities reflects a broader lack of local control over energy provision and energy infrastructures in the country. For instance, in the small northern port city of Nacala, the Scottish temporary generation firm Aggreko has built an 18MW power plant to increase capacity and will sell the higher-cost electricity to EDM. At Ressano Garcia, near the border with South Africa, EDM has begun purchasing power from the 175MW thermal power station built in partnership with South African petrochemicals giant Sasol. Also in Ressano Garcia, Aggreko is involved in gas-fired power generation under an agreement between EDM, NamPower of Namibia and Eskom. EDM pays 1,080 MZN (US$28.1) per megawatt hour from Cahora Bassa, but power from Aggreko costs over four times that amount (Nhamire and Mosca 2014).

These dynamics suggest that while fostering enhanced energy provision, the state is stretched thin in its capacity to manage electrification, with persistent energy poverty and a broad neglect of citizens' needs, particularly in rural areas.

In the following section, we examine the experiences of rural energy provision and links with state power in off-grid contexts.

Statecraft and the practice and discourse of rural electrification

Attempts at rural electrification and expanding energy access through off-grid technologies represent additional ways electricity has been institutionalized within the wider project of development in Mozambique. Since the 2000s, the state has turned to decentralized provision of electricity in rural areas, given the high unit costs of extending the grid to dispersed rural populations, along with increasing donor support and social and environmental concerns over climate change (cf. Calvert 2016). There has been a corresponding rise in the uptake of small-scale renewables, which provide electrical power at or near the point of use, usually less than 100 MW in size.

In part, these efforts suggest neoliberal influences in the electricity sector in African contexts (McDonald 2009). Across the global South, governments have unbundled and privatized large public utilities, facing pressure to reduce corruption and clientelist distribution of services. Yet it is often unclear that political influence in the sector has been reduced; in some cases, the constellation of actors has expanded following privatization (Maclean and Brass 2015). In contrast to the jubilant era of the 1960s, when developmental states in Africa were the primary actors responsible for increasing access to electricity by expanding a highly centralized, national electric grid, the contemporary juncture of neoliberal globalization and privatization has seen a growing range of private, non-state actors becoming involved with electrification 'NGO-business hybridisation' in the sector is increasing (Maclean and Brass 2015, 59). Moreover, with decentralized and privatized solutions to energy poverty, it increasingly becomes the household's responsibility to install renewables such as solar panels in homes, with the state withdrawing from energy provision (McDonald 2009). Also, for all the talk of decentralized and sustainable energy systems, the Mozambican state and World Bank continue to prioritize large-scale, centralized and export-oriented power systems.

The institutional actor shaping the roll out of small-scale renewable energy in Mozambique is the National Energy Fund (*Fundo de Energia*, FUNAE). Established in 1997, it operates under MIREME as the agency in charge of supporting energy access in rural areas, including electricity and fuel. Initially supplying diesel generators and kerosene, FUNAE's focus has shifted to financing and supplying renewables, principally through solar photovoltaic (PV) systems and a small number of mini-hydro and pilot wind projects. FUNAE is funded through the state budget, with revenues from taxes and levies from petroleum and electricity concessions, along with donor support from the World Bank, the European Union, several European countries and, more recently, India (interview with Mario Batsana, FUNAE, 3 November 2013).

Through its involvement in rural electrification initiatives, the agency fosters the links between energy and development while narrating the benefits of sustainable energy. Since the 2000s, FUNAE has partnered with several donor agencies in deploying renewable-energy technologies (RETs) in projects for the provision of electricity for social uses in off-grid environments, such as school lighting, water pumping and vaccine refrigeration. These projects use localized mini-grids or stand-alone systems that supply electricity for public services, including clinics, schools and teachers and nurse's residences. FUNAE operates, however, in a centralized fashion, with its headquarters and decision-making located in Maputo. FUNAE's procurement and supply-based model has succeeded in expanding geographic coverage. The approach focuses on connecting rural institutions, such as government offices, health centres and primary schools, rather than providing direct access for households. FUNAE considers households connected if they live within a 20km radius of these connected institutions (interview with Mario Batsana, FUNAE, 3 November 2013).

During fieldwork, we observed that despite the use of decentralized technologies, these projects featured top-down management structures with limited local participation in design and implementation. In Mavonde, a town in Manica province, local residents explained that most households who live far from the town centre, in order to be close to their *machambas* (cultivated fields), are unable to repay loans offered by FUNAE for installation equipment for solar home systems and remain disconnected from the project. In Chinhambuzi, a solar PV mini-grid, supported by Belgian finance and technical support, supplies several hours of electricity in the evenings for schoolteachers' residences and shops, but ordinary residents of the town remained disconnected. Several residents told us they considered making 'spontaneous connections' to the mini-grid without FUNAE's support, but the system's capacity would not support it.

Similarly, in Majaua-Maia in Zambézia province, which hosts an European Union (EU)-funded mini-hydro project that has rehabilitated an abandoned hydraulic system used on a plantation in the 1960s and 1970s, there was little participation in decision-making among residents in the delivery of electricity. For instance, the system did not link to a local mill used by local women to grind corn for *xima*, a staple food. Interviewees explained that this was a local priority, as women must travel long distances to use a diesel generator–powered mill. In these cases, FUNAE supplies solar units from its Maputo headquarters, drawing criticism for impeding independent enterprises insofar as it receives state subsidies and donor funds, crowding out competition (interview with Boris Atanossov, FUNAE, 17 September 2013). Moreover, FUNAE's model does not address the consumption of charcoal and firewood, despite their continued use in many of the communities hosting RET projects.

FUNAE projects typically involve installations with capacity ranging from 250 to 500 watts, with systems tendered to pre-qualified companies and host communities, which are selected based on feasibility and population size (Interview with Mario Batsana, FUNAE, 3 November 2013). Yet decisions about which energy resources to prioritize and where to build infrastructure are not based purely on technical terms of feasibility or numbers of beneficiaries. Rather, we suggest that FUNAE's initiatives also aim to strengthen rural state institutions and galvanize support in contested rural peripheries. With Renamo and a newer party, MDM (*Movimento Democrático de Moçambique*) taking on the mantle of opposition, Frelimo seeks to extend its presence through FUNAE's projects.

Yet, in some ways, FUNAE is itself a peripheral actor in the country's energy sector. Its focus on RETs is regarded as less significant, and lucrative, than MIREME's pursuit of hydrocarbon revenues. An EU evaluation in 2014 found that FUNAE tends to be excluded from national energy planning, which has sometimes led to unnecessary projects or investments out of synch with gridextension initiatives. Set up primarily as a financial institution, FUNAE is poorly equipped to implement off-grid projects (EU, 2014). Relative to other state actors concerned with energy, FUNAE is chronically under-resourced and dependent on donor funding, while it has been criticized for inadequate maintenance and repair of equipment in its projects. With high import content; dependence on external actors for technology, capital and expertise; and limited presence in the most isolated regions, some question whether FUNAE's approach can meaningfully address energy poverty.

FUNAE's projects have financial support from donors who, along with the state, depict rural electrification as an enabler of rural development, propelling activities in agriculture, trade, industry, health and education, attracting new investments and improving livelihoods. What is rarely discussed explicitly, however, by FUNAE, is *who* and *how many* benefit from rural electrification in districts and villages as they are connected to off-grid energy. Further, the state has very little understanding of the micro-scale energy geographies that shape the take-up of RETs in rural spaces. Off-grid energy provision is afflicted by challenges similar to those faced by grid-based energy, and FUNAE's limited number of decentralized systems 'gloss over' a more typical centralized management approach.

The electricity infrastructures installed by EDM or FUNAE generally serve local elites and local state administrations rather than the rural poor as intended beneficiaries. Furthermore, FUNAE's interventions do not engage with the energy needs of the *urban* poor, given its rural remit. The current installation process also often overlooks local conditions and contextual knowledge, as the goal is often to bring electricity to the district capital or centres of state administration (*postos administrativos*[4]), to appear in government statistics that claim electrification as more inclusive than it is in practice.

Conclusion

Access to electricity, both socially and spatially, remains acutely uneven in Mozambique. Alongside the growing cross-border trade in electricity, the state has ambitious plans for improving grid connectivity centred on large-scale power generation from fossil fuels and hydropower. Yet many of these projects exhibit a 'post-colonial amnesia' (Isaacman and Sneddon 2003), and it is unclear if they can transform the path dependencies within the country's energy system that have been created by centuries of colonialism and extractive mercantilist capitalism or help to move beyond the 'colonial electrical geographies' that characterize much of the Southern Africa region (McDonald 2009).

Through an analysis of recent grid-connected and off-grid electrification efforts, we have suggested that energy infrastructure materializes state power and authority in Mozambique. This infrastructure and its electricity flows are monopolized by the ruling Frelimo Party, exercised though its state agencies including MIREME and FUNAE and parastatal companies, EDM, which operate as intermediaries between the state and international interests and between the party and national elites. Electricity infrastructures are largely geared to facilitating resource extraction and the international circulation of capital, enriching elites in league with multi-scalar alliances and actors. The monopolistic nature of grid-based electricity has enabled rent-seeking, as energy provision supports patronage networks and petty corruption. In this way, the configuration of elites in Mozambique has constrained energy access while electrification serves as a tool to maintain political power.

It cannot be assumed that the energy needs of the poor will be delivered through ambitious expansions in generation and distribution capacity. Even in urban neighbourhoods that obtain grid access, connections often occur regressively and poor households can remain without electricity for years, as they are unable to afford the connection charges. Further, the normative assumption is that all individuals *should* be connected to the grid, but the necessity and desirability of life on the grid are seldom questioned (Gupta 2015). While connecting all citizens to the grid is regarded as an index of the modernity by the state, questions of affordability are frequently overlooked, and energy 'access' is often understood in technical terms without fully understanding the micro-scale energy geographies that shape it along with the wider uptake of RETs. Given the current social and material relationships within Mozambique's energy sector, the scope for rapid and socially inclusive increases in access thus appears limited, notwithstanding the state's aspiring plans and targets.

We have shown that state ideologies and practice in Mozambique have shaped its electricity infrastructure, reflecting wider geopolitical imaginaries of development, territory and nation. The process of electrification aims to buttress the power of state institutions and expand the scope of state activity while countering the spread of ethnic or regional fragmentation. Yet, this projection of state power has in many ways been largely symbolic. The slogan '*Cahora Bassa é nossa*' rings hollow amid continuing exports to South Africa and local disarticulation of its hydroelectricity flows. There is a separation between the state's rhetoric and current sociopolitical realities. Further, the everyday spaces of state power and electricity are not uncontested. As we have shown, specific social and material relationships shape energy access, whether it is through Renamo's resistance to the national political order, neighbourhood-level negotiations around electricity and charcoal usage, the management of off-grid energy services in rural communities or some residents' plans to circumvent the system and connect 'spontaneously'.

The extension of grid-based electrical power aims to bring more centralized influence over people and places, while local communities are often regarded as passive recipients of energy and supporting infrastructure that is planned and delivered for them by the state and investors. In some communities that have been bypassed by planned grid extension or where access is unaffordable, disadvantaged residents address their own needs, such as through charcoal provisioning. Yet such efforts are fragmented, partial and inevitably local in scale (cf. Nielsen 2010). Furthermore, participation among users in shaping electrification – on- or off-grid – often entails local communities and users being consulted, or asked to give consent to an initiative, rather than actively shaping it (Castán Broto, Salazar and Adams 2014). As a result, thus far, citizens have enjoyed little influence over systems of energy provision, and there is a pressing need for an open public debate about *who* and *what* energy is ultimately *for* (Ribeiro 2015). Electrification in Mozambique is subject to what Li (2007, 7) calls the practice of 'rendering technical', where those concerned with improvement exclude the structure of political–economic relations from their diagnoses and prescriptions – the 'anti-politics' machine that Ferguson (1990, 270) speaks of that 'insistently repos[es] political questions of land, resources, jobs or wages as technical "problems" responsive to the technical "development" intervention' in ways that are subliminal and routine. Yet as we have shown, electrification is a profoundly political process that shapes state–citizen relations in multiple ways and that enables the state to order, arrange and make legible its territory as a key component of the everyday spaces of state power.

Notes

1 Data were gathered through semi-structured interviews with representatives of the national electricity utility, Electricidade de Moçambique (EDM), the National Rural Energy Fund (FUNAE), several ministries, donors, small businesses and NGOs. The research also included site visits to six off-grid energy projects in Maputo, Manica and Zambézia provinces and a newly built solar-panel assembly plant outside the capital, Maputo.
2 Baptista (2016) notes that EDM plans to ease prepayment by using ATMs and mobile phones.
3 Mozambique needs 300,000–400,000 new customers, apart from those being connected by EDM, if it is to achieve universal access by 2030 in keeping with the SDGs (World Bank 2015).
4 The districts of Mozambique are divided into 405 *postos administrativos* (administrative posts).

References

Agência de Informação de Moçambique (AIM). 1981. Information Bulletin, 58: 13.

Baker, L., P. Newell and J. Phillips. 2014. 'The Political Economy of Energy Transitions: The Case of South Africa', *New Political Economy*, 19(6): 791–818.

Baptista, I. 2015. 'Taming Uncertain Livelihoods in Urban Africa: Electricity Infrastructure in Colonial and Postcolonial Maputo', Presentation at symposium on 'African Dreams: Imaginations of Urban Life and Infrastructure in the African Metropolis', Oxford University, June 8.

Baptista, I. 2016. '"We Live on Estimates": Everyday Practices of Prepaid Electricity and the Urban Condition in Maputo, Mozambique', *International Journal of Urban and Regional Research*, 39(5): 1004–19.

Bertelsen, B. E. 2016. *Violent Becomings: State Formation, Sociality and Power in Mozambique*. New York and Oxford: Berghahn.

Boyer, D. 2014. 'Energopower: An Introduction', *Anthropological Quarterly*, 87(2): 309–33.

Brew-Hammond, A. 2010. 'Energy Resources in Africa: Challenges Ahead', *Energy Policy*, 38(5): 2291–301.

Bridge G. and P. Lebillon. 2013. *Oil*. Cambridge: Polity.

Büscher, B. 2009. 'Connecting Political Economies of Energy in South Africa', *Energy Policy*, 37: 3951–8.

Calvert, K. 2016. 'From "Energy Geography" to Energy Geographies': Perspectives on a Fertile Academic Borderland', *Progress in Human Geography*, 40(1): 105–25.

Castán Broto, V. 2017. 'Energy Sovereignty and Development Planning: The Case of Maputo, Mozambique', *International Development Planning Review*, 39(3): 229–48.

Castán Broto, V., D. Salazar and K. Adams. 2014. 'Communities and Urban Energy Landscapes in Maputo, Mozambique', *People, Place and Policy*, 8(3): 192–207.

Castel-Branco, C. N. 2015. 'Growth, Capital Accumulation and Economic Porosity in Mozambique: Social Losses, Private Gains', *Review of African Political Economy*, 41(1): 26–48.

Cipriano, A., C. Waugh and M. Matos. 2015. *The Electricity Sector in Mozambique: An Analysis of the Power Sector Crisis and its Impact on the Business Environment.* Maputo: USAID Mozambique.

Club of Mozambique. 2015. 'Mozambique Electricity: New Tariffs Are Low and Well below Market Prices', http://www.clubofmozambique.com/solutions1/sectionnews.php?secao=mining&id=2147492940&tipo=one (accessed 15 November 2015).

European Union. 2014. *Final Evaluation of Projects under the 9th Energy Facility in Mozambique, Final Report*, February.

Ferguson, J. 1990. *The AntiPolitics Machine: Development, Depoliticization and Bureaucratic power in Lesotho*. Cambridge: Cambridge University Press.

Ferguson, J. and A. Gupta. 2002. 'Spatializing States: Toward an Ethnography of Neoliberal Governmentality', *American Ethnologist*, 29(4): 981–1002.

Fine, B. and Z. Rustomjee. 1996. *The Political Economy of South Africa: From Minerals Energy Complex to Industrialisation*. Boulder, CO: Westview Press.

Gandy, M. 2004. 'Rethinking Urban Metabolism: Water, Space and the Modern City', *City*, 8: 363–79.

Geffray, C. 1991. *A Causa das Armas*. Porto: Afrontamento.

Gupta, A. 2015. 'An Anthropology of Electricity from the Global South', *Cultural Anthropology*, 30(4): 555–68.

Huber, M. 2015. 'Theorising Energy Geographies', *Geography Compass*, 9(6): 327–38.

International Energy Agency (IEA). 2014. *Africa Energy Outlook – A Focus on Energy Prospects in Sub-Saharan Africa*. Paris: IEA.

Isaacman, A. and C. Sneddon. 2003. 'Portuguese Colonial Intervention, Regional Conflict and Post-colonial Amnesia: Cahora Bassa dam, Mozambique 1965–2002', *Portuguese Studies Review*, 11(1): 207–36.

Isaacman, A. and B. Isaacman. 2013. *Dams, Displacement and the Delusion of Development: Cahora Bassa and its Legacies in Mozambique, 1967–2007*. Athens: Ohio University Press.

Labban, M. 2012. 'Preempting Possibility: Critical Assessment of the IEA's World Energy Outlook 2010', *Development and Change*, 43(1): 375–93.

Li, T. 2007. *The Will to Improve: Governmentality, Development, and the Practice of Politics*. Durham, NC: Duke University Press.

Luque-Ayala, A. and J. Silver (eds). 2016. 'Introduction', in *Energy, Power and Protest on the Urban Grid: Geographies of the Electric City*, 1–18. London: Routledge.

McDonald, D. (ed.). 2009. *Electric Capitalism: Recolonising Africa on the Power Grid*. London: Earthscan.

Maclean, L. M. and J. Brass. 2015. 'Foreign Aid, NGOs and the Private Sector: New Forms of Hybridity in Renewable Energy Provision in Kenya and Uganda', *Africa Today*, 62(1): 56–82.

Meehan, K. 2014. 'Tool-Power: Water Infrastructure as Well Springs of State Power', *Geoforum*, 57: 215–24.

Ministério da Energia. 2014. *Estratégia de Energia 2014–2023*. Maputo.

Newell, P. and D. Mulvaney 2013. 'The Political Economy of the "Just 'Transition'"', *The Geographical Journal*, 179(2): 132–40.

Nhamire, B. and J. Mosca. 2014. *Electricidade de Moçambique: Mau serviço, não transparente e politizada*. Maputo: Centro de Integridade Pública.

Nielsen, M. 2010. 'Mimesis of the State: From Natural Disaster to Urban Citizenship on the Outskirts of Maputo, Mozambique', *Social Analysis*, 54(3): 153–73.

Ockwell, D. and R. Byrne. 2016. *Sustainable Energy for All: Technology, Innovation and Pro-Poor Green Transformations*. Abingdon: Routledge.

Painter, J. 2006. 'Prosaic Geographies of Stateness', *Political Geography*, 25: 752–74.

Practical Action. 2016. *Poor People's Energy Outlook: National Energy Access Planning from the Bottom Up*. Rugby: Practical Action.

Ribeiro, D. 2015. 'Mozambique: Energy for Whom and for What?' Presentation at Energy for Development in Mozambique, workshop hosted by Durham University and University of Eduardo Mondlane, Maputo, 17 March.

Scott, J. 1998. *Seeing Like a State: How Certain Schemes to Improve the Human Condition Have Failed*. New Haven, CT: Yale University Press.

Shamir, R. 2013. *Current Flow: The Electrification of Palestine*. Stanford, CA: Stanford University Press.

Söderbaum, F. and I. Taylor. 2010. 'State, Region and Space in Africa', in U. Engel and P. Nugent (eds), *Respacing Africa*, 45–70. Leiden and Boston, MA: Brill.

Star, S. L. 1999. 'The Ethnography of Infrastructure', *American Behavioral Scientist*, 43(3): 377–91.

Sumich, J. 2010. 'The Party and the State: Frelimo and Social Stratification in Post-Socialist Mozambique', *Development and Change*, 41(4): 679–98.

Sumich, J. 2016. 'The Uncertainty of Prosperity: Dependence and the Politics of Middle Class Privilege in Maputo', *Ethnos*, 81(5): 821–41.

Ulsrud, K., T. Winther, D. Palit and H. Rohracher. 2015. 'Village-level Solar Power in Africa: Accelerating Access to Electricity Services through a Socio-technical Design in Kenya', *Energy Research and Social Science*, 5: 34–44.

von Schnitzler, A. 2013. 'Traveling Technologies: Infrastructure, Ethical Regimes, and the Materiality of Politics in South Africa', *Cultural Anthropology*, 28(4): 670–93.

Winner, L. 1980. 'Do Artifacts Have Politics?', *Daedalus*, 109(1): 121–36.

World Bank. 2015. *Mozambique Energy Sector Policy Note*, Report No: ACS17091, Washington DC.

9

Big grid: The computing beast that preceded big data

Canay Özden-Schilling

Introduction: Little bulb, big grid

There is a light bulb in Livermore, California, that has been burning almost continuously since 1901.[1] The bulb was one of the many produced in the late 1890s in Ohio's Shelby Electric Company; merchants brought it to the California market, and one businessman donated it to the Livermore fire station. It originally hung in the fire station's hose cart house for the convenience of night-shift firefighters. The bulb remained on, without a power switch, through the fire department's relocations and renovations; its service interruptions remained limited to hours or a few days at most. In 1973, it caught the attention of a local journalist who traced and confirmed the bulb's longevity and secured its place in the Guinness World Records.

Ever since, the bulb, now rebranded as the 'centennial light', has had a growing group of fans. In 1976, while it was transferred to the fire station's new location two streets over, it was escorted by the police, and its reconnection to a power supply was watched by dozens who held their breaths before it came back on. (The interruption of service clocked in at twenty-three minutes during the transfer.) The Centennial Light Committee, a group consisting of Livermore's firefighters and history buffs, threw a party for the bulb's hundredth birthday in 2001, which was picked up by the news media and attended by hundreds more people than originally anticipated. Today, the bulb still hangs from the Livermore fire station's high ceiling and frequently receives visitors. Reduced to a mere 4 Watts from its original 60 Watts over the span of the twentieth century, it is not able to illuminate much more than itself. If you need reassurance that the bulb is still going, its dedicated webcam posts pictures of the defiant bulb online every thirty seconds.

Our imagination is often captivated by such tiny technological relics of a time past, like the little bulb that has inspired documentaries and children's books. They are *little engines that could*, dependable beyond the call of duty, antidotes to planned obsolescence. While the celebration of the little light bulb as a solid piece of engineering is not necessarily misplaced, however, its continuous operation should perhaps be credited to the continuities in the infrastructure into which it is plugged. Between 1901 and its move in 1976, the bulb was connected to mains electricity – what I will call here 'the grid'. The electricity that powers the bulb today is the same frequency and voltage that powered it in 1901.[2] The continuity is in the grid as much as in the bulb hooked up to it – it is a result of the grid's momentous growth over the twentieth century, which necessitated lasting standardization and synchronization of materials and procedures across large swaths of territory. In other words, what keeps the tiny bulb going, I suggest, is anything but tiny. In this chapter, I theorize the infrastructure behind the electric devices, like the centennial light, that often capture our attention, the electric regime in which most citizens of industrialized countries live – a structure I call the 'big grid'.

I define the big grid as a system of intense and broad electric interconnectedness that relies on structures of data collection and analysis. In anthropology and daily life, we associate 'data' with contemporary times all too easily, but the big grid is nothing new: it is a persistent feature of the electric histories of both the twentieth and the twenty-first centuries in the United States, and, as I will suggest in this chapter, an instance and a precursor of the contemporary phenomenon of data abundance and dependence, which anthropologists and other scholars of digital life have called 'big data'. I argue that our electric futures, which have been recently depicted in engineering circles as hinging on an axis of intelligence (i.e. future smart grids vs. contemporary analogue, or 'dumb', grids) depend, in fact, on understanding where the big grid came from and what alternatives it might have. This *longue durée* argument draws on my reading of the history of electrification and electrical engineering, as well as my ethnographic research with electricity traders, grid engineers, regulators and citizen activists in the United States.

The big grid has a metonymic relationship with big data: it is both a precursor and an instance of it. This chapter unpacks this relationship in two sections. In the first section, I give big data a prehistory – one rooted in specific material histories, in which the practice of big data appears not as the motivator but as the outcome of assembling infrastructures. In the second, I show an infrastructure of big data at work, giving anthropologists an opportunity to criticize constructively the arrangements upon which big-data practices stand. Focusing on its incarnation in the United States, I suggest that the big grid is a centralized infrastructure that only grants access to experts – and experts of particular kinds – and excludes users from decision-making mechanisms. I give voice to the critics of the big grid who find in current efforts of renewable-energy integration an infrastructural continuation of the old regime – a continuation of exclusive expert access to data management and decision-making. While celebrated new energy technologies might convey a sense of a radical break with the grid's analogue past, the analytic of the big grid may help us see the persistence of large infrastructures, be they physical or digital, like the electric grid and big data, through episodes of technological and political change.[3] Throughout the chapter, I call for the exploration of new avenues of thinking about electricity alongside current objects of interest in anthropology – data, infrastructures and expertise.

Big grid was before big data

One must begin with a definition of the grid. I take the electric grid to be the entirety of the hardware and software equipment that enables electricity's movements – an infrastructure made up of stronger and weaker transmission lines and intersection points where electricity can be injected and withdrawn. While often referred to in the singular, the electric grid is an amalgamation of multiple, overlapping, coexisting grids. What scale one chooses to focus on depends on what economic, political or metallic connections one chooses to bring to attention. For instance, the North American grid (which covers all of the continental United States along with parts of Canada and Mexico) is simultaneously three separate grids (the Western Interconnection, the Eastern Interconnection and the Texas Interconnection), each of which sustains synchronized frequency within itself and is weakly connected to the other three by a few direct current (DC) transmission lines, only to be used in emergencies. Each interconnect, in its turn, hosts several grids – this time understood as administrative and economic units called 'independent system operators' (ISOs), which run competitive markets and oversee electricity trade within their territory and, to a lesser extent, with each other. As this bird's-eye view account of the grid might reveal, the entire continental US grid is interconnected but run by different administrative units that have separate, overlapping jurisdiction.

The grid is what makes electricity the commodity we know: a service that we receive at end points of the grid and pay for on a periodic basis, as opposed to, for instance, a good that can be bought in bulk or anonymously in the marketplace.[4] Neither the grid nor the electricity we know has always been there. Entrepreneurs in the nineteenth century sought to commoditize electricity without necessarily transmitting it through a grid – they produced battery-powered novelties like doorbells and clothes and tried their hands at electric medicine (Nye 1992). In the meantime, Thomas Edison and, gradually, other rival entrepreneurs started building individual grids (e.g. Edison's Pearl Street Station in Manhattan) to sell electricity as a service, relying on smaller amounts of revenue collected from larger customer bases (Hughes 1993). What became known as the 'war of currents' between Thomas Edison, who built a DC-based grid in New York, and George Westinghouse, who, with help from Nikola Tesla, built an AC-based grid in the American Midwest was, in fact, a battle for the expansion of their respective system's reach – a direct result of a business plan that relied on reaching small consumers in ever-increasing numbers (Hughes 1993). By the 1930s, utilities across the country had mostly connected their grids through automatic relays to share their customer pool when it was more profitable to do so (Nye 2010, 39). Electricity was organized into a 'big grid': a grid that operates through the transformation of citizens into consumers and the concentration of wealth at the hands of a few producers. It has remained a big grid ever since.

In many ways, the big grid was a precursor of what scholars have called the age of 'big data' – the age in which gathering and deploying massive amounts of information has become key to the work of scientists, engineers and activists (Boyd and Crawford 2012). 'Big data' signifies the drive to acquire and store information in massive quantified data sets and the belief that the analysis of these data sets has a superior potential to yield meaningful answers to research questions (Mayer-Schönberger and Cukier 2013). Anthropologist Genevieve Bell speaks of a 'reassertion of empiricism' across the communities of practice that are driven by the big-data approach – a conviction that gathering more data is the necessary path to the discovery of the truth (Bell 2015, 24). She poses the following questions for anthropologies of data to explore: 'What is it about this particular historical moment that makes so compelling the need to return to an empirical point of view? What is going [on] right now that makes us say we need data, more and more and more of it? Why is [data] so comforting and so seductive, or, why is it that this is the moment in which more data seduces?' (Bell 2015, 14).

These questions are certainly key for future anthropologies of data. However, an exclusive focus on 'this moment' as *the* moment of big data runs the risk of ahistoricity – it might cloud the fact that we have come to the moment of big data through specific, material histories that directly influence our current experience of it. I agree with Bell that we are surrounded by a desire for more data, yet it should not follow from this observation that the desire for more data precedes and drives the supply of it. The case of the big grid, I argue, demonstrates that scientific and engineering concerns around managing and supplying public goods, in this case electricity, necessitated and brought about early forms of big data; big data, as the abstraction that we now understand, is embedded in histories of science and engineering. In other words, the big grid, as a concept, might give big data its much needed (pre)history. The big grid is a precursor to big data in two interrelated ways: 1) The environment in which big data can flourish, namely, digital computing, was inspired by the big grid; 2) The management of the big grid brought about the computational methods that are prevalent in the age of big data.

A brief history of electrical engineering is where we need to start tracing the twin histories of the big grid and big data. 'The early electrical community' of the United States came to being in the 1830s; it was made up of inventors and entrepreneurs interested in developing electromagnetic telegraphy systems and telephony (McMahon 1984, 17). Yet the real boost for electrical engineering came with the emergence of the lighting industry in the 1870s and grid builders, like Edison and Westinghouse, who conceived of lighting as a service transmitted through the grid (McMahon 1984). The first electrical engineering departments in the United States were heavily funded by the same industrialists who sought to expand their individual grids. They directed their attention to solving the issues of stability that the industry was experiencing – issues around synchronizing the voltage and frequencies of the various elements connected into a given system and thus reducing power surges and outages (Mindell 2004). The first electrical engineers consisted of 'mathematically literate and scientifically trained' (Mindell 2004, 141) engineers with backgrounds in phenomena related not necessarily to electricity but feedback and control in general. They set up analogue grid simulations where different components were represented by miniscule versions of grid devices, like power plants, substations and transmission lines.

At electrical engineering departments like that of the Massachusetts Institute of Technology (MIT), the study of the grid came to inspire fundamental research in addition to serving practical purposes over the course of the 1920s and 1930s. Vannevar Bush, a former employee of General Electric and an electrical engineering PhD from MIT and Harvard, ran a laboratory at MIT which hosted thoroughly practical grid projects funded by industry giants. 'Steeped in the culture of electric power systems' (Mindell 2004, 162), Bush and colleagues invented the differential analyser, an analogue computer designed 'to assist in the solution of equations associated with large electric power systems' (Edwards 1996, 46). The notable mathematicians of the campus, including Norbert Wiener and Claude Shannon, who frequented the lab were instrumental in turning grid-specific computers into general-purpose machines open to the use of other scientists and engineers on campus who studied other feedback and control phenomena, like aircraft tracking. Grid study at Vannevar Bush's lab helped stimulate theories of information and, eventually, Norbert Wiener's cybernetics, whose origins in the studies of the grid have become less than conspicuous over the years. Historian Hunter Crowther-Heyck writes, 'the rapidity of internal communication within electrical systems made it possible to think of ever-larger conglomerations of machinery as being single, unified systems' (2005, 187). Cybernetics was a project in turning practical concerns, like voltage synchronization in electric grids, into a 'general approach to the world' (Bowker 1993, 116; also see Bowker 2005).

Theories of information and communication, the appeal of which grew over wartime and came to underlie the emerging field of operations research, could not be contained in the confines of grid study for long. Wiener himself wrote prophetically, 'There is in electrical engineering a split … which we know as the distinction between [electric] power and communication engineering. It is this split which separates the age just past from that in which we are now living' (1948, 39). The post-war years saw intense government investment in computers and the work of dedicated mathematicians to free 'communication engineering' from the confines of grid studies – within a couple of decades, digital computing had become the premise of a separate field: computer science. Meanwhile, in electrical engineering departments, grid studies fell out of popularity; large industrialists had resolved stability issues and settled into a regulation regime where they were guaranteed to recover costs and were thus less motivated to fund research to improve efficiency. A new division of labour between computer science and electrical engineering came into being; with digital circuits becoming prevalent, computer science would become the study of software, leaving the study of circuit design, and electronics in general, to electrical engineering (Ceruzzi 1989). Big grid, as a research interest at electrical engineering departments, started fading, but only after it had given big data a promising home in computer science research.

Over the second half of the twentieth century, systems researchers gradually moved towards big data partly out of a desire to improve upon the limitations of grid studies at electrical engineering departments. For instance, Jay Forrester, who pioneered the field of system dynamics and promoted the application of systems approach onto social phenomena, maintained that analogue computers used in modelling complex phenomena, like electric grids, were only moderately successful because analogue computers were not able to address the non-linearity and uncertainty necessarily embedded in systems like electricity transmission (Edwards 1996). Digital computing would become host to the study of increasingly more complex, non-linear phenomena. While the electric grid itself was no longer studied widely in the second half of the twentieth century, many diverse subjects, from urban housing to world population, were studied *as if* they were grids; solipsistic analyses of individual components gave way to analyses of the interactions between different components. Complex systems researchers hoped to improve predictability based on repetitive, continuous observations instead of discovering causal relationships, drawing on the research culture of the early electrical engineering labs. Big data inherits grid studies' reliance on observation-based empiricism and diminished interest in causality. Put differently, big data originated in complex systems researchers' efforts to improve the study of systems like the electric grid, while staying true to the empirical spirit of the early electrical-engineering labs.

The big grid, I argue, posed certain questions for scientists and engineers in various disciplines to transfer to digital computing, reformulate, scale up and, hopefully, solve. Take optimization – a prevalent technique across big data communities referring to the minimization or maximization of a function while observing certain constraints. Grid operators and professional engineers running power plants have been interested in solving optimization problems since very early on for the practical purpose of cutting their companies' operation costs. But, in the absence of today's digital computers, they solved their optimization questions by hand, 'using judgment [and] rules of thumb' (Cain, O'Neill and Castillo 2012, 7). Optimization problems were solved as infrequently as a few times a year (Happ 1977). Grid operators and industrialists have welcomed the improvement of computerized optimization techniques; today, they solve optimization questions very similar to those invented in the early twentieth century but as frequently as every five minutes and automatically, thanks to digital computers. The questions and methods of how to study complex phenomena, in many instances, have preceded digitalized techniques. Equally importantly, they are rooted in questions of governing public infrastructures like the electric grid.

To be sure, the big grid is absolutely not the only precursor of big data. Yet recognizing that big data is a generalized, non-subject-specific approach which is, in fact, rooted in specific infrastructural histories, like that of the electric grid, is a productive start for the anthropological critique of the arrangements upon which big data practices stand. Grid researchers, with the help of incipient forms of big data and funds from electricity industrialists, created a regime where producers and consumers could interact safely while keeping producers' infrastructures intact and their costs down. Under this regime, electricity users, at the time a growing segment and eventually the entirety of the US citizenry, had to assume the role of mere consumers. Electric citizenship is now synonymous with electricity consumption in industrialized societies running on big grids. As the next section explores in more detail, citizens, who have been transformed into consumers from an electric perspective, find their political concerns about the grid reduced to a matter of consumer rights. As this infrastructural history reveals, big data has been complicit in the disenfranchisement of electric citizenship.

In the next section, I start sketching an anthropological critique of big data by focusing on the contemporary moment in which digital computing is welcomed back into the management of the big grid. This time, the big grid appears as yet another *instance* of big data, one that we can study while keeping its alternatives in perspective. Electrical engineers who give shape to the contemporary grid pursue what they call a 'smart grid' – a grid that relies much more explicitly on practices of big data, such as widespread and continuous digital communication and complex forms of optimization. Despite what the sense of novelty around it might suggest, I show that the smart grid, just like big data, is a continuation of the big grid and an instance of big data – one that shows us the limitations of what big data can offer in terms of the governance of our everyday lives.

Big grid is an instance of big data

A major trial of the big grid's desirability came in the summer of 2003.[5] On the afternoon of 14 August, in Walton Hills, Ohio, a 345 kV transmission line sagging in the summer heat came into contact with an overgrown tree and tripped. What happened next was a chain reaction known as 'cascading failures' in electrical engineering. In an intensely interconnected system, when a transmission line trips, its load shifts to other lines following the physics principle of the path of least resistance: these other lines might quietly carry the additional burden until the original failure is fixed or they may get overloaded and fail themselves. On that day, the line known to grid operators as 'Chamberlin-Harding' took out a number of other 345 kV lines within a matter of hours. The dated software in the control rooms of FirstEnergy, the corporation that operates transmission lines in northern Ohio, failed to record the failures in time. Faced with a sudden black hole of electricity demand, power plants across the Midwest automatically shut down one after another as required by their security protocols. Power-plant and transmission line failures spread to Pennsylvania, Michigan, Ontario and New York, eventually resulting in what is now known as the Northeast Blackout of 2003 – a two-day service interruption that affected fifty million people across the United States and Canada and demonstrated the potentially fatal vulnerability of electricity-dependent infrastructures, from health care to water supply to transportation.[6]

The sequence of events that I have summarized here was in no way apparent in the immediate aftermath of the Northeast Blackout. While governors and utility operators across the US–Canada border put the blame on a lightning strike in New York State or a power-plant failure in Pennsylvania,[7] it took investigators a few days to narrow the origin point down to Ohio; in a report published in April 2004, an American and Canadian government-led task force definitively traced the blackout back to the sparks between Chamberlin-Harding and a tree. For government officials, grid engineers and citizens alike, it was alarming that grid failures could travel hundreds of miles before being traced and contained. The task-force report catalogued the shortcomings or the absence of communication channels between control rooms across the American Midwest and Northeast – channels that would have been critical to avoid the Northeastern Blackout and that are generally necessary to run what the report called 'one large, interconnected machine' (US–Canada Power System Outage Task Force 2004, 5). Despite dissenting voices, it has been commonplace throughout the twentieth century to refer to the bigness of the North American grid as an asset; as the report also asserted, intense interconnectedness could trivialize small failures, with high-voltage lines 'absorb[ing]' surges in voltage or current (US–Canada Power System Outage Task Force 2004, 83). After the blackout, the big liability of bigness became hard to disavow.

As Susan Leigh Star (1999) famously wrote and most ethnographers of infrastructures repeated afterwards,[8] infrastructures have a tendency to become more visible to users upon breakdown. Historian David Nye (2010) reminds us that by the 1930s, the term 'blackout' had come to refer to the temporary shutting off of the electric grid; the emergence of the term indicated that the normalization of artificial light across the urban United States had been completed and darkness itself had become anomalous or artificial (as in the case of city-wide wartime blackouts to misdirect enemy aircraft). By the 1930s, when utilities had largely connected their grids to each other's through automatic relays (as opposed to through the work of technicians), grid failures became prone to cascade (Nye 2010, 39). The Northeast Blackout of 2003 serves as a milestone for the grid engineers I encountered during my fieldwork; they cite it as the main motivator of the contemporary smart-grid research agenda. Since 2007, the Department of Energy has hosted a Smart Grid Task Force and funds available for smart-grid research across the United States have proliferated. Today, the dominant opinion in the research and operation of the electric grid is that the grid's bigness has long been a mismanaged asset and that the management is to be improved in two interrelated ways: by making the grid smarter, or data-laden, and even bigger.

When the US Department of Energy officials,[9] academic electrical engineers[10] and utility companies[11] speak of a 'smart grid', they, by and large, refer to a version of the current grid upgraded with communication and automatic sensing technologies. The smart grid does not refer to a wholesale replacement of the current grid; rather, it is a research agenda – the totality of the efforts to produce software and hardware to reorganize the grid digitally and to reconnect it with information bits travelling in real time and spontaneously.[12] The smart grid is often touted as the welcoming of the digital age into the study of the electric grid – ironically so, since the electric grid inspired the lines of research that ushered in the digital age. While the invasion of the grid, like everything else, by big data was only predictable in the general context of an ever-growing reliance on data abundance, anthropological critique might guide us to see that it was not the only possible outcome of the Northeastern Blackout. In fact, responding to blackouts and failures by unleashing big data on the grid leaves critical voices out of the conversation of how we might imagine our electric futures.

In the twenty-first century, the efforts towards developing a big grid and a smart grid have sustained each other in the United States.[13] The end of the twentieth century saw a government push for a multiplicity of electricity providers to share grids and compete – a process commonly known as 'deregulation' (or 'restructuring'). Restructuring began in 1992, when the Energy Policy Act allowed states to break up electricity monopolies. In 1996, the Federal Energy Regulatory Commission proposed Independent System Operators (ISOs) as entities that would run competitive markets and operate their designated grids based on daily market results. ISOs have been in charge of, and generally favourable towards, the grid's continued expansion. They played an important role in reconciling the perils of intense interconnectedness, which were exposed starkly by the Northeastern Blackout, with the assumed benefits of the big grid. Mending the grid with superior communication and self-repair technologies, the logic went, could offset problems associated with long-distance transmission; transmission freed up of communication issues then becomes a necessity to increase reliability. Thus, the grid was to grow both physically and digitally. Recently, companies that specialize in building transmission services have constructed miles and miles of new transmission lines and expanded the North American grid both laterally (i.e. by increasing the connection between separately administered grids) and in place (i.e. by intensifying the volume of already existing connections within individual grids). Transmission companies have found strong allies in ISOs, perhaps because their boards are populated by representatives from the industry – including the very transmission companies whose projects are subject to ISO approval.

When ISOs approve new transmission lines as necessary for reliability purposes, the lines' cost gets socialized across the ISO territory (i.e. added to consumers' electricity bills), and utility companies collect a fixed profit from distributors for usage. This risk-free business model incentivizes grid expansion tremendously. For instance, ERCOT, the ISO that runs the Texas grid, is known to be a particularly aggressive transmission builder, having approved more than 8,500 miles of transmission lines since 1999.[14] Researchers and industrialists applaud this development as a positive step towards the integration of renewable energy into the grid. They point out that, while renewable resources, like wind from northern Texas, cannot be transported to urban demand centres like Houston, the electricity generated from renewable resources can, thanks to hundreds of miles of transmission lines. Transmission expansion buttressed by smart communication technologies is now commonly believed to be the future of an environmentally friendly grid. But does transmission expansion, or a continuation of the big grid, have to be the only environmentally friendly electric future available to us?

A critical voice belongs to citizen groups habitually derided in the industry – those assumed to boast a 'not-in-my-backyard' (or NIMBY) attitude and to oppose transmission expansion, and thus reliability, on self-interested grounds. Two of these groups that I have studied in rural Illinois and West Virginia believe that ISOs frequently approve the addition of long-distance lines to the electric grid, not because these lines are necessary for reliability purposes but to expand the geography of profitability for electricity companies (Özden-Schilling 2016). This is perhaps not a radical suggestion to industry players and experts. During my fieldwork, I encountered market participants trading in ERCOT's market who welcomed ERCOT's substantial transmission expansion as it made their market more open to possibilities of arbitrage and, hence, in their words, 'more exciting'. It is no secret that an increased number of routes for electricity to travel translates into enhanced opportunities of profit for market participants.

In a similar vein, the US–Canada Task Force report on the Northeastern Blackout briefly drew attention to the potential effect of the then-emergent electricity markets on service reliability; some contributing researchers have relayed their concern, the report points out, that electricity trade might be encouraging transmission that spans longer distances than the grid could handle (US–Canada Power System Outage Task Force 2004, 148). To voice such concerns, which often get side-lined in the industry, citizen groups educate themselves in ISOs' obscure regulations and the physics of electricity transmission – often through dedicated, online research. They counter ISOs' arguments around reliability by invoking a different electrical engineering principle – that the shorter a transmission line is, the more reliably it works. They point out that electricity generation near resources and demand is routinely discouraged in favour of the construction of new transmission lines[15] and that the big grid does not have to be the only transmitter of renewable energy across society.

It might be counter-intuitive to consider the continuations between the big grid and the smart grid. After all, the smart grid evokes the decentralization of electricity production and consumption, as well as a proliferation of all things small – solar panels on rooftops that bestow a measure of energy independence on consumers, tiny digital devices (e.g. smart metres) that allow precision in transactions between consumers and utilities and a diverse array of new, environmentally friendly energy resources – all of which stands in contrast with the insignia of the big grid – massive structures housing nuclear and coal power plants, the metal bulk towering over vast landscapes,[16] energy corporations that expand their territorial monopolies by buying out smaller utility companies.[17] Besides, the smart grid evokes progressivism. In fact, the smart-grid researchers whom I studied work with undeniable dedication to their sense of the public good; the alternative grids that they model in their computers are meant to accommodate more consumer choice, more renewable energy and less critical failure.

While the smart grid may depart from the big grid in its preferred materials – say, copper wires might be gradually dropped to make way for super-conducting ones – I argue that it might be resting upon the big grid in its politics as much as in its reliance on data. In 1882, when Thomas Edison, the disputed inventor of the incandescent light bulb and undisputed progenitor of the big grid, started charging the customers of his Pearl Street Station for electricity service rather than the equipment for its production (Rudolph and Ridley 1986), citizens were indefinitely transformed into passive consumers; from an electric perspective, 'citizen' and 'consumer' became interchangeable terms. Today, such interchangeability is scarcely challenged in smart-grid visions. In imagined smart-grid futures, our refrigerators, electric cars and air-conditioners are to interact constantly to reduce collective operation costs and failures; but when our devices make equal participants of a large system, do we vicariously become equal participants in the grid as well?

The smart grid's purportedly superior communication channels are meant to circulate specific types of data – for instance, those that relate to the availability of renewable energy and real-time electricity prices – but exclude communication between citizens as to how the grid might be governed. The decision-making centres where the resources and vehicles of the grid are determined, such as ISO boards, do not correspond to the decision-making centres where citizens have traditional participation rights, like voting. The big grid's exclusion of citizen input once provoked citizens to rise up.[18] The smart grid might plead guilty to the same political handicaps that haunted the big grid and continue to conflate consumption with citizenship. The challenge ahead is to identify and intervene in the political vision that the smart grid is meant to enact so we can begin to conceive of our electric futures as active citizens.

This brings us back to the political vision enacted by big data and its handicaps. If the age of big data entails a 'reassertion of empiricism' (Bell 2015, 24), the belief that more data gets one closer to the truth, it is 'only *one* kind of empiricism' (Bell 2015, 25) – one that needs 'critiquing' and 'countering … with our own' (Bell 2015, 24). Projects in big data, like the big grid, often promote a particular kind of communication – one whose success is assumed to correlate with the amount of data available and with data's ease of travel. In countering big data's empiricism with our own, it is imperative to consider what other avenues of communication between humans might need to be built into the infrastructures we inhabit – how we can make data into our allies, as opposed to our stand-ins, in our endeavour to share public resources and services fairly. We must interrogate what new roles we, the citizens of the grid, are assigned as the grid grows to accommodate the travels of data bits alongside electricity.

Conclusion

Our intensely interconnected electric grid, what I theorized in this article as the 'big grid', is important for anthropologists to explore for two reasons. The first has to do with the big grid's theoretical relevance. The big grid is in the roots of big data – an object of interest to anthropologists that has been deemed to define the contemporary moment but has yet to be given an origin story. The history of the big grid might illuminate the lineage of the desire for lives steeped in data, while its present moment, problematic for the reasons I outlined in the last section, might provide scholars with the opportunity to critique the political ramifications of big data's presence in the governance of everyday lives. The second reason for the big grid's relevance carries both empirical and political weight. It has to do with how our electric futures will shape up and how we, as anthropologists *and* citizens, will continue to inhabit one of the most ubiquitous infrastructures in contemporary existence. The big grid is the vehicle for a sizeable portion of the overall primary energy resources used to power life in industrialized societies[19] – energy resources that have a direct bearing on the progression of anthropogenic climate change. In addition, it is an infrastructure that is difficult to participate in politically and even more difficult to opt out of. In its ubiquity and indispensability, there is a unique opportunity for anthropologists to understand and productively intervene in the inequalities rampant in the governance of public infrastructures.

The light bulb known as the centennial light was switched on in a formative moment for the grid: industrialists were at work taking steps that foreshadowed that the future of electricity lay not in producing eccentric novelties for the rich but in growing grids to carry electricity to the masses. Rusty and dim, the bulb is now supported by a digitalizing grid that is bigger than ever. The big grid, in all likelihood, will outlast the tiny bulb. For a more just electric future, we will have to investigate different ways in which we can plug into electric grids, big and otherwise.

Notes

1   To assemble the following story, I drew on the following sources: the Centennial Light Committee's website, an 'All Things Considered' segment about the bulb on NPR and a 2011 documentary by Christopher Leps called *Century of Light*. Accessed 12 October 2018, http://www.centennialbulb.org/ and http://www.npr.org/templates/story/story.php?storyId=1124201. Accessed 12 March 2019, https://vimeo.com/113518437.

2   After the move, it was hooked up to a separate power supply (presumably also connected to and charged by the grid) to minimize the effect of potential outages. The other thing that keeps the bulb going is that it has been in the custody of a public organization, the fire department of the city of Livermore, that has been in operation continuously since the bulb was lit. Other bulbs from the same collection manufactured by the Shelby Company are still available and function well (in fact, they have become collector's items since the bulb's ascent to fame), yet few have been sheltered from the vicissitudes of private enterprise to enjoy a prolonged life in the same location. (The manufacturer itself was bought out by General Electric in 1914.)

3   In a similar vein, anthropologist Stephen Collier (2011) argues that most material qualities of the Soviet heating infrastructure persisted from the socialist era through the transition to the post-socialist period, which resisted the kinds of neoliberal governance that post-Soviet planners hoped to install.

4   See also Gretchen Bakke's chapter in this volume for an analysis of the existential interdependency between electricity and the grid.

5   In reconstructing the following story, I largely rely on the 'Final Report on the August 14, 2003 Blackout in the United States and Canada: Causes and Recommendations', a publication of the US–Canada Power System Outage Task Force (2004), appointed by US president George W. Bush and Canadian prime minister Jean Chretien in the fall of 2003.

6   Political scientist Jane Bennett (2005) offers an account of the Northeastern Blackout of 2003 to develop a theory of agency centring on assemblages and making room for non-humans. While I agree with Bennett on the distributed, composite and equally non-human nature of agency in general and the grid in particular, I am wary of a kind of materialism that treats non-human agency as somehow prior to human agency and only accessible to the probing of physical sciences, which, I believe, often mystifies the work of assemblages more so than describes it (for an extended critique, see Paxson and Helmreich 2013). The grid does not speak for itself, as Bennett might argue (2005, 462), but generates diverse, controversial conversations, such as the one about the value of built-in communication channels, as discussed in this section.

7   See CNN's coverage on 14 August 2003. Accessed 12 October 2016. http://www. cnn.com/2003/US/08/14/power.outage/.

8   In a review article, Brian Larkin (2013) accurately observes that anthropologists may have repeated this assertion too often and taken it for granted. Infrastructures can be as visible as invisible; they can exist as highly visible symbols and spectacles.

9   See the Department of Energy definition of 'smart grid'. Accessed 12 October 2016. http://energy.gov/oe/services/technology-development/smart-grid.

10 See the Institute of Electrical and Electronics Engineers' definition of 'smart grid'. Accessed 12 October 2016. http://smartgrid.ieee.org/about-ieee-smart-grid.

11 See, for instance, Duke Energy's definition of 'smart grid'. Accessed 18 March 2019. https://www.duke-energy.com/our-company/about-us/smart-grid.

12 Elsewhere, I detail the similarities of this idealized grid structure with the structure of free markets according to neoliberal economics (Özden-Schilling 2015).

13 To be sure, smart grid research is extensive and diverse across the United States. Some research groups actively investigate the possibility of smaller grids. In this chapter, I mainly refer to 'smart grids' as understood and promoted by government offices and grid operators.

14 See ERCOT news release. Accessed 12 October 2016. http://www.ercot.com/news/releases/show/475.

15 Once again, the industry would not necessarily disagree with this point. The US–Canada Task Force's report suggests that the origin point of the Northeast Blackout was a 'transmission constrained load pocket with limited generation' (2004, 24). The report does not address the larger repercussions of the fact that transmission expansion in the absence of generation expansion may create undue pressure on the grid.

16 For many residents of the United States, high-voltage transmission lines had become an eyesore by the 1960s; utility companies undertook extensive public-relations campaigns to make them palatable to Americans, such as design contests open to the public (Levy 1997).

17 Samuel Insull, who built a utility empire based out of Chicago after serving as Thomas Edison's consultant, became synonymous with corporate corruption in the 1930s after he suffered a major bankruptcy and erased the savings of thousands of stockholders. Before its bankruptcy, the high rates that Insull's Commonwealth Edison charged in the absence of competitors led to consumer protests; Franklin Roosevelt's presidential campaign publicized the issue across the country (Rudolph and Ridley 1986).

18 See note 17.

19 According to the Energy Information Administration statistics, in the United States, about 39 per cent of primary energy sources (e.g. oil, coal, natural gas) are converted to electricity. Accessed 12 October 2016. http://www.eia.gov/energyexplained/index.cfm.

References

Bell, Genevieve. 2015. 'The Secret Life of Big Data', in Tom Boellstorff and Bill Maurer (eds), *Data: Now Bigger and Better!*, 7–26. Chicago, IL: Prickly Paradigm Press.

Bennett, Jane. 2005. 'The Agency of Assemblages and the North American Blackout', *Public Culture*, 17: 445–65.

Bowker, Geoffrey. 1993. 'How to Be Universal: Some Cybernetic Strategies, 1943–70', *Social Studies of Science*, 23: 107–27.

Bowker, Geoffrey. 2005. *Memory Practices in the Sciences*. Cambridge, MA: MIT Press.

Boyd, Danah and Kate Crawford. 2012. 'Critical Questions for Big Data: Provocations for a Cultural, Technological, and Scholarly Phenomenon', *Information, Communication, and Society*, 15: 662–79.

Cain, Mary, Richard O'Neill and Anya Castillo. 2012. 'History of Optimal Power Flow and Formulations', *Federal Energy Regulatory Commission (FERC) staff paper*. Accessed 18 March 2019. https://www.ferc.gov/industries/electric/indus-act/market-planning/opf-papers/acopf-1-history-formulation-testing.pdf.

Ceruzzi, Paul. 1989. 'Electronics Technology and Computer Science, 1940–1975: A Coevolution', *Annals for the History of Computing*, 10: 257–75.

Collier, Stephen. 2011. *Post-Soviet Social: Neoliberalism, Social Modernity, Biopolitics*. Princeton, NJ: Princeton University Press.

Crowther-Heyck, Hunter. 2005. *Herbert A. Simon: The Bounds of Reason in Modern America*. Baltimore, MD: Johns Hopkins University.

Edwards, Paul. 1996. *The Closed World: Computers and Politics of Discourse in Cold War America*. Cambridge, MA: MIT Press.

Happ, H. H. 1977. 'Optimal Power Dispatch: A Comprehensive Survey', *IEEE Transactions on Power Apparatus and Systems*, 96: 841–54.

Hughes, Thomas. 1993. *Networks of Power: Electrification in Western Society, 1880–1930*. Baltimore, MD: Johns Hopkins University Press.

Larkin, Brian. 2013. 'The Politics and Poetics of Infrastructure', *Annual Review of Anthropology*, 42: 327–43.

Levy, Eugene. 1997. 'The Aesthetics of Power: High-Voltage Transmission Systems and the American Landscape', *Technology and Culture*, 38: 575–607.

Mayer-Schönberger, Viktor and Kenneth Cukier. 2013. *Big Data: A Revolution That Will Transform How We Live, Work, and Think*. New York: Houghton Mifflin Harcourt.

McMahon, Michal. 1984. *The Making of a Profession: A Century of Electrical Engineering in America*. New York: IEEE Press.

Mindell, David. 2004. *Between Human and Machine: Feedback, Control, and Computing Before Cybernetics*. Baltimore, MD: Johns Hopkins University Press.

Nye, David. 1992. *Electrifying America: Social Meanings of a New Technology, 1880–1940*. Cambridge, MA: MIT Press.

Nye, David. 2010. *When the Lights Went Out: A History of Blackouts in America*. Cambridge, MA: MIT Press.

Özden-Schilling, Canay. 2015. 'Economy Electric', *Cultural Anthropology*, 30: 578–88.

Özden-Schilling, Canay. 2016. 'Expertise in the Grid: Electricity and Its Publics', *Limn*, 7: 101–6.

Paxson, Heather and Stefan Helmreich. 2013. 'The Perils and Promises of Microbial Abundance: Novel Natures and Model Ecosystems, from Artisanal Cheese to Alien Seas', *Social Studies of Science*, 44: 165–93.

Rudolph, Richard and Scott Ridley. 1986. *Power Struggle: The Hundred-Year War Over Electricity*. New York: Harper and Row.

Star, Susan Leigh. 1999. 'The Ethnography of Infrastructure', *American Behavioral Scientist*, 43: 377–91.

U.S.-Canada Power System Outage Task Force. 2004. 'Final Report on the August 14, 2003 Blackout in the United States and Canada: Causes and Recommendations', http://energy.gov/sites/prod/files/oeprod/DocumentsandMedia/BlackoutFinal-Web.pdf (accessed 12 October 2016).

Wiener, Norbert. 1948. *Cybernetics or Control and Communication in the Animal and the Machine*. Cambridge, MA: MIT Press.

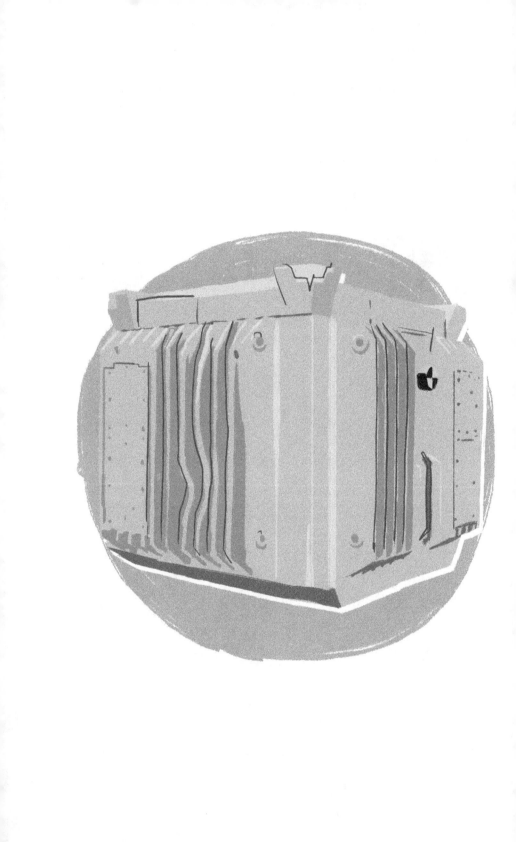

10

Touring the nuclear sublime: Power-plant tours as tools of government

Tristan Loloum

Going on a guided tour in a nuclear power station doesn't sound like a first choice for a holiday destination. The mere mention of such an excursion often triggers reactions of surprise and sarcasm ('You can actually visit these places?', 'Did you come out glowing?'). Indeed, many people ignore the fact that most nuclear stations are open to visitors, whether through information centres, guided tours or open days. In France, the electric utility company Électricité de France (EDF) has long been 'the most visited company', with more than 400,000 visitors every year. The largely state-owned company has always been a leading actor[1] in the promotion of so-called 'industrial tourism' (Otgaar 2010) and 'company visits' (Morice 2006), conferring to nuclear power plants a central part in the touristic display of the nation's *fleurons de l'industrie* ('industrial jewels'). In Great Britain, nuclear stations have had information centres since their early days, but most of them closed in the 2000s because of British Energy's financial troubles and anti-terrorist restrictions. Guided tours and visitor centres eventually reopened in 2013, four years after EDF Energy (EDF's subsidiary in the UK) took control of British Energy and its eight nuclear power plants. They are today one of EDF's main public-relations apparatus.

This contribution focuses on guided tours and visitor centres in two EDF Energy power plants in Northern England (Heysham 2 and Hartlepool), analysing the underlying communication process at stake in the encounter between the public and a sensitive industrial infrastructure.[2] A first set of arguments exposed in this chapter examines these tours as a 'sublime experience', defined here as an aesthetic of grandeur that transcends beauty, with mixed feelings of awe and wonder, perplexity and fascination. Just like the 'agreeable kind of horror' that filled Joseph Addison's mind when his Grand Tour went through the Alps (Addison 1773), David Nye (1994) has applied the 'technological sublime' to the sensation of vertigo experienced when facing great man-made monuments, like the Golden Gate Bridge, the Hoover Dam or Fifth Avenue. My main hypothesis is that power station guided tours aim to frame this sublime experience in order to defuse the fear of atomic risk while emphasizing popular fascination for industrial gigantism and engineering achievements. I show that most important messages are delivered during the visits through non-verbal communication: for instance, through gazing devices installed in the factory both for surveillance and aesthetic contemplation, through repeated security checks that inspire a sense of authority and control, through company-supplied protective clothing and equipment that conveys a sense of familiarity and empathy with the factory and its workers and so on.

A second point developed in this chapter suggests that EDF's visitor policy is part of a wider public-relations strategy – interpreted by French anthropologist Sezin Topçu (2013) as an 'art of governing a contested technology' – that consists in 'internalizing' anti-nuclear criticism (instead of avoiding or confronting it) by recruiting social science and environmental experts. Guided tours follow the same kind of governmental logic in the sense that they stage a paradoxical concern for 'transparency' and 'openness', suggesting to visitors that the company has 'nothing to hide'. This is a suggestion that seems contradictory, as safety measures and industrial secrecy do imply significant informational and access restrictions. Besides, how could we – as mundane visitors – make an objective assessment of such complex issues (and invisible to the eye) as radioactivity or carcinogenic hazard?

While exploring the concepts of nuclear 'sublime' and 'governmentality', the touring of a nuclear power plant reminds us of the ambivalence of tourism. On the one hand, there is its productive relation with enchantment, the imaginary and the sacred: tourism as a 'modern magic' (Picard 2013). On the other, there is its power of conformation, commodification and control: tourism as an apparatus of surveillance (Hollinshead 1999). More than a mere communication tool for corporate discourse, it should be noted that 'energy tourism' lays on a variety of cultural meanings, embodied emotions and material interests (Winthereik, Maguire and Watts 2019).

The technological sublime

The sublime is a fugitive emotion, based on mixed feelings of 'awe and reverence' (Marx 1964) but also a historically and socially situated frame of mind. What is astonishing for one person may be commonplace for another; what was yesterday's enchantment may become tomorrow's banality. Electricity lends itself very well to this complex of emotions: it is almost invisible, yet it lights millions of homes; it is formless, made of infinitely small moving electrons, yet it flows through gigantic static structures; it is destructive when passed through the body, yet it breathes life into cities and states.

In the *American Technological Sublime* (1994), David E. Nye analyses the American transference of the notion of the sublime from nature to technology and infrastructure. While nineteenth-century naturalists and artists have drawn extensively upon the 'natural sublime' – an emotional reaction to a natural landscape so impressive as to render a spectator speechless before its startling transcendence of ordinary experience (Burke 1909; Kant 1914) – Nye argues that twentieth-century Americans have repeatedly experienced sublimity through great technological achievements like bridges, dams, railroads or the atomic bomb. Unlike the natural sublime, the technological sublime is seldom experienced in solitude but rather as an event 'organized for crowds of tourists' (Nye 1994, 43). As such, the collective semiotics and embodied experience of the technological sublime can 'weld society together' (Nye 1994, xiii). It is no accident that in the United States, most impressive engineering works are inaugurated on the Fourth of July holiday. More than a matter of aesthetics, the technological sublime served as a specific kind of semiotics that shaped the American national identity:

> Where Kant had reasoned that the awe inspired by a sublime object made men aware of their moral worth, the American sublime transformed the individual's experience of immensity and awe into a belief in national greatness. (Nye 1994, 43)

In his previous work, *Electrifying America* (1990), David Nye referred to the 'electrical sublime' as the spectacular illumination of world fairs and civic ceremonies, the embellishment of nocturnal cityscapes and the highlighting of singular buildings, bridges and emblematic avenues ('Great White Ways'):

> The illumination was at once a marvelous tourist attraction, an advertisement for electrification, and a new form of the technological sublime, one in which a technology did not displace or conquer nature but rather intensified it ... striking the public dumb with amazement. (Nye 1990, 391)

Electricity is here equated to one of its most visible outputs: lighting. The production of electricity itself is covered in another chapter on the 'industrial sublime' (Nye 1994, 109–42), in which Nye develops the idea that each form of power generation bears a distinct relationship to the sublime. Unlike the grimy, fuming, coal-fired, steam-driven factories, located along railway lines and run by cohorts of industrial workers, electrified (hydropower and nuclear) plants seemed to require 'virtually no workers' while being much larger and more productive, suggesting a 'quiet, streamlined, antiseptic industrial landscape' (Nye 1994, 133). Filled with anti-utilitarian meanings, hydropower dams soon became 'major tourist sites'. The Hoover Dam, probably the most emblematic hydro-infrastructure in the United States, was given evocative names like 'the Great Pyramid of the American Desert' or the 'Ninth Symphony of our day' by the American writer Frank Waters. Dams have always had a strong connection with tourism in mountain regions, not only because they enabled the opening of remote valleys through access roads and electrification but also because integration with scenic landscapes has always been a key element of their design (Rodriguez 2012). By combining the natural and technological sublime, they have become cornerstones of mountain imaginaries, major tourist attractions and places of aesthetic wonder.[3]

Sublime tourists and nuclear power

The 'nuclear sublime' has often been associated with the atomic bomb and nuclear accident sites and, to a lesser extent, with civil nuclear energy. For Frances Ferguson (1984), the essential attribute of the sublime is that it allows oneself to 'think the unthinkable' (Ferguson 1984, 5); it is in the 'thing that is bigger than any individual, and especially bigger in terms of being more powerful and usually, more threatening'. What distinguishes beauty from sublimity is therefore the possibility of control over the observed object: 'We love the beautiful as what submits to us, while we fear the sublime as what we must submit to'. Because atomic power includes the possibility of our own annihilation (the 'nuclear holocaust'), our fascination with the nuclear is an ontological paradox. Just like suicide, 'taking one's own death into one's own hands', the nuclear sublime is 'the outcome of the subject's search for self-determination … the achievement of a freedom from the conditions of existence by means of one's nonexistence' (Ferguson 1984, 6).

Conversely, David Nye rejects the possibility of a nuclear sublime precisely because its annihilating power contradicts Burke's classic definition of the sublime, which presupposes a sense of personal security: 'One was exposed to the power of the hurricane, but nevertheless one saw it in relative safety' (Nye 2014, 255). Even with civil nuclear energy, 'it proved difficult to separate attitudes toward reactors from fear of the bomb' (Nye 2014, 235). He therefore considers nuclear tourism as 'implausible'. And when acknowledging that 'Three Mile Island became a popular tourist site in the 1980s', he views it as a 'curious irony' and a momentary craze of tourists 'on the outlook for novelties' (Nye 2014, 237).

Nick Rush-Cooper (2013) takes another path in his research on the tourism experience in Chernobyl. First, in relation to the notion of safe distance and subject/object separation, he argues that it is the embodied experience of radioactivity that triggers the reflexive 'Chernobyl Sublime', as tourists measure it through the exclusion zone with a Geiger counter. He shares this point with Goatcher and Brunsden's *Chernobyl and the Sublime Tourist* (2011), in which the sublime lies in an experience of place, a 'disenfranchisement of the senses' (Beck 1995) that cannot be captured by photographs. Next, while following Nye's analysis of the sublime as a historical object (rather than a universal feeling, according to Burke and Kant), Rush-Cooper deviates from Nye's dismissal of tourists as being sublime-seekers and tourism being anything other than an 'art of imitation'. For Rush-Cooper, tourism is 'performative' in the sense that it participates in the production of place, and therefore the production of sublimity – apart from being (and not contradictorily so) 'an interesting and fun day out' (Rush-Cooper 2013, 150).

As we can see, tourism has an ambivalent relationship to the sublime. For Daniel Boorstin (1964), tourism is presented as the antithesis of the modern encounter between travellers and nature. Pointing out that 'travel' came from 'travail', hence a necessary troublesome and laborious engagement with the landscape, Boorstin decries the passive stance of the contemporary 'packaged' tourist, who avoids risk and expects everything to be done for him or her. Unlike the sublime experience, a momentous experience which 'fills the mind with grand ideas and turns the soul in upon itself' (Nye 1994, 6), tourism is presented as a succession of 'pseudo-events', artificial scenes whose only purpose is mundane consumption. To some extent, David Nye shares this denial of tourism as an 'authentic' experience. Drawing on reports of early travellers to Niagara Falls and the Grand Canyon, he suggests that 'excessive tourism' leads to an 'erosion' and an 'eclipse' of the sublime (Nye 1994, 8). The main reason for that is the preconceptions disseminated by the tourism industry:

> Ordinarily, the visitor does not see the Grand Canyon or any other site with unprepared eyes. Most sublime objects have become tourist sites. Their existence has been well advertised in advance, their appearance has been suggested by photographs, and their meaning has been overdetermined. As a result, in many cases tourists do not experience the sublime at all. (Nye 1994, 13)

Instead, they experience 'like many modern tourists' what he calls an 'inversion' or an 'egotistical sublime' (Weiskel 1986), a disjunction between expectations and reality, 'leading to a disappointment' (Nye 1994, 14).

This common disdain for tourists has already been called into question by early tourism anthropologists like Dean MacCannell (1976), whose neo-Durkheimian interpretation of tourism as a modern day 'quest for authenticity' tends to reconcile tourists with the sublime. In a world that is increasingly desacralized, the enchanted encounter with new Others and new landscapes is presented as a way to reinvest daily life with transcendent significance. Nelson Graburn (1978) associates tourism with a 'sacred journey' because it mimics the three-stage symbolic structure of any *rite de passage*: departure, liminality (or communitas), reintegration. The tourism sublime may therefore happen in these liminal moments, emerging from the collision of a well-adjusted daily routine (the *profane*) and the anomic context of holiday-making (the *sacred*) fuelled by spectacular views, unfamiliar sensations and ontological alterity. Obviously, not all tourists invest the same sensibility in this 'sacred journey', and just as it seems unfair to presume that 'in many case tourists do not experience the sublime at all', it would be somewhat naive to believe that every single traveller is a full-blown aesthete, struck by awe-inspiring visions in every getaway. It also seems unfair to consider that tourism necessarily impoverishes aesthetical experience by 'staging authenticity' (MacCannell 1973) or by marketing landscape and culture. Just as there is a plurality of tourist types, there is a plurality of ways of organizing tourism, and much sublime experience is made possible because of tourism itself and the efforts of creation made by its promoters.

The genealogy of openness

In France, the first 'nuclear tours' date back to the 1970s, when the government officially launched its nuclear programme. Welcoming visitors into the nuclear factory was part of a new public-relations strategy aiming to build the image of a friendly and transparent company. At that time, civil nuclear energy was a flagship of the post-war French industry, and industrial accidents had not yet tarnished its image. 'It was a time of nuclear enthusiasm, if not nuclear utopia', comments Fanny Lopez (2014, 70), who traced the genealogy of public access in EDF nuclear stations. This open policy resonates with the architecture of nuclear factories. Unlike hydropower dams located in spectacular landscapes, which made hydraulics engineers more sensitive to architectural design, the first nuclear stations were built by heat engineers applying the model of thermal power stations, that is, in a purely utilitarian way. In 1974, the Executive Board launched the 'Plan Architecture' in order to develop a 'specific language of nuclear architecture' (Bouvier and Parent 2005, 7). For the first time, architects worked alongside engineers on the design of future power plants. Instead of hiding industrial facilities behind slopes and vegetation, the first architect involved in the Plan, Claude Parent, bet on industrial symbiosis: 'the station was not aimed to disappear, instead it had to participate in creating a new landscape' (Bouvier and Parent 2005, 7). Some projects based on industrial ecology promoted the development of farming around nuclear sites (including aquaculture at the mouth of heated effluents). Tourism and leisure activities near the stations were an integral part of this strategy, affirming nuclear energy as a rightful element of the territory. Claude Parent's designs had inspiring titles that were evocative of the symbolic power of nuclear technology: for example, *Tutankhamun's Feet* and *The Tiger's Pawn*. At that time, nuclear architecture echoed a certain form of sacralization of the atom – typical of the post-world-war context as well as the sublime – that identified power stations as 'cathedrals of the twentieth century' (Bouvier and Parent 2005, 7).

But this enthusiasm was soon cooled by a growing anti-nuclear protest and the 'anthropological shock' (Beck 1987) caused by the Three Mile Island (1979) and Chernobyl (1986) accidents. As mentioned by Sezin Topçu in her monograph *La France Nucléaire* (2013) on the government of nuclear energy in France, some EDF communications experts considered that such sacralization served the cause of anti-nuclear movements by reinforcing the idea of nuclear energy as a Promethean technology, fundamentally uncontrollable by ordinary humans. Specialists advocated a 'desacralization of nuclear issues' so as to normalize its role in the electricity supply chain and reduce the perception of nuclear risks. It was also in this period that EDF mandated research groups of linguists, semiologists and sociologists to think about the most efficient communication strategies. Gone were the 'cathedrals'; nuclear power stations were renamed 'steam engines of the twentieth century'. Still, according to Topçu, 'guided tours in nuclear power stations are launched in this context, in order to break with the idea that nuclear plants are inaccessible "sanctuaries" to the public. They will give birth to a proper nuclear tourism with approximately 300,000 visitors a year' (Topçu 2013, 200, my translation). Ever since, visits have become an important public-relations tool to produce a controlled yet 'open and transparent' image of the nuclear industry. In the 1990s, terrorist threats[4] and economic difficulties experienced by the group (in a context of market deregulation) caused other problems. Today, visitors must book at least three weeks in advance and send copies of their ID for a 'security check'.

British power plants experienced a similar shift. According to Mandy, a guide at Heysham 2 since the 1990s, 'people used to just show up and we would take them on a tour. Some were just wearing flip-flops' (Mandy, participation observation September 2016). Information centres closed in the early 2000s, when British Energy was under great financial stress. The Hinkley Point C[5] project was apparently the main reason to reopen visitor activities in UK power plants, now the property of EDF Energy: 'First they wanted to focus on Hinkley Point and build a big information centre there, but then they extended it to all power stations. Because it's a national project' (Mandy, participation observation September 2016). Three years after reopening, the number of visitors is increasing. According to Martyn Butler, EDF external communications manager for the Northern Region:

> Hartlepool and Heysham were celebrating their 20,000th visitor in October 2016. After Hinkley, they are the second and third most visited centres across the network. As of the end of August we were at 33,208 visitors – however, this is across the whole fleet of eight visitor centres. By year end we are on track to achieve 50,000 visitors. (Martyn Butler, interview September 2016)

For the public-relations expert, an important reason for attracting tourists is 'to inform the general public on the importance of nuclear power in the energy mix of the UK' (Martyn Butler, interview September 2016). In the information centre, panels praise nuclear energy by comparing it with other sources (1 kg of coal lights up a lamp for four days, while 1 kg of uranium lights it up for 140 years) and by putting forward key figures for energy supply (5.5 million customers, 20 per cent of UK total energy), for the economy (15,000 jobs in EDF Energy, 6,600 jobs in nuclear power plants) and for the environment (30,000,000 tons of CO_2 saved). In a context of market deregulation and increasing competition among energy suppliers, all means are important to woo customers. Although many clients remain 'captive', the liberalization of markets implies that customers should be able in the future to choose the kind of energy that they want to consume. For now, as the country faces difficult decisions (namely, the Hinkley Point project), EDF's marketing strategy aims to influence public opinion.[6]

Demonstrative safety and the controlled gaze

Another key objective of guided tours, according to Martyn Butler, is 'to show that we are open and transparent, especially after Fukushima. We wanted to reassure people.' Safety is indeed omnipresent during the visit. When entering the site, the tone is set by a police car parked on the access road and a 5-foot concrete sign displaying EDF's corporate motto: 'Safety is our overriding priority'. On arrival, people must sign a visitor's book in the information centre. Apart from the visitor centre, photographs are prohibited everywhere, including in the parking lot. The first 10–20 minutes of the tour are exclusively dedicated to 'press the safety button', as our guide puts it. After delivering the opening remarks about safety ('How will you show commitment to nuclear safety?'), the guide invites us to put on the safety equipment: a reflective vest, a helmet with hearing protection, safety gloves and plastic glasses. This array of safety equipment gives the impression of a zealous initiation to the security-centred world of a working nuclear plant; even though some workers move about without specific safety equipment, we are instructed to keep our helmets and glasses on at all times. At Heysham, there was particular vigilance because of a planned shutdown for maintenance.[7] I wasn't even able to bring a pen and a paper on the tour because of extra security measures. The demonstration of EDF's concern for safety isn't just a matter of speech, it's a demonstration at work, and visitors experience it personally. They must be given a perfect example of the company's commitment to security. After depositing any metal belongings in a safe, a security agent double-checks our IDs and searches us with a metal detector; after that, we are given an electronic pass and required to go individually through a safety revolving door.

Within the working sectors of the factory, the path is marked with signs and yellow lines painted on the floor. Safety messages and reminders are posted everywhere. Some of them explicitly address workers, advocating a faultless 'nuclear professionalism'. Other educational panels are specifically designed for visitors. In one of the corridors, a 20-foot-long timeline traces the history of the power plant (with photographs of women guides from 1985); another highlights some EDF merchandizing (such as the group's mascot, Zingy, and the electric Mini Cooper). Visitors are taken across footbridges which allow them to enjoy the spectacle of the station without interfering with its functioning. Unlike Hartlepool and Heysham 1, Heysham 2 seemed to have been designed with a particular concern for visitors. Apart from the fact that the whole factory was built in the shape of a massive ocean liner, at least three bay windows allow visitors to gaze upon the most sensitive and scenic elements of the station: one facing the sea and the pipes used to pump and eject the cooling water, another one over the reactor chamber and the final one over a control room reminiscent of a scene from a vintage science-fiction movie. As French anthropologist Saskia Cousin noted, these gazing devices are also devices of control, similar to the Foucauldian panopticon:

> Like the panopticon, the footbridge allows control over individuals: hanging over the working areas, far off, often glazed, hence soundproof, it allows visitors to see 'what's going on' in the factory while avoiding unwanted communications. (Cousin 201, 56, my translation)

While walking out of the security office, we encounter a heavily armed policeman. Like any high-security deployment, the omnipresence of safety precautions has an ambivalent effect. On the one hand, it is reassuring to see that safety is taken seriously, often to a point that no one could ever imagine. But on the other hand, the obsessive concern with security acts as a worrying reminder of the awe-inspiring potentiality of nuclear hazards.

The paradox of nuclear transparency

As Sezin Topçu puts it, transparency is 'an identity-discourse of nuclear energy' (Topçu 2013, 160). Since Chernobyl, EDF has chosen to adopt a proactive strategy towards nuclear safety, by communicating in real time on the severity of industrial incidents and by making public the results of inspection measures made on the facilities. The point of issuing a press release for every incident, even the most anecdotal ones, was to better control the information, set the pace of nuclear reporting and defuse controversies upstream. Through its communications services, EDF develops a genuine nuclear pedagogy aiming 'to accustom little by little the population to the idea of an incident, to its *banality*, to the fact that it becomes commonplace in a risk society' (Topçu 2013, 160).

The internalization of criticism also involves new institutional forms of relationship with anti-nuclear protesters and residents, such as the *Commissions Locales d'Information* (CLI). Part of the criticism of nuclear energy has evolved towards a more scientific discourse. The experts-versus-laypeople divide is progressively reconfigured, as many residents develop a challenging expertise. This expertise is based on a long-term cohabitation with nuclear industries, a highly informed opinion on sanitary risk and the involvement of many independent scientists with anti-nuclear movements (de Carvalho 2013). Much could be said about the limits of such a joint expertise approach and the incompleteness of the type of transparency implemented by nuclear actors. For Sezin Topçu, there is a 'permanent paradox' – if not a certain 'hypocrisy' – behind the discourse of a 'transparent and controlled atom', as it seems impossible to communicate serenely and objectively on matters like cancer occurrences, nuclear accident scenarios and nuclear waste disposal (Topçu 2013, 182–93).

This paradox also applies to guided tours in nuclear power stations. While the possibility of a visit suggests that EDF has 'nothing to hide', there are obvious limits to such openness. We have already mentioned questions of safety, which restrain access to many parts of the factory, but we could also mention questions of industrial secrecy. Especially in a context of market pressure and strategic investments (e.g. Hinkley Point C), it is understandable that industrial managers want to filter the kind of information – beginning with photos – that come out of the visits. Other limits are cognitive and psychological; even if the company was ready to fully play the game of transparency, many aspects presented during the tour remain unintelligible for the average person without proper measurement tools. How can one be transparent when dealing with an invisible matter like radioactivity? Metaphorically, one could argue that the clear water of the spent-fuel storage pond doesn't say anything about its toxicity. Transparency is performed but never complete. The strict standards of cleanliness everywhere in the station, supposedly for safety reasons, support the idea of a clean, antiseptic industry, a 'symbol of modernity and the future', especially if compared to the dusty 'smoke-billowing coal-fired factories' (Nye 1994, 133–4). During the tour, attention is focused on the engineering aspects of the station, the spectacular arrangement of sophisticated machinery and highly skilled workers who busy themselves before our eyes like bees in a massive super-organized industrial hive. All of this is thrilling, not only intellectually but also sensorially. Eyes are filled with uncommon scenes; the labyrinthic profusion of footbridges, tubes, machinery and sectorial divisions has a disorienting effect, accentuated by the near absence of natural light and the overwhelming space of engine rooms, the persistent smell of concrete and the deafening noise of the turbines, attenuated by the veiled silence of ear-itching protections, and so on.

Humanizing the industrial monster

While from a tourism experience point of view, all this seems very convincing, the over-emphasis on the technicalities of the factory conveniently prevents the visitor from addressing the general issues of nuclear energy. Understandably, a nuclear power station isn't the best place to make a case against nuclear energy, but it is interesting to note that not one controversial comment or question was formulated by the visitors (including myself) during the tours. It felt inappropriate or 'taboo'. Controversial questions – such as questions relating to technological faults in new generation reactors, the company's economic difficulties and so on – were also carefully avoided in the permanent exhibition of the information centre. However, guides did not seem uncomfortable with 'political questions'. In fact, one of the first interactions I had with a guide in a nuclear station started with a 'political discussion'. I met Ray – a sixty-nine-year-old guide and a former engineer at Hartlepool station – while shuffling between the information panels in the visitor centre. When I told him I was a social scientist interested in the tourism display of energy facilities, he immediately asked me if, in my opinion, 'All this [the visitor centre] is a political thing' (Ray, participant observation May 2016). As I awkwardly avoided the question by arguing that he was probably in a better position to answer that question and that such initiatives may have many purposes (including political ones), he stated that the most important thing for him was to pass on knowledge: 'I chose to work here [as a guide] because I like sharing what I believe in … and also because my wife kicks me out!'

This short anecdote suggests that the guides aren't necessarily uncomfortable with engaging in 'political' arguments; it is more often the visitors who are. As permanent workers in the nuclear industry, the guides have had plenty of time to think about the ethical dilemmas of their activity and prepare themselves for awkward questions. And although our group seemed too polite to engage in a controversial discussion, other visitors don't always share the same embarrassment: 'we are constantly subject to criticism', another guide told me during an informal encounter. By exposing itself to detractors, guided tours are part of EDF's strategy of openness and transparency, which consists in pre-empting criticism rather than avoiding it (Topçu 2013). The passionate-humoristic spin of Ray's response (the passion of sharing and the tyranny of spouses) also demonstrates his ability to depoliticize a debate. While the self-censorship and the persistence of taboos suggest that nuclear stations continue to transmit a feeling of 'sacrality' among visitors, we could argue that the guides' familiarity with the factory's environment has a 'secularizing' effect.

EDF guides have close relations with the factory they work in; most of them are retired nuclear engineers (like Ray) or relatives of nuclear workers (Mandy is married to a technician). This double-familiarity – with the plant and the workers – is reassuring. The nuclear reactor is not just a cold monster of steel, graphite and plutonium; for the workers, it is simply another 'sector' among many, a few doors away from the cafeteria. Their affective relationship with technology raises empathy: Mandy calls the reactors 'she' ('because they're ladies!') and jokes about her husband's 'other wife', the diesel generator where he works. The same thing happens with safety: the guide's usual ease with the many procedures helps de-dramatize the situation. At Hartlepool, when we come across an armed policeman, Ray cracks a joke to soften the atmosphere: 'Don't worry, I told him not to shoot you. But if he does shoot you, just start running in a zig-zag!' The guides allow a certain intimacy between workers and visitors: While walking through the station, they hail and greet their colleagues; to explain radioprotection and radioactivity measurement routines, Ray gives one of the co-workers a pat on the back and asks him to show us his electric personal dosimeter (EDP). All these little attentions contribute to humanizing the station. They make the 'awe-inspiring' confrontation with the nuclear sublime become a banal promenade among friendly co-workers.

As we are impressed by the magnitude of the infrastructure, the casual manner of the guide takes us back to its banality; her familiarity with the place makes us 'kin' with the power plant (Haraway 2015; Wintbereik, Maguire and Watts 2019). When standing at the foot of the first high-voltage pylon located at the mouth of the transformer, Mandy explains that this is the first pylon of the network after the station: 'That's where it all begins.' In the blink of an eye, my imagination travels back and forth between the far-off corners of the national grid and the concealed walls of the nuclear reactor. She says that the latest maintenance work cost more than several hundred thousand pounds. As I ask her if this pylon has a 'special name' among workers, expecting some kind of collective devotion to such an emblematic piece, she just replies in a teasing tone, 'Yeah, the big pylon!' and moves on to the next feature, laughing.

Managing human resources

Mandy is happy to have interested and disciplined visitors: 'The vast majority are children, it's difficult to get their attention. And we must always keep an eye on them: you don't want to have kids getting lost in the turbine room'. Schools are the main source of visitors for EDF information centres. At Heysham, they represent approximately 70 per cent of the public. In the exposition, the colourful panels seem specifically designed for the children. Dispersed around the room, experiments invite visitors to discover electricity in a playful manner: by producing current with a wheel, testing different conductive materials or wiring a staircase switch. One terminal – 'On the Waves of Radiation' – is composed of two wheels that look like wheels of fortune and allows visitors to measure the radiation of commonplace radioactive materials (a camping gas light, granite, fertilizer) with a dosimeter and to compare the insulating capacity of different shield samples (wool, cloth, glass, aluminium). In another corner of the room, a video game in an arcade cabinet consists of replacing uranium bars with a handling machine as quickly as possible. Near the main entrance, flyers and brochures advertise the many EDF education programmes: The POD (EDF Energy's online education programme), apprenticeships, early careers, trainee programme and so on. With more than 13,000 employees and a growing demand for qualified engineers, visitor centres and guided tours are key instruments to attract future workers.

Company visits also fulfil internal communication purposes. From the workers' point of view, it seems that they enjoy being an object of curiosity. Some of them wave and smile as we look through the bay window above the control room or as we pass by in the corridors. As I sign the visitors' book at the entrance to the information centre, I notice the names of professionals from many partner companies. When speaking with the manager, I learn that visits are a common way to spend time after a business meeting with a client or a contractor. It is also an important opportunity for the workers' families to discover what their work environment is like. Each year the visitor centre organizes special open days for them. The transformation – even temporarily – of an industrial environment into a visitor attraction can have a legitimizing effect: the fact that people outside the organization show interest in their work may increase their self-esteem as workers and their confidence in the company's mission. Although this may appear anecdotal if compared with the many factors that influence life quality in the workplace, building a friendly united image of the company is useful for suggesting unity among a diversified and numerous workforce.

Conclusion

The genealogy of visitors' access to nuclear power plants shows that touring has been a problematic issue, not only for safety and economic reasons but also because popular representations of nuclear energy have evolved, ranging from national pride and technological vanguard to atomic disaster and sensitive target for terrorist attacks. Due to the complexity of nuclear engineering, imagination is often an intellectual 'crutch' that helps laypeople to make sense of it. The way people react in relation to nuclear energy is necessarily imbued with meanings and images, a touch of 'awe and reverence' typical of Leo Marx's (1965) first definition of the 'technological sublime'. They ascribe to it an imaginary that has been fuelled by a history of military testing, atomic bombing and nuclear accidents but also by a sense of industrial grandeur, scientific novelty and technological prowess.

Ever since the first world fairs, promoters of electricity have had an ambivalent attitude towards the sublime, not only using its enchantments to sell services and spread new technologies (cf. Raoul Dufy's *Fée de l'Electricité*), but also trying to demystify its risks and reassure the population about its dangers. From a commercial and political point of view, the sublime is a double-edged sword: on the one hand, it can 'weld society together' and speak directly to the heart through the language of emotions (in a 'subliminal' way); on the other, it reminds us of the ontological vulnerability of the self in the face of uncontrollable forces of nature or technology. In the case of nuclear energy, this ontological insecurity seems incompatible with the ideal of a faultless safety record promoted by experts. And, while some nuclear architects have intended to build upon the sacred-leaning nuclear imaginary to conciliate the atom with a sense of aesthetic beauty (that is, controlled beauty), the efforts made by communication managers have focused on the diffusion of a secularized, rational image of nuclear infrastructure.

From the point of view of the company, visits fulfil many purposes: they serve to consolidate the role of nuclear energy in public opinion, build the image of an open transparent company, reassure local residents and attract new recruits. But this is done in a peculiar way, by passing over the mere discursive dimension of corporate communication to propose an embodied experience, a physical interaction with the factory and its people. Because tourism involves emotions and imagination, it is particularly helpful for the company to get the message across. EDF's guided tours tend to counter this sublime feeling by transmitting a sense of control and safety. By allowing visitors to experience the daily routine of nuclear workers, the company depicts the factory not only in functional and dispassionate terms but also in a friendly way, transforming the nuclear sublime into a banal excursion and a 'fun day out'. By exposing itself willingly to the public's curiosity and potential criticism, EDF presents itself as a 'transparent' company, while always staying in control of the terms of dialogue and the limits of accessibility. It is precisely this proactive, productive and even 'friendly' response to nuclear rejection that makes guided tours an efficient tool of government.

Notes

1 EDF published the first *Guide du Tourisme Industriel et Technique* in 1992, and three years later, it launched the 'Industrial and Technical Tourism Trophies' that rewards private companies for outreach initiatives towards the general public.

2 Fieldwork was conducted between May and September 2016 through participatory observation (guided tours, visits in EDF information centres) and interviews with guides and external communication managers from EDF. Most of the ethnographic material is based on two guided tour experiences: one made at Hartlepool with four fellow social scientists from Durham University, and another one at Heysham 2 with a retired couple from California who had planned a stop at Heysham while on holiday, as the husband had participated in the zoning of the second reactor when he was still working as an industrial consultant. I also benefited from complementary fieldwork in France at EDF's *Hydrélec* national museum, where I was able to interview the cultural mediator and to consult some of the company's archives as well as a valuable literature on EDF's history of public relations.

3 It is no coincidence that dams are regularly used as spaces for art exhibitions. It is because they raise questions about the nature/culture divide (wilderness versus domestication, landscape versus industry) and challenge our common perceptions of the landscape.

4 Visits were stopped on several occasions in the 1990s because of the anti-terrorist plan 'Vigipirate'.

5 Hinkley Point C is a project to construct a new 3,200 MWe nuclear power station with two European Pressurized Reactors (EPR) in Somerset, England, next to the Hinkley Point B station. The construction cost is estimated at £18 billion

(£24.5 billion including financing costs) and should be assumed by EDF together with a Chinese state-owned company (CGN). In exchange, EDF has negotiated a guaranteed fixed price – a 'strike price' – of £92.50/MWh (in 2012 prices). After several years of harsh negotiation on both the French and the British sides, the proposal was finally approved by the EDF board in July 2016 and by the UK government in September of that year.

6 Using energy tourism as a lobbying tool is not uncommon among energy groups. Once, at another guided tour in a Swiss hydropower dam, I had the opportunity to observe similar comparisons. In one of the explanatory panels, the group states that to produce the same amount of electricity, 570 wind turbines would be necessary (34 times the surface of the water dam's reservoir). On the next one, it is said that the hydroelectric factory can be started in only 200 seconds, while a nuclear station requires weeks to be entirely switched off. Here, too, guided tours are a way to 'share the group's concerns with the public in a critical political moment' (Sarah Falcinelli, communication manager, interview May 2016), as Swiss hydropower actors are pressing the government to help the hydropower sector overcome the financial crisis caused by low energy prices (Loloum 2016).

7 Approximately every two years, nuclear stations are shut down for several weeks for maintenance. This is a busy period when many contractors converge on site. At Heysham, the parking lot was nearly full that day. This planned maintenance shutdown of the Heysham 2 reactor occurred after 940 days of continuous operation, a 'world record' according to the guide, which judging by her enthusiasm, is seen as a good thing. At Hartlepool, visits are suspended during the shutdown, probably because it is an older generation of reactor (just like Heysham 1, built in the same period).

References

Addison, Joseph. 1773. *Remarks on Several Parts of Italy, &c. in the Years 1701, 1702, 1703*. Dublin: Printed for T. Walker.

Beck, Ulrich. 1987. 'The Anthropological Shock: Chernobyl and the Contours of the Risk Society', *Berkeley Journal of Sociology*, 32: 153–65.

Beck, Ulrich. 1995. *Ecological Politics in an Age of Risk*. Cambridge, MA: Polity Press.

Boorstin, Daniel J. 1964. *The Image: A Guide to Pseudo-Events in America*. New York: Harper & Row.

Burke, Edmund. 1909. *On the Sublime and Beautiful*, The Harvard Classics (Vols. 1–51, Vol. 24). New York: P. F. Collier & Son.

Cousin, Saskia. 2001. 'Industrie de l'évasion ou entreprise d'encadrement? Le cas du tourisme industriel', *Quaderni*, 44(11): 45–71.

de Carvalho, Lucie. 2013. 'Le complexe nucléaire de Sellafield au cœur des controverses: le fait technologique entre experts et profanes', *VertigO - la revue électronique en sciences de l'environnement*, 13(2), doi:10.4000/vertigo.14187 (accessed 20 April 2017).

Ferguson, Frances. 1984. 'The Nuclear Sublime', *Diacritics*, 14(2): 4–10.

Goatcher, Jeff and Viv Brunsden. 2011. 'Chernobyl and the Sublime Tourist', *Tourist Studies*, 11(2): 115–37.

Graburn, Nelson H. H. 1978. 'Tourism: The Sacred Journey', in Valene L. Smith (ed.), *Hosts and Guests: The Anthropology of Tourism*, 17–31. Oxford: Basil Blackwell.

Haraway, Donna. 2015. 'Anthropocene, Capitalocene, Plantationocene, Chthulucene: Making Kin', *Environmental Humanities*, 6: 159–65.

Hollinshead, Keith. 1999. 'Surveillance of the Worlds of Tourism: Foucault and the Eye-of-Power', *Tourism Management*, 20(1): 7–24.

Kant, Immanuel. 1914. *The Critique of Judgement*. London: MacMillan and Co.

Loloum, Tristan. 2016. 'La vie touristique des grands barrages hydroélectriques', *Mondes du Tourisme*, 12. http://tourisme.revues.org/1360 (accessed 20 April 2017).

Lopez, Fanny. 2014. 'Les touristes du nucléaire: l'enjeu de l'accessibilité des sites de production EDF, 1974–1991'. *Annales Historiques de l'Électricité*, 12(1): 65–75.

MacCannell, Dean. 1973. *Staged Authenticity: Arrangements of Social Space in Tourist Settings*. Chicago: University of Chicago Press.

MacCannell, Dean. 1976. *The Tourist: A New Theory of the Leisure Class*. New York: Schocken Books.

Marx, Leo. 1964. *The Machine in the Garden: Technology and the Pastoral Ideal in America*. New York: Oxford University Press.

Morice, Jean-René. 2006. 'La visite d'entreprise en Europe: un champs à explorer', *Cahiers Espaces*, 92: 10–15.

Nye, David E. 1990. *Electrifying America: Social Meanings of a New Technology, 1880–1940*. Cambridge, MA: MIT Press.

Nye, David E. 1994. *American Technological Sublime*. Cambridge, MA: MIT Press.

Otgaar, Alexander H. J. 2010. *Industrial Tourism: Where the Public Meets the Private*. Rotterdam: Erasmus Research Institute of Management (ERIM), Erasmus University Rotterdam.

Parent, Claude and Yves Bouvier. 2005. 'Architecture et paysage du nucléaire: La centrale crée le site', *Annales Historiques de l'Électricité*, 3(1): 7–17.

Picard, David. 2013. *Tourism, Magic and Modernity: Cultivating the Human Garden*. New York: Berghahn Books.

Rodriguez, Jean-François. 2012. 'Hydropower Landscapes and Tourism Development in the Pyrenees. From Natural Resource to Cultural Heritage', *Journal of Alpine Research*, 100(2): 2–15.

Rush-Cooper, Nicholas. 2013. *Exposures: Exploring Selves and Landscapes in the Chernobyl Exclusion Zone*, Durham theses, Durham University. Available at Durham E-Theses Online: http://etheses.dur.ac.uk/8490/ (accessed 20 April 2017).

Topçu, Sezin. 2013. *La France nucléaire: l'art de gouverner une technologie contestée.* Paris: Éd. du Seuil.

Weiskel, Thomas. 1986. *The Romantic Sublime: Studies in the Structure and Psychology of Transcendence.* Baltimore, MD: Johns Hopkins University Press.

Winthereik, Brit Ross, James Maguire and Laura Watts. 2019. 'The Energy Walk: Infrastructuring the Imagination', in D. Ribes and J. Vertasi (eds), *Digital STS: A Field Guide for Science & Technology Studies.* Princeton: Princeton University Press.

11

Afterword: Electricity as inspiration – towards indeterminate interventions

Sarah Pink

Rethinking concepts that prevail in the social sciences and humanities through an encounter with electricity is a complex and exciting task. The editors and contributors of this volume have skilfully opened our eyes to the new horizons this offers for scholarship and practice in research. The new agenda that their collective work maps out provides an opportunity to consider more than simply the question of what a social sciences- and humanities-driven study *of* electricity might look like. It also offers three other possibilities. The first is to ask what role social sciences and humanities approaches to electricity might play in an interdisciplinary research agenda together with engineering, design and policy approaches. The second is to ask what it means to reflect back on academic disciplines through the demands that the study of electricity, as something that is so complex in its qualities and affordances, indeterminate in its meaning and indiscrete in its being. The final implication is to invite us to consider how social science and humanities approaches to electricity, with an interdisciplinary orientation and shaped through the critical encounter with electricity itself, might be honed into an interventional agenda that implicates electricity in the making and imagining of possible futures. In this afterword, I explore these questions with particular critical reference to the example and prism of the discipline of anthropology; however, the implications this raises are relevant to a range of different disciplines that inform the chapters of this volume.

The first set of reflections this volume invites stresses the need to shape disciplinarily informed approaches to understanding electricity in the social sciences and humanities, as well as approaches that are interdisciplinary within this field. For instance, in the case of anthropology, the proposition of an anthropology of electricity brings to the fore the capacity of anthropology to shed new critical light on things that are not usually visible; that is, anthropology, often but not always combined with ethnography, offers us ways to encounter those elements of everyday life, history and imagined or anticipated futures that are not within the theoretical or methodological grasp of other disciplines. For me, as someone who is critical of the conservatism and inward-looking nature of the past-oriented project of much – but not all – contemporary mainstream anthropology as a whole (e.g. Pink and Salazar 2017), this capacity to reveal and theoretically advance through the analysis of not always apparent phenomena is one of the key strengths of the discipline. It is also, I argue, a significant way in which anthropology could, and indeed should, participate in interdisciplinary debate, practice and research. I return to this point later through a consideration of possible routes for this to be achieved. However, initially with regards to the social science and humanities study *of* electricity, my concern is with two aspects of the benefits of scholarly engagement with electricity.

First, as outlined in the introduction to this volume, social science and humanities research about electricity is different to research about energy. While electricity can be seen as an (important) element of contemporary energy research, it is also, as the chapters here demonstrate, much more than this. A focus on electricity is, on the one hand, more precise because it calls on us to interrogate the qualities and affordances of one thing that is in energy research bundled under a wider category. This is, as the book shows, better undertaken as an interdisciplinary task. However, on the other hand, electricity, when studied within one discipline, cannot necessarily be encompassed under the concepts that researchers in cognate disciplines tend to use for energy. For example, the sociological focus on the social practices surrounding energy use or demand for energy and psychology research about human behaviour relating to energy use (both discussed in Pink et al. 2017b) are discipline specific. While they provide insights that are of interest to anthropologists, they cannot be extended across all other disciplines. For example, when taking a critical anthropological approach to electricity, we see how anthropology distinguishes itself from a sociological approach, specifically because it reveals how tricky the concepts we use to define, speak and write about such 'things' are. Whereas sociologists and psychologists have been content to think with already existing concepts of practices or behaviours respectively in order to comprehend energy use, anthropologists of electricity, as well as other scholars contributing to this book, have torn apart most of the existing concepts that might have been used to define electricity – both academically and societally. Instead, they emphasize the difficulty of fitting electricity into categories and demonstrate the historically and contemporary contingencies of any definitions that might come about.

Taking anthropology as the example again, we can see how, on the one hand, an anthropological interrogation of electricity illuminates where anthropology stands in relation to its sister disciplines. The same might be said for history, STS and other approaches represented in this volume. However, on the other hand, it becomes clear that an anthropological analysis situates its perspective in relation to those of technological and engineering disciplines, policy and business. While it is important not to render the prism through which any of these perspectives may think too stereotypically or as being singular, there is clearly a need for social science and humanities perspectives in this broader interdisciplinary arena. As the contributors to this book demonstrate, the ways of knowing and insights generated through these disciplines can play a role in interpreting corporate, engineering, policy and legal approaches to and attempts to define and regulate electricity, turn it into a commodity, and market it. Here, the critical perspective of anthropology shows up very well how these systems work, how they have emerged historically and how they are ongoingly emergent in both national and cultural contexts where they are established already and where they are in progress. However, there are also limitations to the disciplines, one being their tendencies towards insularity and the development of internal discussions and debates – being what the anthropologist Marilyn Strathern referred to as 'communities of critics' (2006, 204). When scholars write in and to their own disciplines, they often tend to fall into a default traditional role of offering theory, explanation and critique without working towards future societal interventions. Anthropology is a good example of this tendency. This is not to say that anthropology needs to be a problem-solving discipline but that instead we need to continue to press on with the task of rethinking it as a discipline that seeks to create possibilities for what might play out in as-yet unknown near and far futures. Electricity provides a fertile field for such an interventional anthropology to grow up in, and this is not least because it is already something around which an interdisciplinary field of research, scholarship, practice and intervention is being constituted. The table at which such questions are debated is one where anthropology needs to have a place and where it might work towards interventions towards alternative possible futures. The same applies to other social science and humanities disciplines. I return to this point later.

The third implication of bringing together electricity with academic disciplines that have not conventionally studied it is to invite questions about what electricity might do to/for the social sciences and humanities. As the contributors to this book brilliantly show, interrogating electricity leads us to examine how we understand a series of old and new core concepts in the social sciences and humanities which are all part of interdisciplinary theory building in this field, even where they are articulated differently through specific disciplines – including agency, power, materiality, thingness and data. As the contributors show, a focus on electricity can entail a critique of how human agency has been neglected by the recent theoretical turn to new materialism or can serve as a reference point in recent discussions of big data.

This book sets us on an important path for inquiry in the social sciences and humanities precisely because it applies their perspectives to and examines something that has often been treated as if it were invisible but is in fact a fundamental element of society, culture and the ongoingly changing materiality of our everyday worlds. It simultaneously leads us to question how disciplines construct their objects, units or topics of analysis – by confronting scholars with an object that cannot be constructed easily. Indeed, each chapter of this volume demonstrates a different way that electricity might be constructed as an object of analysis while, conversely, reflexively recognizing the complexities of such a procedure in itself. This inescapable quandary of having to construct a way to catch hold of something that cannot necessarily be captured and defined in any singular way is a perennial problem for all disciplines in the social sciences and humanities, exemplified by everyday life studies in its quest to study everyday lives and configurations that are in continuous flow (Pink 2012). The study of electricity yet again brings it to the fore in a way that both demonstrates the problem and emphasizes the need to be reflexive about how objects of study are constituted and constructed. Yet it seems that the study of electricity makes this questioning relevant in further ways because, as I discuss next, we are not only dealing with a body of academic scholarship but also with a question and issue that inevitably invokes an applied, public and interventional agenda, one that calls on us to take responsibility for how electricity will be part of our as-yet unknown and always uncertain futures. To continue with the example of anthropology, I argue that opening up such a research agenda calls for an interventional anthropology that is prepared to and capable of imagining as yet unknown, and potentially never known and unknowable, futures. This also means going against the grain of what scholarly disciplines conventionally do.

Anthropology is however a good example of what might be possible since it is a discipline that has, particularly in recent years, emerged as a leader in the development of innovative and successful collaborations with design. I next elaborate on the relevance of this relationship and, in doing so, suggest how a design anthropology approach might become the next step, to build on the critical ways of knowing that can be accessed through an interdisciplinary social science and humanities electricity research agenda.

At the core of a design anthropology approach (e.g. Smith et al. 2016) are concepts of intervention, emergence, possibility and collaboration. Some of these challenge traditional mainstream anthropology, particularly in their attention to intervention and possibility, and in implying an alternative temporality to that conventionally applied to anthropological work. That is, by bringing anthropology together with design, new ways of activating the discipline are created. These go beyond the techniques of applied anthropology, which has itself been seen as an 'impure' (see Wright 2005; Roberts 2005) rendering of the discipline, to challenge anthropological practice further. Elsewhere with colleagues, I have argued for a *blended* practice (Pink, Akama and Fergusson 2017a; Akama, Pink and Sumartojo 2018) that brings together the techniques and differing temporalities of anthropology, ethnography, design and documentary. This is what I would like to propose as a next step in the relationship between anthropology and electricity – that is, a development of the theme that not only creates new opportunity for theoretical critique but also one that calls for the reconstitution of anthropological practice. This would be a form of anthropological practice that is *open* – open to negotiating with other disciplines in ways that might shift its practice, open to the future-focused temporalities of design and open to researching the unknowable rather than clinging to the specificity of what we have witnessed having already happened and writing this into the past. The approach to electricity as developed by the editors and contributors to this book shows a starting point for this, since it has identified electricity as an indeterminate yet underpinning element of contemporary worlds. In doing so, it demands a certain openness to attending to something that is so obviously difficult to conceptualize in any single way. In my experience, such difficult subjects already lend themselves to blended practice – for example, when using ethnographic documentary techniques to research usually invisible and difficult to define things like everyday energy (see www.energyanddigitalliving.com) or the contingencies through which hidden ways of knowing about laundry emerge (see www.laundrylives.com). Video as a mode of moving forward through the world (Pink 2011) and design as a future-focused discipline (Gunn, Otto and Smith 2013) inspire us to keep going into the as-yet unknown future and to open up possibilities rather than stopping at the edge of the present and allocating the knowable to the past. This means seeking modes of intervening in uncertain futures (Akama, Pink and Sumartojo 2018), and in particular here refers to acknowledging the uncertainty that an indeterminate thing like electricity presents us with. Keeping this as a focus could indeed be useful, since uncertainty is no stranger in the areas of research that contributors to this volume have drawn our attention to – for instance, in science, particularly in the context of climate science research which anthropologies of electricity (as energy) will inevitably become implicated in (see Akama, Pink and Sumartojo 2018 for further discussion of this); and in big data analytics, where social-science and humanities critics have highlighted the similar liveliness (Lupton 2016) and brokenness of data (Pink et al 2018). Whether or not future forms of blended practice in research and intervention involve those techniques I have noted above, my experience suggests that these are most interestingly played out at the interface between conventional scholarship, practice-based disciplines and improvisatory approaches to creative practice. When we begin to interface these with policy, science and engineering fields, exciting new possibilities open up – but we also need to be open to those possibilities.

Anthropology is not the only discipline that has begun to open up to and whose practitioners have begun to develop collaborations with design and engineering disciplines. Indeed, it is interesting to note that such collaborations have often been in the field of energy research. My own work with designers and engineers is one example of how anthropological approaches can become part of an energy demand reduction agenda (see http://www.leedr-project. co.uk/). Another example is the collaboration that the sociologist Mike Michael has developed in the field of speculative design (e.g. Michael 2016). Energy, as discussed, is not synonymous with electricity. Yet these collaborations and the new future-oriented concepts, categories and insights they are able to generate have carved a way ahead and, I believe, ease the way of an interdisciplinary electricity agenda.

This book therefore emerges at a key moment in research and scholarship and signifies an important first step into a way of understanding the invisible and indeterminate agencies and materialities of our everyday worlds and into creating a new openness. While the approaches here begin with some clear theoretical premises, at the same time what is significant about the way that this book develops is that it invites forms of rethinking based on the empirical and theoretical investigation of a shared question-space – that of electricity. It is precisely such moves that form the basis from which we might continue to reshape both interdisciplinary and discipline-specific theory building towards an agenda that articulates what elsewhere I have called an 'ethics of responsibility' (Pink 2017b). In the example of anthropology, which I continue here, we can see the importance of this, since it offers a way forward that evades the discipline's tendency to fall back on a critical isolationist stance that seeks ethical refuge in past temporalities of ethnographic writing (Pink 2017a). The challenge now is to continue this work and to push the agenda on through disciplinary and interdisciplinary approaches led by the social sciences and humanities and that activate interventions.

Such interventions call on an ethics of responsibility because they are indeterminate in two ways: first, because the thing/non-thing we would follow as our route into the world – electricity – is indeterminate; second, because following an understanding of the world as ongoingly emergent (Akama, Pink and Sumartojo 2018) the future is similarly indeterminate – that is, it involves moving into an uncertain future with an uncertain thing. This, I believe, captures very accurately the way that we might conceptualize the work of interventional anthropology at least, and potentially that of other social science and humanities disciplines. The analysis of electricity articulated in this book makes it very clear that these might be the conditions under which we work. However, my comments here are not intended to sweep the ground from under our feet by arguing that it is pointless to intervene in an uncertain world – in fact, quite the opposite. They are simply a warning that we need to be mindful of these circumstances and, if there is anything we can grasp onto, it should be the ethics of responsibility I have called for here.

References

Akama, Y., S. Pink and S. Sumartojo. 2018. *Uncertainty and Possibility: New Approaches to Future Making*. London: Bloomsbury.

Gunn, W., T. Otto and R. C. Smith (eds). 2013. *Design Anthropology: Theory and Practice*. London: Bloomsbury.

Lupton, D. 2016. *The Quantified Self*. Cambridge: Polity Press.

Michael, M. 2016. 'Speculative Design and Digital Materialities: Idiocy, Threat and Com-promise', in S. Pink, E. Ardevol and D. Lanzeni (eds), *Digital Materialities: Anthropology and Design*, 99–113. London: Bloomsbury.

Pink, S. 2011. 'Sensory Digital Photography: Re-Thinking "Moving" and the Image', *Visual Studies*, 26(1): 4–13.

Pink, S. 2012. *Situating Everyday Life: Practices and Places*. London: Sage.

Pink, S. 2017a. 'Ethics in an Uncertain World: Between Theory and Practice', in S. Pink, V. Fors and T. O'Dell (eds), *Theoretical Scholarship and Applied Practice*, 13–51. Oxford: Berghahn.

Pink, S. 2017b. 'Technologies, Possibilities, Emergence and an Ethics of Responsibility: Refiguring Visual-Digital Research Techniques', in E. Gomez Cruz, S. Sumartojo and S. Pink (eds), *Refiguring Techniques in Digital Visual Research*, 1–12. Cham, Switzerland: Palgrave Pivot.

Pink, S. and J. F. Salazar. 2017. 'Anthropologies and Futures: Setting the Agenda', in J. Salazar, S. Pink, A. Irving and J. Sjoberg (eds), *Future Anthropologies*, 3–22. Oxford: Bloomsbury.

Pink, S., Y. Akama and A. Fergusson. 2017a. 'Researching Future as an Alterity of the Present', in J. Salazar, S. Pink, A. Irving and J. Sjoberg (eds), *Future Anthropologies*. Oxford: Bloomsbury.

Pink, S., K. Leder Mackley, R. Morosanu, V. Mitchell and T. Bhamra. 2017b. *Making Homes: Ethnographies and Designs*. Oxford: Bloomsbury.

Pink, S., M. Ruckenstein., R. Willim and M. Duque. 2018. 'Broken Data', *Big Data and Society*, 5(1): https://doi.org/10.1177/2053951717753228.

Roberts, S. 2005. 'The Pure and the Impure? Reflections on Applying Anthropology and Doing Ethnography', in S. Pink (ed.), *Applications of Anthropology*, 72–89. Oxford: Berghahn.

Smith, R. C., K. Tang Vangkilde, M. G. Kjærsgaard, T. Otto, J. Halse and T. Binder (eds). 2016. *Design Anthropological Futures*. London: Bloomsbury Academic.

Strathern, M. 2006. 'A Community of Critics? Thoughts on New Knowledge', *Journal of the Royal Anthropological Institute*, 12(1): 191–209.

Wright, S. 2005. 'Machetes into a Jungle: A History of Anthropology in Policy and Practice, 1981–2000, in S. Pink (ed.), *Applications of Anthropology*, 27–54. Oxford: Berghahn.

Index

Printed in the USA
CPSIA information can be obtained
at www.ICGtesting.com
LVHW021649271223
767455LV00005B/95

9 781350 102644